METROPOLIS
TO
METROPLEX

METROPOLIS TO METROPLEX

The Social and Spatial Planning of Cities

JACK MELTZER

THE JOHNS HOPKINS UNIVERSITY PRESS

Baltimore and London

THE JOHNS HOPKINS UNIVERSITY PRESS, Baltimore, Maryland 21218

THE JOHNS HOPKINS PRESS LTD., London

Library of Congress Cataloging in Publication Data

Meltzer, Jack.
  Metropolis to metroplex.

  Bibliography pp. 177–96
  Includes index.
  1. City planning. 2. City Planning—United
States. 3. Metropolitan areas. 4. Urban pol-
icy. I. Title.
HT166.M428 1984   307′.12   83–49195
ISBN 0–8018–3152–0
ISBN 0–8018–3153–9 (pbk.)

Contents

Acknowledgments

A series of acknowledgments is in order. At the outset, a Ford Foundation Study and Travel Grant helped me mobilize my energies and act on a long-held desire to write this book. In the earliest stages, William Swenson, who had been a research assistant at the University of Chicago Center for Urban Studies during my term as its first director, and who subsequently became my colleague and friend, helped me for a brief period in organizing my material and my thoughts.

I owe a special debt of gratitude to a group of my students who helped me assemble, review, and refine the citations in the selected bibliography, which appears at the end of the book. John Condas, Joy Swanson, and Thomas Delapa, working separately, undertook the task of assisting me in assembling the references. Ellen Meltzer and Eric Schneider took on the elaborate task of reviewing, classifying, and refining the references and completing the final associated tasks. Rosemary LaGrotte prepared the citations for word processing.

Gwen Graham, of the University of Chicago, typed the first full draft of the manuscript. Kristy Nabors, my secretary at the University of Texas at Dallas, produced the entire manuscript—text and selected bibliography—in record time and literally without error.

The editorial skills of Janice Feldstein and Mary Lou Kenney enhanced this effort. My appreciation also to Henry Tom, the Johns Hopkins social sciences editor, for his confidence and counsel. The index was prepared by Judith Hancock.

My wife was, as always, my close companion and support, my most constructive and trusted critic, and my best friend and respected colleague. But beyond all of this, her insightfulness, her probing mind, her persistence, and her patience proved invaluable. Her intellectual instinct, imaginative influence, and sense of balance and direction are literally reflected in every word.

Finally, I express my appreciation to all of my former students, to my friends and colleagues, to my adversaries, and to the known and unknown authors of everything I have ever read. The exchange and interchange of ideas and the ferment that they generated underlie this product.

My inspiration, which sustained me, was my children, Richard, Marc, and Ellen, their spouses, Judy and Lynn, and their marvelous children, Andrew, Nora, Cassie, and Lauren. I thank you all.

METROPOLIS
TO
METROPLEX

Contemporary Issues in Policy and Planning

The outmigration of population from the central cities of the United States began on a massive scale after World War II. The population movement was accelerated by the great demand for housing and by an increase in the number of family formations, which had been deferred by the war. These changes were accommodated and facilitated by federal housing and public works policies tilted markedly toward development in the areas outside the central city. They were reinforced more by the obsolescence in the central city than by the deterioration, and by the real and perceived social problems associated with racial change and with increases in the dependent population. They were speeded by the attractions of the less dense and newly developed outlying areas.

During the 1950s and 1960s, the population movement took on a strongly negative character. Northern and large city "havens" witnessed an influx of people from the South, the farms, and the smaller places, while city dwellers sought to escape from the large and older central cities to outlying segments. Thus, the nation saw both the suburbanization and the metropolitanization of its urbanized areas. The older central city was presumed to have retained its dominance, albeit with a large hinterland. It was not uncommon to characterize the hinterland as parasitic, dependent upon the central city, availing itself of the city's benefits yet bearing few, if any, of its burdens.

The central city that has emerged in the 1980s, however, is not a "tree trunk" with "social and pathological infirmities" accompanying the aging process and spawning the growth of suburban limbs and branches that have ostensibly sapped its recuperative capacity. Rather, the older central city has a reconstructed urban profile resulting from a profound transformation in the whole pattern of human settlement.

1

During the immediate postwar period, public and private intervention in the inner city focused on eliminating slums and blighted housing and overcoming historical obsolescence to create a balanced and healthy environment—a desirable and constructive goal, it was thought, for society. Society would benefit from the upgrading of its plant and facilities, and the people forced to live in deteriorated structures and neighborhoods would be aided if their circumstances were improved. Further, people with economic choice would thereby be encouraged to remain in the city or be attracted to it, thus making it possible for the city to retain its diversity and socioeconomic heterogeneity.

It became clear, however, that the surgical removal of slums and blight was a simplistic remedy. The elimination of structures or the clearance of areas was neither remedial in itself nor an assured restorative prescription. In addition, it soon became apparent that the needs, and accordingly the programmatic responses, of each socioeconomic group affected or to be served were different. For example, lower socioeconomic groups placed a higher value on the support services and material benefits on which their survival largely depended, whereas higher socioeconomic groups placed greater value on external and environmental benefits that had to be facilitated by complex institutionalized devices. Market factors also had a differential impact on various socioeconomic groups. The greater the stress on market considerations, the more extensive the measures introduced to sustain or create the area's market appeal. The more extensive the measures thereby introduced, the more devastating the effect on the most vulnerable populations. Furthermore, the interdependent relationship between social and spatial goals and components became self-evident. Consequently, no single-minded professional approach was adequate to the mission. The restoration of the city required a fusion of professional approaches and program measures to serve both the newly emerging social and population groups and the dependent populations looking to the city to reinforce and fulfill their aspirations.

By 1980 there were also sharp evidences of further profound change in the regionalization of the nation as a result of: the redistribution of people and activities to newly expanding areas of the South, Southwest, and West; the growth of the low-density and "museumlike" states; and the increasing magnetism of the smaller metropolitan areas.

Developing a Framework for Change

The intent of this volume is to connect the diverse territorial, substantive, and contextual strands that are shaping the twenty-first–century city.

These strands provide the context for understanding and intervening in the urbanization process and for enhancing the public and private decision-making capacity. The dominant pattern of human settlement (which will likely continue into the twenty-first century) reflects the regional redistribution of metropolitan and central-city populations and activities. The diminishing supply of resources and the increased pressure to secure access and a more equitable distribution of goods and services make it necessary to modernize systems and to make vastly expanded bodies of knowledge applicable over extended spaces. New hierarchical organizational arrangements and new transportation linkages and living and activity centers must reflect the increasingly specialized character of the central city, the changes in family and social organizations, and the shifts in the size of the dependent population. Administrative and strategic planning must cut across and integrate diverse functions and activities, drawing on scientific management approaches aimed at achieving a unified plan for the system. The significant factors in community and economic development related to participation and microgovernance build on and reinforce human service–delivery networks. Policy and planning are not neutral forces in the urban (or social) "revolution" but must represent a synthesis of social welfare and environmental approaches.

The historical tendency in the theoretical and professional literature to place the dominant stress on developing a blueprint for intervention and action needs revision and replacement by a commitment to developing a framework for change and for setting in motion a process by which change is achieved. Such a shift in approach is found to affect professional policy, theory, and conception, as will the attempts to narrow the gap between science and humanism and to reconcile environmental and social welfare approaches.

We have moved through a series of historical stages—since before the turn of the century through the 1920s, from the City Efficient to the City Beautiful and to the City Achievable; since the 1920s, from the City Governable to the City Manageable; and since World War II, from the City Possible to the City Tolerable.

Planners must think in terms of process, not blueprints. They must recognize that the potential of systems approaches and other methodologies and new technologies, including the computer, exceeds the human capacity to make the most of them. Scientific and technological models and systems are predicated on closure, and since most urban and settlement-related issues are dependent on, or are influenced by, human behavior, they either defy closure or are not met—at least currently—by the knowledge or wisdom to achieve it. Further, with quantification, decision making becomes the captive of, rather than the instrument of, change. Commonly, in the face of a technological emphasis, services to clients and users are viewed as a cost, whereas the introduction of administrative procedures is viewed as a saving.

These redirections are affecting the primacy and role of the professions engaged in urban and settlement-related interventions and activities. The redirections are also likely to alter the status of professions such as social work, particularly with respect to their policy, planning, and community components. The social work profession's stress on the beneficiary and consumer, accounts in part for both its past weakness and its potential strength. The profession focuses on connecting the critical components of the urban and metropolitan system so as to provide and distribute needed and valued benefits and services. A major characteristic of the profession is its role as facilitator and as linchpin in the more general human support system and network. Rather than asserting power, the profession lubricates the system and thereby enhances its functioning and interaction. These very factors have given the social work profession a special distinction. The stress on process and on facilitation and accommodation rather than on an identifiable set of functions, while perceived to be a weakness historically, has heightened the profession's usefulness and potential by narrowing the distance between the service and the recipient and the provider and the consumer.

We look to the legal profession to mesh the gears and make the system operable. Lawyers are the "Switzerland" of professionals—the honest brokers, the communicators, and the exchange agents. These facilitating and reinforcing roles account for the substantial number of key nonlegal positions held by lawyers, and the growing dependence on lawyers for advice and counsel. Law is the only profession we permit to be "neutral" and available to each and all of the adversaries, without being saddled with defending or rationalizing its positions. Accordingly, it is hardly surprising that lawyers have assumed a significant role in connection with urban and settlement-related activities.

In the face of massive changes in the pattern of human settlement, accommodation depends on the introduction of systems, policies, and practices to facilitate a historical transition. These are programmatic, rather than ideological, challenges. Ideology is generally fed by hope or conviction. But during periods of massive change and disruption, there is usually little hope and almost no conviction. Survival tends to be the order of the day, and survival and ideology are rarely happy companions. Survival normally engenders not compassion but, rather, tough-mindedness and often meanspiritedness. We may have, for example, a positive attitude toward aging, yet hostile attitudes toward the aged.

Ideology in the face of the compulsion to survive is viewed as a luxury that society can ill afford, and it is not uncommonly perceived to be a challenge and an obstruction to survival. Self-interest is consequently the governor: the principal measure of success is who can deliver the goods. Management stresses efficiency and facilitation. It encourages an emphasis on cushioning the effects of change, rather than on effecting change. A statement by an executive of the Department of Health and Human Services in the Reagan administration makes the case. He was quoted in the *New York Times* as saying that the early managers of the health maintenance organizations (HMO's) were "more concerned with doing a social good than with providing a return on investment," pointing out that they were not well suited to managing multimillion-dollar enterprises. The cliché that the way to achieve success is by lowering expectations may not be far off the mark. As a matter of fact, our most exciting recollections are often of magnificent failures, particularly since successes rarely fulfill our expectations and are often achieved by depressing or at least practical and unexciting compromises, which are usually dull and unsatisfying.

It is clear that people tend to be influenced more by their fears than by their hopes and, consequently, fear may be a stronger organizational force for action and unity than hope, which inspires loyalty and commitment. This may explain in part the excessive self-interest of populist (antipolitician) politicians who inflame popular fears and in fact represent a threat to the system.

The complex political climate of these final decades of the twentieth century has resulted in and has also precipitated a number of phenomena and dilemmas. The very complexity of society and its political system has created a "catch 22" in which individual freedom depends on, and can only be expressed through, group identification and through actions set in motion from within institutions and systems, which, in turn, sharpen the conflict faced by individuals seeking to assert and retain their identity. This suggests that individuality and freedom may not be synonymous. Changes have also emerged in the nature of coalitions. In the past, coalitions collected amenable partners in natural and relatively compatible partnership arrangements. Currently, coalitions are frequently unhappy and tenuous collections of disparate, sometimes angry, partners, huddling to govern or survive. While we are governed locally and nationally by majorities and seek to conform to collective behavior, we are influenced by special-interest minority groups, and frequently seek their approbation and support.

A comparable dilemma is created by the consumer and client control issue. Conflict is frequently created rather than controlled in the face of competing constituent preferences—as in the case of community, parent, or teacher interests. Similar conflicts are reinforced and universalized as institutions assume traditional family functions, and secondary contacts supersede primary contacts. One comes to live one's life through surrogate instruments. From another perspective, this conflict and accompanying dilemma are played out on a further important stage as we observe loyalties to professions and occupations taking precedence over political and territorial considerations.

Related to these phenomena is the tendency in a society such as our own, which is increasingly consumer- rather than citizen-oriented, for a privilege or benefit, once granted, to be perceived as a right that subsequently cannot be withdrawn without impunity. Seniority, civil service status, tenure, and other job protection devices, which are introduced in part to provide freedom and maintain individuality, are in the final analysis used to preserve security.

In the wake of the initial evangelistic fervor for an accelerated rate of involvement to overcome technological and bureaucratic detachment, and as a programmatic measure to increase productivity and enhance quality control, consumers and workers have reduced their demands. What they ultimately accept as desirable and workable is the opportunity to comment on, react to, and exert influence over the process and product through participation and through creating a sense of community as the means to achieve satisfaction and improve performance, rather than through seeking either an exercise of authority or the right of decision making. Consequently, it is not power that is at stake. At issue are method, process, performance, service, and product. From this vantage point, process, policy, and planning precede sanction and inform decision making, in contrast to the more traditional assumption that policy, planning, and programming follow and flow from sanction. In this spirit, decision making becomes a democratic and participatory process, with clear, undivided, and fixed authority.

A number of patterns have been established to achieve administrative and management control, as well as to reconcile the relative advantages of large- and small-scale organization for encouraging new technologies and preserving individual influence over the massive systems that affect them. To achieve these purposes, some countries—France being a dramatic illustration—have tended toward centralization and nationalization of public activities and enterprises and decentralization of the private sector. In the United States, as well as in many other countries, the reverse tendency has operated. The private sector has tilted nationally and centrally, and the public sector has begun to reverse a historic centralizing trend.

The social implications of slums and blight may be more significant than their structural and spatial connotations. In a substantial number of instances, the slum designation is applied to areas with presumed social disorganization, and less frequently to areas where social organization is present and potent, even though the respective areas have comparable rates of physical deterioration. This may account for the fact that ethnic areas are generally left intact.

Poverty is like cancer—it is a word describing and characterizing the unknown. Many common symptoms obscure differences and blur distinct diverse causes, effects, and remedies. The understanding and treatment of poverty require more sophisticated classification and diagnosis, which, in turn, would permit careful and appropriate prognosis and response. Additionally, there is a national ambivalence and schizophrenia about ways of remedying poverty in the U.S.; proposed policy, plan, and program approaches are alternately based on John Kenneth Galbraith's *Affluent Society* or on Michael Harrington's *Other America*. The ambivalence is reflected in programmatic responses that seek either to build bridges or to build walls among and between territorial groupings, communities, socioeconomic classes, organizations, and activity systems. Critical ambivalences also exist between public- and private-sector approaches to problem resolution. Increasingly, however, the gap between these alternatives is narrowing, if not closing. Further, it is becoming apparent that removing institutional and systemic obstacles and blockages to individual and group self-improvement may be more important than programmatic interventions to create and promote affirmative opportunities.

Another commonly held view requires refinement in the face of a growing national experience. Upon careful examination, integrated communities are likely found to be biracial, i.e., made up of racial groups residing in segregated modules or subunits, living side by side but in isolation from each other. The instances of integration on a building-by-building or block-by-block basis, as in the case of Hyde Park–Kenwood in Chicago, are indeed rare.

The issues discussed in this book are organized around themes reflecting the local and regional patterns of settlement, and the forms of social, spatial, and administrative organization likely to shape and influence the character of urban development going into the twenty-first century. The focus and stress are on public and private intervention and on the changing relationships among these sectors; on the interplay between the bodies of available knowledge and human service mechanisms and instruments introduced to enhance their delivery; and on the means by which governing capacity, and citizen and consumer roles, can be strengthened and reinforced.

This volume incorporates and seeks to integrate the demonstrably relevant themes that increasingly comprise the policy and planning agenda and challenge, by drawing on the planning, social welfare, and urban-regional fields. These themes are of concern to faculty and students; to public and private practitioners in administrative, managerial, and policy and planning positions at various geographic levels; to those engaged in the human services, social welfare, and economic and community development activity areas; and to thoughtful citizens, public officials, and lay leaders.

The book deals with the range of public and private interventions and the changing character of human settlement patterns, issues that are woven throughout the ensuing chapters. The chapters synthesize and reflect on the form and quality of change, on its widespread relevance and applicability, and on the emerging urban and metropolitan realities.

The Dictionary of the Social Sciences (1978) as well as other dictionaries generally define *metropolis* as the largest city of an area having economic and social dominance. This contrasts with the term *metroplex*, which is widely used in the Dallas–Fort Worth area. The term apparently surfaced in connection with the vast communications network fanning out from Dallas–Fort Worth. Recently it has been used to describe the highly urbanized counties and contiguous areas including and surrounding the central cities, along with the urbanizing collar counties and adjacent hinterland. This volume builds on the latter usage in both a metropolitan and regional context with particular stress on the associated spatial and social systems.

CHAPTER 2

The Urbanization Mosaic

The Development of the Modern Metropolis

The origin of the modern city can be traced to the latter part of the nineteenth century, and more particularly to the industrial age. Dramatic and spectacular changes in the economy created new institutional forms and occupations as well as new divisions and consolidations of labor. Fresh relationships emerged in the character of development and of ownership, in the distribution of power, and in and among spatial, economic, and social activities and patterns. The demands and problems created by the expanding populations and industries that flocked to the cities outstripped the solutions provided by governmental, political, social, and institutional facilties that attempted to cope with their effects and consequences. The virtual absence of infrastructure and of any semblance of order in residential and work locations and relationships and in community support systems compounded an increasingly desperate situation. In only the most elementary sense did a city exist: it was merely a collection of people and activities concentrated in a given place at a fixed moment in time.

The industrialized city, with its belching smokestacks, open sewers, and tenements, led to the birth of a distinctive "culture." The dramatic effects of urbanization gave rise to a growing consciousness and capacity seeking to bring order out of chaos. Governmental institutions were created and strengthened to extend and consolidate the range of municipal government. In New York City, for example, public works and public-health measures were introduced; fire and housing regulations were adopted and enforced by stages; mass transit began to influence the distribution of population and create new patterns of human settlement;

9

social and other related support services emerged largely through voluntary efforts such as settlement houses; and public education took root, as did other institutions that combined to forge and develop the culture of the contemporary city. It was during this period, before and after the turn of the century, that large waves of immigrants who helped fuel and sustain the insatiable demands of industrialization flowed into the cities and were socialized there, imprinting the demography and the political, social, and occupational structures for decades to follow as well as contributing in profound ways to the process of urbanization.

The major economic and propertied interests treated the city in large part as a wasting asset, a neglect that only exacerbated the obsolescence and deterioration of its spatial environment, its buildings, and its capital value. These circumstances provoked an increasingly militant social and political reaction to the human condition in the cities and to the inequities of the economic system. Governmental policies and practices designed to alleviate slum conditions and address economic inequities seemed inadequate and unresponsive to the problems they attempted to solve. The private plant and the public plant were both in disrepair, and the modest sums being expended in both sectors fell far short of the amount needed for modernization. Nevertheless, people continued to live in the cities, with only small-scale movement to the periphery of an as yet undefined metropolitan area.

An increase in immigration from the South to the North and from rural to urban places, a process that would continue and grow, exerted new pressures on the central city. At the same time, first-generation American offspring of the earlier massive waves of immigration added to these pressures in their desire to achieve financial success, break out of ethnic enclosures, and establish traditional relationships and living arrangements in marriage, family, and neighborhood.

Neither the local nor the federal government was prepared to meet the demands and expectations of the growing urban population, nor could they remedy the increasingly evident social and economic dysfunctions of an industrial society. In addition, the government seemed incapable of stimulating the private sector to do its part in making the cities livable and economically viable. The Great Depression that followed the 1929 economic collapse turned the growing problems of the cities into a national crisis and created a readiness to challenge and modify traditional social relationships and values. The rights, functions, and responsibilities of citizens, business and industry, government at all levels, and voluntary associations such as unions had to be rethought.

Of the many changes that evolved during the long years of the depression in the 1930s, the most important for the future urbanization in America was the great expansion of the role of the federal government under the leadership of President Roosevelt. His New Deal won the general support of the public in this time of crisis, and the new government programs enabled the country to cope with its growing population and other pressures bearing down on it. Immigrant and first-generation Americans were given a much larger measure of hope for access to the new middle class. During the 1930s the government fundamentally altered and enlarged its functions and substantially modified inter-relationships among individuals, the private sector, and the public sector. Though a relatively orderly revolution in fundamental social relations was accomplished within the democratic framework of the government, unforeseen consequences—not to be recognized until after World War II—were generated.

The government, especially the federal government, had fashioned a series of new public interventions, approaches, and strategies. These initiatives shifted the balance of power toward government and individuals organized in voluntary associations, and away from industry and business. By strengthening the means and increasing the opportunities available to the individual to operate as part of a union or other voluntary group, government policies had altered the duties and powers of individual citizens. Now there were new social groupings, new relationships among federal, state, and local levels of government. Not only did the federal government take vigorous initiative in these activities, but in the process, government at the local level was strengthened at the expense of the states. In the more than fifty years that have elapsed since 1930 we have had ample opportunity to experience, if not fully to understand, the transformations in our society and in the process of urbanization that in large measure were accomplished by the forces set in motion during the New Deal.

From the perspective of urbanization, the New Deal created a more active and interventionist role for the central government in restoring the collapsed economy and in sustaining and extending its recovery. The new mechanisms established to perform these functions were large bureaucracies that would soon become in practice a fourth branch of government. Expanded old departments or newly created bureaucracies with major responsibilities in the life of the nation attracted people with the professional skills and personal characteristics needed to accomplish a peaceful revolution in the most ethnocentric nation on earth. The result was a new alliance, if not an amalgamation, among the professional governmental employee, the academic specialist, and the expert bureaucrat. This professional-intellectual-governmental-political coalition has been largely responsible for urban-related programs in the last forty years. Part of the complexity and confusion that exist in current metropolitan policy results from the diverse intervention strategies worked out by competing administrative-professional groups and operational sub-specializations. These bureaucrat-professionals now constitute a number of pressure groups that have a significant effect on urban and metropolitan policy.

The New Deal's stress on public works as a job-creating device had an immediate and lasting effect. Most of these public works were urban oriented and thus helped to modernize the urban plant, add to the supply of housing and other critical facilities, and focus attention on the city itself and on its needs for social action. Related to these public-works measures were the programs for home financing, stimulating economic recovery and family and community support. Public-works and housing programs, introduced to combat the economic depression, later became important linchpins in an emerging national urban policy that fostered metropolitan-wide development and suburbanization to serve the needs of the wave of veterans returning from World War II.

When the war ended, vast numbers of veterans came to the cities in search of opportunities, full of hope and energy. The educational programs made possible by the G.I. Bill of Rights helped retrain them and served to delay their entry into the labor markets. Many potential problems related to the sudden demobilization of millions of servicemen were avoided by the programs set up at the conclusion of the war. These programs, especially the housing and suburban developments that directly affected the cities, also helped to stimulate the economy. The housing assistance programs helped create an effective demand, and in speeding people from the old central city into outlying areas, they did relieve some pressures and help to create modern living environments that met market demand at the time. These and other government programs enabled people to act on their ambitions, and as a result of the spectacular increase in family formation there was set in motion a process of expectation and action, of unfilled need and demand, that led to even more support for massive public-works programs, school construction, consumer goods, new consumption patterns, and the like.

The decline of the cities that had begun prior to World War II continued after the war. Some central-city locations proved to be exempt, however. These areas, often near major institutions and other valued central-city areas, in many cases received federal and local support and frequently were home to homogeneous ethnic or upper-middle-class communities.

By the 1950s a national urban-suburban policy had evolved. Its four directives called for: (1) reconstruction of the central city; (2) stimulation of suburban development in the metropolitan area surrounding the central city; (3) facilitation of metropolitan growth and expansion through financial support, assistance, and outright subsidies to consumers, builders, and financial institutions; and (4) the creation and extension of supportive services and facilities through the availability of substantial aid to individual localities. All four tasks were enmeshed in an administrative and political network that accomplished much but created a legacy of complicated practices and policies.

The social and economic pressures on the cities resulting from the new population mix were perceived as dysfunctions according to the traditional urban models and norms. No doubt the city's physical plant was outmoded; it was obsolete and unsatisfactory as either a good residential environment or as efficient industrial and commercial space. When it could not provide low-density housing and adequate facilities the population eventually turned to areas outside the central city. Though these negative circumstances in fact provided positive opportunities to reshape the central city, the changes were generally seen as problems rather than opportunities. The traditional theoretical views tended to emphasize the negative impact of the deteriorating urban environment rather than to look positively toward a new metropolitan urban system.

Now people were sorting themselves out across a metropolitan-wide spectrum of geographic areas and social groupings. Physical movement and social mobility combined to aid in the formation of new neighborhoods and communities, new subsettlements, and new living and working arrangements. The traditional governmental and administrative structures and policies lagged behind. Inadequate attention was paid to the abandoned and bypassed areas (and populations) in the historically dominant homestead and central-city heartland. The processes that were modifying and altering the patterns of city life which had reached maturity over the preceding seventy years were also generating new social and spatial groupings imprinting the future metropolitan city. Different interventions were also emerging, and particular professions, including planning, were assigned pivotal roles in dealing with the problems of the new metropolis.

The New Subregional Reality

The population shifts that took place within the nation's metropolitan areas in the decades immediately following World War II were part of a continuum—stages integral to the urbanization process.

The postwar period saw a concentration of the population in the three major coastal areas of the United States as well as in the Great Lakes region, the growth of the major metropolitan areas, and an increase in population in the parts of the metropolitan areas that lay outside the city. These phenomena began to moderate, however, and by the 1970s the modifications became statistically significant. People were beginning to seek out new, less developed areas offering growing job opportunities. Changes in value systems were refashioning public and private policies, and new forms of transportation and communication were not only shortening travel time and cutting costs, but were also combining to alter traditional locational preferences.

A new urban profile was taking shape. Population flow was no longer dominated by earlier directional movements. New job-generating facilities and installations were attracting people to the sun belt—often to landlocked areas of the country—to the low density and mountainous states, and to the relatively smaller urban metropolitan areas. These locations no longer mean withdrawal to a "bucolic" existence; in most cases they provide easy access either to the individual's former metropolis or to a nearly equivalent substitute. As transportation and communication improve, the psychological distance will shrink further, especially as distance comes to be defined as the energy consumed rather than the travel time elapsed.

The new locations provide a substantial diversity of activities, and new options in housing, jobs, and recreation. They have often become part of a galaxy of related centers, often less than 100 miles apart (about 1½ hours on the interstate highway systems). Each center assumes specialized and distinctive roles that are to some extent comparable to the multicentered character developing within the major metropolitan areas themselves. The collection of small urban centers and the multinucleated metropolitan subcenters is the twenty-first–century metroplex that provides citizens with opportunities to develop different lifestyles in new environmental settings. In the metroplex the new arrivals do not have to abandon their careers or interests.

These population shifts have exacerbated the problems of the older regions of the country, particularly the Northeast and the Middle West, and have had an especially negative impact on the major central cities, which are their prime victims. A metropolitan/metroplex configuration has been emerging which will constitute the urban spatial profile for much of the next century. The scale and complexity of the problems of the older central cities began to emerge with the mass movement of population from the central city to the outlying areas. In part, the consequences of the movement were obscured by the influx of new lower-income population, and when even this flow stopped, the problems in the inner city became painfully visible. Public programs (highways, urban renewal, etc.) that displaced central city neighborhoods and residents were a traumatic experience for the relocatees and sometimes even worsened the problems by increasing the flow of financially viable families and businesses out of the city. The general migration into the major metropolitan areas overshadowed the huge losses of central city populations to the outlying sectors of the metropolitan areas that were occurring almost simultaneously. In addition, the disparities between the central city and the outlying areas were observable and demonstrable with respect to nearly all social, economic, and fiscal yardsticks: individual and family income, educational years achieved, per capita tax yields, welfare and dependency, etc.

The financial and administrative crises faced by major cities in the late 1970s included a relative loss of tax-yield and income-producing sources; a continuing need to maintain, replace, and expand capital plants and facilities; an increase in costs of housekeeping services; and a heightened demand for services reflecting both rising levels of expectation and the pressing needs of the impoverished new arrivals. These fiscal burdens were not offset by compensating inflows of reliable and consistent new revenues that could attract and sustain the necessary political support. The situation was exacerbated by outmoded administrative, fiscal, and management practices; sweetheart agreements between the financial institutions and city hall; and the frequent use of public employment as an instrument of welfare policy to promote equity rather than governmental and institutional efficiency. The sheer magnitude of the population movement from the central city to the suburbs, and even from the older, close-in suburbs to more distant ones, was of critical importance. The movement was even more telling because the people leaving belonged to a relatively more affluent population—better educated and trained, family-oriented people at the productive period of their lives. The aged and other dependent populations became a larger percentage of those left in the city, and they were augmented by needy in-migrants from the farms, the small places, and the South, all seeking to make their way. Thus by the 1970s (and certainly by the 1980s) in many older urban areas of the country, population in the outlying metropolitan areas either matched or exceeded that of the central city, and job opportunities increased in the outlying areas in dramatic numbers. For many metropolitan areas in the 1970s, jobs were moving out of the central city faster than people. On the whole the city became the place of residence (work was either not available or available only by a reverse commute) for blacks, for the aged, for the lower-income and poor, and for middle- and high-income populations living in selected communities. Further, the black communities faced the prospect of a rising percentage of teenagers, very high black teenage unemployment rates, and a higher rate of crimes committed by teenagers. An increasing number of dependent families in the central city were locked into the welfare syndrome.

The basic shape, function, and character of the historical central city was taken as the standard that had to be preserved, revived, or re-created at all costs. The social scientists who put forward this view found ready advocates among the urban practitioners, especially the planners. Urban social science presented a theoretical model lodged in the past; the actual changes that were occurring were so far-reaching in scale and character that they simply could not be explained by or adapted to prevailing theory and practice. The result frequently was a perception of metropolitanization as proof of the decay of the central city and as serving no good purpose; it was often a call to action to extend public works and redevelopment facilities in pursuit of a city vanishing into history.

Until well into the 1970s, a persistent and continuous conflict was generated between two powerful antagonistic urban constituencies. On one side were the legislators, bureaucrats, and private developers seeking to serve a large part of the population that was creating the suburban housing market. On the other side were large numbers of wage earners and their families seeking housing, facilities, and an environment within the existing central city, but demanding new laws, policies, and developments to enhance the quality of life. Soon the vast numbers of people who voted with their feet and their wallets in favor of the suburbs became too powerful to be ignored. The partisans of the old central city perceived this migration as a tremendous danger and sought to restore the city to its former glory. They continued to conceive of the city and respond to its problems as if it were still the focal point, the spatial, social, and functional center of the metropolitan area. But a new metroplex world and a new function for the old central city were in the making.

Federal and local public policies and the private marketplace fed and fostered the concept of metropolitanism, flying in the face of the prevailing academic and practical wisdom that focused on the old central-city model. Public measures and generous financial aid tended to champion metropolitan initiatives, while central-city programs generally attracted only modest and occasional public interest, and therefore drew only limited and narrowly targeted financial support. The metropolitan transformation has continued until it is no longer deniable.

The new metropolitan/metroplex city represents a dramatically different pattern of urbanization in the face of an evolving twentieth- and twenty-first–century welfare and technological age and a sharply changing spatial, demographic, economic, social, and political landscape. Academics have now begun to turn their attention toward understanding the new metropolitan/metroplex reality by creating theories that assign new roles to what was formerly the central city. It has become clear that to look forward to a new future with only a backward-looking theoretical stance will not help us to understand the new forms of human settlement that we are creating.

The long-held assumption was that the movement of population and activities out of the central city simply multiplied and thickened the concentrations in the outlying areas, without altering the fundamental nature of the central city or its outlying parts. From this fiercely held assumption the view persists that while the redistribution of people and activities has created a beleaguered city being bled socially and economically, the central city has maintained its pivotal position. The redistribution has simply complicated the task of central-city command and control of the region. From this perspective the city continues to oversee a vastly expanding and complex empire, but with fewer weapons and assets. Consonant with this point of view, the central city is seen as requiring new and improved administrative and management forms and structures to guide and influence growth over areas extending beyond its traditional corporate limits and power on the assumption that it continues to sustain and spawn suburban jurisdictions. The very pairing of the words *city* and *suburb* embodies this view and reflects the outdated perception of the relationship between the central city and the outlying areas.

The small suburban enclave no longer exists as a semiautonomous political jurisdiction with narrow concerns over limited facility requirements and municipal housekeeping provisions and maintenance. Rather, what has begun to take shape as people and activities have moved outward are a series of relatively self-contained and self-sufficient decentralized regional units. Each of these regional units approximates a modified city; all are linked together in a galaxy of interdependent relationships and are inexorably dependent one upon the other. Although each such "subcity" has no fixed and definable boundary or outer limit, since one bleeds into another, they are all generally organized around a major regional shopping center and increasingly include the entire spectrum of uses conventionally associated with a city.

The major regional shopping centers are located concentrically, at each of the strategic points of the metropolitan compass; they contain fine department stores and specialty shops and constitute a decentralized mini-downtown. In nearly every major city the first ring of land development has been completed, and frequently the second and even the third ring as well. Each of these regional subcities constitutes a focal point encompassing a substantial number of small suburban jurisdictions. Each of these mini-downtowns creates a market shed and an orbit of influence. Within each subcity universe residential growth occurs, and industrial development and job opportunities either newly created or drawn from the central city continue to increase. These subregions, while continuing to be dominated by single-family homes, are beginning to provide a range of housing types that includes high-rise buildings and dense multiple-housing compounds. The areas include hotels, office buildings, hospitals, and colleges. They provide commercial and community theaters, orchestras, newspapers, and nearly all of the activities and characteristics customarily associated with a city.

It is the collection of these subcities that constitutes the metroplex—the new form of human settlement in the United States. The pattern is of a multinucleated central place. The new regional centers are either located along interstate highways or at principal interstate interchanges already in existence or especially created for that purpose. While it is rarely possible to establish the outer limits of a particular subcity, their basic form and reach are clear and demonstrable. Increasingly, each of these subcities includes a spectrum of age groupings. No longer are they made up exclusively of families with young children; they contain high schoolers, single persons, childless couples, and the aged as well. Further, as each of the subregions takes on the character of a diverse city, each assumes distinctive functions that over time will more sharply differentiate them. Each is developing its own modified labor market, reflecting differences in socioeconomic status, educational achievement, economic and job-generating activity, etc. Local jurisdictions (towns, villages, and cities) now represent lower-echelon cells within the subregions themselves. The subregional configuration offers a special set of governance problems and presents an imposing challenge to functional integration, service delivery, and administration.

Special problems of communication and transportation are posed both by the scale of metropolitan development and by its decentralized and multinucleated character. No economic and efficient systems have yet emerged to accommodate these new patterns with feasible mass transit solutions, given the scope, diversity, and distribution of functions and activities. To develop a transportation network for a monolithic and highly centralized region with a prevailing central city orientation requires substantial augmentation if it is to accommodate the flows between neighborhoods and communities within the central city and the outlying subcities (particularly those connecting inner-city populations with new job-generating facilities); the flows among subcities, the new regional shopping centers, and the office, commercial, and industrial service and employment centers; and the flows within each of the subcities themselves. The transportation network and infrastructure, as in the case of nearly all other capital works and support services, either do not exist at all or exist only primitively and are not joined into a unified and workable system. The concern with jobs and energy has underscored the necessity of finding workable and financially feasible solutions. It is not surprising that transportation represents a first-priority activity in a number of metropolitan jurisdictions. Additionally, even though there is resistance from the taxpayers of many localities, mass transit agencies have been created in a number of metropolitan urban areas, sometimes with the power to tax and to legislate. The crucial question of transportation dramatizes the connectiveness of the new metropolitan settlement fabric, whose functioning depends on the flow of people, goods, and services among and between all of its territorial parts.

Beyond the loss in population, and the socioeconomic changes in the character of its distribution, the basic function and role of the central city have been undergoing major changes. Substantial parts of the city's land areas are vacant and bypassed. They are either not needed to accommodate population demands or are in locations that do not generate a market interest. A signficant amount of housing is abandoned or deteriorating, and industries and jobs continue to leave the city. The central city is finding it necessary to make its adaptation, traumatic as the process is, to the new urban and metropolitan pattern of human settlement. Many of its dysfunctions are the by-products of this adaptive process. In a profound sense, the city is not disintegrating, but rather is being reshaped by the forces of urban change.

The city has lost particular kinds of activities that have not been able to survive technologically in their current sites and forms or have been seduced to other more appropriate or preferred locations. The city has been becoming a more specialized place, rather than an all-purpose place. Statistical surveys have confirmed the city's role as a specialized service center. The city's growth industries have been its office, financial, educational, and health- and hospital-related activities. While its retail role has undergone a major change as a result of the growing importance of the regional centers, the city has continued to retain an important specialty role. Even more important, it has been able to take on the characteristics of a regional shopping center with its own captive market shed of service, often at the expense of the older community centers, particularly those within the inner city. The city has been becoming a subcity in its own right, similar in many respects to the outlying subcities—although on a jumbo scale, and with notable distinctions and exceptions.

In lieu of the prior dependent relationship of the suburban jurisdiction on the central city, each of the clusters of suburban jurisdictions comprising a particular subregion exists in an interdependent relationship with the central city. It had been the case, and a popular misconception continues, that while the suburbs could not exist without the central city, the reverse was not true, except insofar as the suburbs constituted a labor-force storage area. With the profound changes in the nature of human settlement, however, the central city—itself now a modified subregion—is as dependent on the outlying subregions as these subregions are on the central city.

Part of this new relationship has also resulted in a shift in the city's historical role from that of importer and consumer of people, to that of exporter of jobs and people. The city is no longer the principal means and ladder by which people fulfill their aspirations. These changes have fundamentally altered the nature of the housing market, as well as the linkage among all other major components of the metropolitan system. The social structure, the economy, and the service delivery network need to be perceived and understood in terms of this metropolitan framework. These phenomena also establish the basis for preserving and restoring the central city. While we hear often about the "planned shrinkage" of the central city, it is more appropriate to say that the city needs to adapt to an achievable threshold of development consistent with these metropolitan realities. It is far more realistic for a city to set its growth and restoration sights on a future consistent with its emerging specialized character than to operate on the basis of its prior commanding role and position.

These facts, combined with the obsolescence and deterioration of its public and private plant, facilities, and infrastructure, as well as its archaic taxing and financing policies and practices, have exacerbated the problems of the central city. The burdens on the one hand have bedeviled the central cities, and on the other hand have prompted rallying cries that have been utilized to create and reinforce existing and new markets. City planners have sought to turn older neighborhoods, areas, and structures into assets, and to help them achieve a certain social distinction. Leaders have pursued a strategy of social specialization to match the city's distinctive and specialized economic strategy. In some locations the city has succeeded in attracting and holding populations at particular periods in their life cycle, making it possible for those with common needs and interests—the singles, childless couples, those with distinctive life styles and behavior patterns—to congregate into islands of mutual support. Concomitantly, the costs of new construction, the decline in energy resources, and changing life styles have combined to provide the city with added opportunities in certain preferred locations to turn its aging plant into a highly inhabitable and marketable commodity.

However, despite these evidences, the efforts are severely limited in scope. The effect of metropolitanization has been devastating. Despite the strong specialized service role for the central city and the very substantial growth and construction thereby generated, the central city has not yet succeeded in making the necessary spatial accommodations to the new form of metropolitan settlement. This despite the restoration and revitalization of the central-city core that are under way in many older localities. These latter activities tend to be taking place in highly distinctive neighborhoods, generally along or near waterfront areas, institutions, mass transit connections, transportation interchanges, open spaces, or in relation to major retail, commercial, or office activity centers. All too frequently, city leaders have adopted policies that have sought to reestablish the central city's former grandeur while failing to accept the new reality and to fashion functional roles consistent with it. City officials have often refused to accept defensible developmental levels of construction and reconstruction consonant with the total metropolitan social and economic market envelope. The restoration and revival opportunities would be enhanced if the changes being experienced were perceived as occasions to modernize and humanize the city, rather than as obstacles to re-creating its prior image. There is the added burden in the central city of replacing worn-out parts and accommodating to new population distributions and social groupings, to new roles and functions, and to spatial adjustments resulting from changes in land, building, density, and use requirements.

The fact is that despite the glamorous construction and restoration taking place in and near the core of the older central cities, deterioration is continuing and social and physical decline are occurring at a pace that is outstripping the capacity and commitment that are necessary to reverse the downward course. It has been suggested, though, that the city is becoming obsolete more rapidly than it is deteriorating. The older central cities have not succeeded in coping with and accommodating to the tremendous population and activity losses which they experienced in the decade of the seventies. The maldistribution of taxation among the diverse levels of government and the inequitable share of revenue available to the central cities are further exacerbated by measures to reduce local taxes as an incentive for private development. The local burdens are compounded by the added inequities borne by the older cities and regions, pyramiding the local encumbrances and further penalizing localities in need.

For some time to come the cities will be forced to modernize and adapt their plant, facilities, and functions while simultaneously servicing and meeting the needs of the poor, the aged, and the unskilled—and to do so in the face of a narrowing economic base, an unreceptive tax and institutional structure, and a resistant market. The inevitable tension that is the by-product of accommodation and modernization further complicates the situation.

The symptoms of change—e.g., abandoned housing and vacant retail space—are perceived to be the causes of the change. In the face of this erroneous perception the course of treatment prescribed seeks to reconstitute the central city through promotions, tax reduction, and programs of population and social control. What went before is endowed with an intellectual validity. These patterns, instead of being perceived as functionally appropriate to their time and adapted to the economic and social circumstances to which they were related, are imbued with absolute value, and changes represent deviations and dysfunctions demanding prescription and remedy. This attitude is further strengthened by the fact that settled prior patterns are at their maturity—in contrast to the inevitable fluidity and uncertainty that change will bring. They are appealing in their seeming logic and degree of refinement. In time the so-called symptoms are recognized as normative. Only then are programs and attitudes refashioned and fresh and creative public and private interventions introduced. But this stage is reached only after the city and its residents undergo a traumatic experience.

Planning for the New Urban Constituency

The blacks and Spanish-speaking groups are taking control of the older central cities. They are largely first- and second-generation populations. They are creating their own institutions and communities and are asserting political power. The blacks and the Spanish-speaking groups are frequently viewed as a threat to the prevailing normative order, as were earlier ethnic groups, and their behavior is often criticized as dysfunctional and in need of remedial action. The fact is, however, that these groups are as important to the city's restoration, adaptation, and modernization as were the earlier waves of immigrants.

The new social agglomerations who make up so much of the central city—the young people, singles, childless couples, and those who share life styles sharply different from those of the general population—are new urban pioneers, valuing inner-city locations and perceiving diversity and heterogeneity as positive market assets. They cluster in particular communities and imprint these communities with their distinctive styles, which in turn attract specialized retail and other services that often have an appeal that extends to the wider market. The areas in which these population groups locate also usually attract an elderly population with limited financial resources. These groups of citizens are joined by families returning to the city for a variety of reasons, and by couples who have completed the task of family rearing. The latter groups compete for space with the "urban pioneers" and, given their financial resources, usually prevail. Some locate in "uncharted" areas, replacing relatively poorer populations in deteriorated, now gentrified structures; others locate in nontraditional settings, as, for example, in loft buildings converted to residential use.

The prospect exists that new political alliances will be forged between the ethnic groups predominating in the city and these new and diverse social groups. Together they hold great promise for the city's future restoration. In the short run, however, the upwardly mobile aspirations of the black and Spanish-speaking populations are in conflict with the forces that threaten to displace them from their neighborhoods and to limit their access to other neighborhoods and communities. The highly successful attempts by more powerful social groups to capture and improve inner-city areas have usually meant the displacement of poor and minority populations, even when there is an effort to maintain or create a heterogeneous community. Private and public attempts to discourage white flight from the central city and to achieve stability and maintain the quality of housing usually take place in blue collar and lower-middle-income areas beyond the inner ring of the central city—the very areas that the upwardly mobile minority populations look to in the desire for self-improvement.

The inner-city communities, with their vacant land and structures, are viable places to develop housing. They are often in attractive, strategic locations. Restoring and re-creating communities can be the occasion to refashion the central city to meet new needs and new missions. The opportunity exists to stress the merit and advantage of diversity and heterogeneity as positive assets and attractions in a creative market strategy, rather than to see them as obstacles, dysfunctions, or threats.

Re-created inner-city communities are likely to be developed as more compact and diverse urban centers, and the activities that emerge in them are likely to reflect new pressures and new patterns. We can anticipate a growth in home occupations, for example, and changes in the arrangement of living space will be an inevitable response.

Territorial sectors with commonly shared market characteristics and defensible geographic limits will deemphasize and replace the traditional neighborhood and community as the operational planning unit. Spatial modules will prescribe or circumscribe activity centers and reconcile administrative districts to achieve economies and efficiencies and enhance governing capacity. These districts may over time assume the characteristics of a community. The immediate problem faced by the central city is the need to add to or modernize its job-generating facilities and to refashion its management and financial practices and systems. In both the public and private sector, plant facilities and infrastructure tend to be obsolete, even when not deteriorated, and they are dependent on labor-intensive use. The city will inevitably seek to reduce its dependence on labor through the introduction of new efficiencies and economies and through an increased reliance on technology and improved management techniques and practices. All these steps are necessary components in a systematic program of survival; however, the brunt of the required accommodation and transformation for the central city—in both the public and private sectors—and the painful effects on its citizens are likely to be extended and intense for some period of time.

Administering the Metropolitan System

Beyond the fundamental changes that have occurred in the nature of human settlement, in the character of the central city, and in the social, economic, spatial, and demographic patterns, it is important to take note of the organizational and administrative forms that have developed to manage, serve, and facilitate the functioning of the newly emergent metropolitan system. These organizational and administrative forms constitute a matrix of relationships across the governmental layers.

Our management capacity is profoundly challenged by our inability to exercise control and to rationalize the system. This is due to the distribution of population and activities over ever-expanding geographies and their consolidation into complex and interconnected configurations. The growth in the knowledge base promises benefits that are tantalizing.

In confronting the spread of population and the growth in functions and services, administration and distribution become imposing tasks. Historically, in this country we have relied on a formal governing system distributed spatially and hierarchically for the performance of these tasks. If we were to place an overlay of existing governing units onto the newly emergent pattern of human settlement, we would be struck by the profound discontinuity between the settlement patterns and the governing instruments that exist to manage the network. It is not surprising, therefore, that the dichotomy between market and functional activity areas is substantial, and that the gap between problem formulation and the governing universe necessary to comprehend and manage these problems is almost unbridgeable. Governance implies a horizontal capacity to assert command and control across the range of functions at each governmental tier, within a system of hierarchically nested governmental layers. The dichotomy and threat to governance are compounded by the growth of the professions, the functional bureaucracies, and the plethora of organizations and administrative agencies that have been created to deliver the benefits promised by science and technology. Elaborate and massive networks have emerged in connection with each major function—health, education, economic development, transportation, and environment, among others. They are fueled by legislative and budgetary enactments and appropriations. Each is supported by political, legislative, and beneficiary and citizen constituencies, and by their own captive professional and lay organizations and publications. Each such functional activity system cuts the range of governments vertically and commands loyalties to the functional system equaling or exceeding the loyalties to the government of which they are a part.

These phenomena undermine horizontal, ergo executive capacity, and make difficult if not impossible the integration of functions to achieve governmental purposes or to serve citizens at each governing tier. This functional and vertical "bias" extends across the new settlement pattern without regard to geography, territory, or political jurisdiction, diluting formal governing capacity. The challenge in government is to affirm political jurisdiction and assert horizontal capacity; the challenge to professional and bureaucratic power is to affirm their functional supremacy and to assert vertical integration. In the case of governance, the question is citizenship; in the case of functional organization, the question is consumerism. The tension between these forces captures the essential conflict posed by government and management control.

As shown in figure 1, it is possible to portray functions, agencies, departments, and other bureaucratic entities vertically, organizing them around particular subjects and activities (health, education, manpower, economic development, etc.) and to show diverse layers of government cutting horizontally across the functions.

The matrix is further complicated if it is perceived as representing an overlay superimposed at the local level on the expanded and nucleated metropolitan urbanization pattern and at the national level on the shifting, extended, and redistributed regional settlement profile. This latter situation, which has enlarged the scope and complexity of territories, has not moderated the impact and validity of the matrix but, rather, has compounded the governing, administrative, and management challenge over vast spaces. Accordingly, the metropolitan and regional patterns have expanded the needed reach of management, administration, and organizational systems and have stretched and tested the limits of governing capacity.

Mechanisms are proposed either to enhance governing capacity across function or to facilitate administration and management within and among functions in the face of governmental diversity. The downward (vertical) pressures culminate in functional service-delivery systems; the linear (horizontal) pressures aim at creating consolidated service-delivery systems.

Each "vertical" activity represents a functional subsystem, just as each "horizontal" governmental layer represents an element in a governing system. The vertical axis is oriented bureaucratically and professionally, frequently making it necessary for administration to be decentralized. Power, however, is retained centrally at the apex, even as roles and

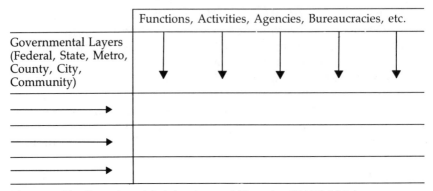

Figure 1. *The Governing, Administering, and Managing (GAM) Matrix*

functions are distributed spatially. The horizontal axis is oriented toward the governing units, with power decentralized "downward" to each governance layer across functions, including as appropriate the neighborhood or community or the suburban jurisdiction.

The vertical and horizontal tugs and pulls can be viewed from a variety of perspectives: as a tension between territory and function, between citizenship and consumerism, between the elective officials and the bureaucrats, between humanism and technology, and between the political and the analytical decision-making processes. These tugs and pulls have complicated the efforts of the executive-administrator, at the top, to comprehend and manage the network and matrix, and those of the consumer-beneficiary, at the bottom, to gain access and navigate the matrix and network and to avail himself of the benefits they promise.

As elaborated in chapter 6, mechanisms have been introduced to facilitate the top-down capacity of the executive-administrator and the bottom-up capacity of the consumer-beneficiary. These include such top-down devices as the coordination, consolidation, expedition, and comprehensive planning of systems and other technologies. Some bottom-up approaches include the use of ombudsmen, advocates, and outreach and information referral programs, and the creation of umbrella devices at the point of service delivery such as neighborhood or community centers, little city halls, and community corporations that sometimes approach a form of microgovernance.

Another means of managing the matrix and overcoming both the horizontal and vertical pressures and the jurisdictional rigidities is to impose an ordering principle on the network that constitutes an organizing theme that by-passes the countervailing pressures portrayed in it. One of four organizing themes is usually adopted to order the system: (1)

a defined territory (a neighborhood or community); (2) a predetermined function assumed to have primacy (i.e., economic development, mental health, education, etc.); (3) a target group to be served (the aged, the young adult, etc.); or (4) a problem or mission (poverty, nutrition, etc.). The selected theme is then imposed on the matrix, and the network reordered to conform to the ordering principle thereby introduced.

While the public sector has been drawn on here to describe and analyze the matrix, and to examine and explore its implications and applications, the matrix and network also have direct applicability to the corporate sector and to the not-for-profit sector, including the major hospitals and voluntary agencies. Comparable illustrations exist in these sectors, and a corresponding experience can be drawn upon to demonstrate the appropriateness of the matrix and network approach.

What surfaces in the efforts to achieve organizational and administrative order and management control is the recognition that while the horizontal and vertical elements are in conflict, constructive efforts at rationalizing the system require that each be addressed and incorporated as critical elements in a unified system. Each are surrogates for valued sets of goals, activities, and desired benefits and end states. The horizontal element represents the democratic will, politics, policy, citizenship, and government without ostensible limits on the absolute right of popular control. The vertical element represents knowledge, professionalism, service, and consumerism, all of which defy containment within governmental tiers or layers. We see the merger between these two forces most dramatically at the point of service delivery. In the public perception, governance and functional performance and delivery intersect and fuse. The range of public and private intervention strategies needs to be considered, and the various policies, plans, and programs must be examined and evaluated within this context.

The discontinuity between our governance structure and the patterns of human settlement at all hierarchical levels is particularly striking. At best, governing units can boast of a chance relationship between their legally prescribed jurisdiction and the actual spatial, social, economic, or market systems. The central city is either too large or too small to make the match between conceptualization and performance; and most of the individual suburban jurisdictions are too small for almost any purpose. The overwhelming number of individual suburbs can at best resist social change, deploy snow plows and garbage trucks, and operate a playground. Schools are the one evident local function performed with skill, largely because of the emotional and financial investment of the parents. However, when suburban bond issues are defeated the school district has no more ability to function without dollars than does the system in the central city.

If the corporate central city is an obsolete form, the corporate sub-urban jurisdiction is an irrelevant one. It is imperative that the problem of governance be examined rationally in the face of the emerging pattern of human settlement. With all of its imperfections, the city generally, over the course of its contemporary history, came close to making itself the functional and governing urban system through annexations and other devices. We now need to define and describe the current metropolitan urban system and its probable course of development and to devise an appropriate governing system. Housing, schools, and all other market issues are out of sync with a city's boundaries. A governing or surrogate form is required that reflects and corresponds to the new metropolitan entity. Formal or informal governing forms are also required—at the outset they are likely to be voluntary and fragmented—to match the subsectors and market sheds within the new metropolitan city. These subsectors will approximate the traditional concept of community. Micro-subdivisions will meet the behavioral, social, and spatial needs that satisfy personal and institutional purposes. The suburban political juris-diction and the central city community already satisfy these require-ments. Macroscales, on the other hand, while important in meeting and solving most problems, tend to be detached and at some distance from the beneficiary. The metropolitan agencies that exist do so at the pleasure of the governing units they seek to influence and coordinate. They are creations of the political constituency they reflect. Generally, they are not a formal part of any single host-governing body, and they have no independent political legitimation. At best, metropolitan planning agen-cies provide a useful platform. As arenas where conflicts can be articu-lated and acted out and differences and interests can be reconciled, they are a force for stability and continuity.

Conclusion

Urbanization is a process as rich as human life and association and is a variety of states, mosaics, and gestalts as well as the portrait of progress. To understand urbanization adequately, it is necessary to expand the limited conception of urbanization and urban areas to include the role played by a wider range of institutions and human activities. Rarely has the city been studied as a total system of complex, interacting parts. Until recently the city was thought both comprehensible and manageable. This was true despite the severity of its problems at any given time, the changes it had undergone at critical historical junctures, and the eco-nomic, social, and political transformations it had experienced during the course of its development. It cannot be narrowly defined in terms of the dominant characteristic of a particular period, like the Industrial Revolution. To limit the study of urbanization to industrial cities is not only to neglect the diversity of the past but to ignore the changes emerging in the "postindustrial" metropolitan/metroplex city systems. Industrialization and urbanization, though intimately associated, can be differentiated across time and place.

The World War II era brought new complexity to American cities. The events and forces at play during the thirties and forties both threatened old social and environmental norms and called forth new policies and principles. Neither the threats nor the policy responses could be easily contained within the limits of theories and conceptions developed through study of the early decades of this century.

The new urban constituencies arising out of the crises of the times and the innovations of the New Deal needed new theories. They found them in a large body of urban scholarship developed by urban theorists drawn primarily from the social sciences. Growing interest in the contemporary industrialized city had been evident in the sharp and dramatic appearance of the field of urban sociology in the 1920s; in the major redirection of attention to the problems of the cities on the part of the fields of anthropology and political science; and in the major leap forward in the scale of intervention and range of attention on the part of the fields of social work, social welfare, and city planning. Ultimately a whole new field of public administration spun off into a set of diversified professions corresponding to the range of public practice areas, including planning, social welfare, public works, municipal finance, taxation, personnel administration, and the like, which not only dealt with the dysfunctions of the city but also sought to influence its growth and directions affirmatively and constructively.

Contemporary studies of cities have generally focused on the factors that have given the city shape or express its character, or on the diverse and varied effects of a constellation of factors at a given moment in time which defined the city at one stage of development. Customarily these studies are approached from various points of view: (1) those of disciplines such as political science, economics, or sociology; (2) of professions such as planning, architecture, engineering, social work, or public administration; (3) of functions or activities such as water or drainage, office or industrial usage, health, education, or transportation; (4) of problems of dysfunction such as welfare and dependency, crime and delinquency, poverty or slums; (5) or of particular populations or institutions such as youth, the aged, or universities.

The critical phenomena that influence urbanization are the parallel and sometimes conflicting pressures to achieve technological change while simultaneously accommodating and responding to human values.

Urbanization phenomena are enmeshed in the sudden shift from an economy of abundance to one of scarcity; from growth to no growth, or controlled and limited growth; and from clearance and redevelopment to preservation, restoration, and conservation. Scarcity and limited resources and capacities sharpen and heighten competition among all activity spheres, between socioeconomic classes, among governmental layers, and between the public and private sectors. Technological achievements are accompanied by rising expectations that create tensions and pressures on the system. The competition for the diminishing supply of resources makes it necessary to develop acceptable allocation instruments to achieve a more equitable, systematic, and objective distribution of resources.

CHAPTER 3

Comprehending and Managing the Urban System

To consider the most appropriate organizational and administrative structures for meeting the problems of "postindustrial" metropolitan city systems is to confront some of the basic issues facing America in the eighties—the need for modernization, the question of allocation and equity, and the form and quality of management and control. In thinking about these questions we confront the specter of "bigness" at every turn. Whether we are dealing with the private sphere or the public sphere—and, indeed, such distinctions are becoming increasingly blurred—it is clear that we must redefine long-held beliefs and free ourselves from symbolic historical attachments to outdated institutional forms.

The challenge is to find viable organizational arrangements able to draw on an ever-increasing pool of knowledge and to stimulate its continued generation, to convert this knowledge into packages of usable goods and services, to develop the administrative mechanisms for their delivery, and to facilitate access to them. This challenge is compounded by the simultaneous need to modernize our "systems" by incorporating and accommodating to continuous change, to respond to the pressure for more equitable allocation of goods and services, and to make defensible allocations of a declining quantity of resources in the face of increased competition for them. These factors sharpen the control questions. They constitute critical considerations that need to be borne in mind when considering issues related to decision making, to questions of centralization and decentralization, to factors involving executive and consumer control, to system and subsystem planning and programming, and to assessing and selecting among quantitative and analytical tools and approaches. To consider either public or private approaches as having inherent merit is a misconception, since neither in their own right provides ready solutions or constitutes easy escape hatches. The public and private sectors are both plagued by these common characteristics.

The Modernization Problem

The issue can be stated simply: how best to modernize without merely safeguarding and sustaining the private sector. Clearly, in the course of determining and adopting the most appropriate path to modernization the private sector has a pivotal role. The private sector represents a set of values that need to be retained and incorporated as an element in both igniting the modernization process and successfully pursuing and undertaking it. But the preservation of the private sector is not a goal in its own right. We have come to recognize that our concerns apply to both the public and the private sectors. The damaging effects that result from scale, specialization, and institutionalization cannot be compartmentalized; they are all-pervasive.

The United States recognized the need to modernize only when it was forced to accept the reality of change and to recognize that its economic position was no longer absolute. The obsolescence that modernization seeks to remedy is largely the consequence of advances in science, technology, and communication, which have become so powerful that modernization has increasingly become the price of industrial and national survival. Competitive pressures, and the need for efficiency and economy, have confronted both the public and private sectors. They have forced governments, agencies, institutions, and private corporations into a massive process of introspection and reexamination, which in many instances has taken on the character of a societal metamorphosis. Despite political rhetoric to the contrary, the obsolescence crisis and the modernization revolution do intrude into all major activity spheres—public, private, and institutional. The costing structure and the survival price can no longer tolerate waste either at the margin due to inefficiencies and irresponsibility or at the core due to the use of outmoded methods instead of new technologies.

The modernization problem that arises from the advance of knowledge and technology is one of the central problems of our time. Responses to the problem through the use of available knowledge and technology are insufficient; many other political and social adaptations are called for. There may be philosophic, tactical, strategic, or pragmatic reasons that suggest a public or private approach to solving modernization problems, but the conceptual and operational dysfunctions stem from the total system and cannot be separated into private or public parts. The requirements for achieving and maintaining environmental quality, and the necessity for conserving and effectively utilizing energy and other pivotal resources that are in diminishing supply, have added to the pressures to modernize. Further, the need to be competitive, and, more fundamentally, the strain to be viable have demanded continued vigilance to eliminate waste caused by inefficiency and to combine cost-saving economies with increases in productivity. Many aspects of modern life show the effects of modernization problems, and as efforts to modernize multiply, ever larger segments of our society will be affected.

Efforts at modernization will continue to affect the size of the labor force needed to keep the system functioning. In addition, it will be necessary to reexamine traditional expenditures in private enterprises and especially in public enterprises to determine what labor costs are not essential and what expenditures have constituted an obscured welfare function to exert either social or political control or have acted to reinforce the upward mobility of segments of the population. It will be increasingly difficult to sustain these practices, and consequently society will need to cushion the probable effects, or can expect to suffer the consequences of increased unemployment.

The need for modernization in the public sector is most clearly evident in our older cities. There the obsolete use of space, the dated physical facilities, the outmoded governmental and organizational structures, and inadequate personnel and administrative practices are matters of general public knowledge. We have come to recognize and accept the fact that if cities are to survive—and the same fact is faced by governments generally—leaders must institute and sustain efforts at restoration, rehabilitation, and preservation; they must question accepted patterns of public finance and be prepared to make necessary changes in tax policy, retirement practices, and lending and payment procedures; and they must generally reexamine and effect necessary changes in personnel practices and management tools. No less important, they must deal with fundamental questions relating to governmental structure, engineering facilities and plant, traffic and transportation, and related problems.

In the so-called private sphere, issues of modernization are also a matter of public knowledge. Private-sector crises have become widely known as a result of recent corporate failures or threatened failures, and the competitive disadvantage of major segments of American business vis-à-vis foreign corporations. The nature of the problems in the private sector, the mechanisms available to deal with them, the conditions and circumstances faced by them as they seek to make needed adaptations and accommodations, the means they are able to draw on, and the terms on which their survival depends if they are to rectify their internal and external dysfunctions are essentially the same as those in the public sector. The differences that distinguish public and private modernization problems are often smaller than those that separate various private enterprises or public agencies.

In both the public and private sectors, the central problems have shifted from arguments over values and broad-gauged goals, to knowledge-related questions. How adequate the knowledge base is for predictive purposes and how to filter, draw from, and integrate a growing and complex body of knowledge to prepare usable information packages are issues open to question. How can policy makers evaluate and select among competing claims of experts promoting diverse approaches based on different knowledge areas? Advocates argue on grounds that assert the prevailing wisdom or the most defensible and documented intervention strategy, or on the assumption that the efficiency of the knowledge base is self-evident and that attention needs to be directed toward securing the popular or political sanctions necessary for its application.

Modernization has meant not only remedying the obsolescence of major types of activity, but profoundly altering fundamental definitions and relationships. Changes are required in all aspects of private and public undertakings, and earlier distinctions such as "private" and "public" are called into question. The specifics of money, time, and energy necessitate making sufficient changes that modify overall systemic relations. Consider the extent of the changes required to introduce new technologies and methods with respect to plant, product, and practice. New physical structures and spatial arrangements, provision for utilities, transportation, and other system components for which the public has responsibility require massive investment. On the private side, modernization in industry or manufacturing demands sophisticated equipment, structural accommodations, and operational and spatial changes affecting efficiency and competitive advantage; in office, retail, and commercial usage and activity it requires location, space provision, and functional arrangement. No industry, commercial or office group, or individual enterprise is unaffected by the need to modernize or is untouched by scientific and technological opportunities.

The pressures on the steel and automobile industries, and even on so contemporary an activity as the space industry, to devote a major part of their effort to a continuous search for an accommodation to technological innovation, demonstrate that stability is no longer a condition of survival and, as a matter of fact, may threaten it. Survival may depend instead on the tension, instability, and uncertainty that result from the continuing search for creative change and the readiness to make adjustments in plant, product, and practice. The implications of such a new reality are far-reaching. They will affect personal, family, and employee freedom and independence as well as institutional continuity and support systems, most particularly in connection with unions and other voluntary associations. Despite their merit, unions, for example, are likely to constrain or obstruct the flexibility and fluidity required by modernization. As a matter of fact, an interesting dilemma is posed by the fact that whereas creative innovation is conventionally assumed to be produced by a stress on the individual or on the small unit with independence and freedom to experiment, to waste, and to fail, modernization and adaptation, on the other hand, are normally more efficiently achieved through highly centralized, more authoritarian organizational forms.

The extensive introduction of scientific approaches to administration in the public, private, and nonprofit sectors is further evidence of the lag that has existed between prevalent practices that have developed over time and the technological innovations and opportunities that demand incorporation and adoption in the face of cost and resource considerations. It is not a coincidence that the M.B.A. and the LL.B. are keys to power, a license to control, and the basis of a new priesthood. Management science and engineering, with their convoluted and complicated methods of personnel selection, programming, and allocation; their mastery of form without substantive knowledge; and their accounting controls and management by objectives (MBO) and cost-benefit and cost-effectiveness measures, are the weapons and rhetoric of the administrative gurus crowding the freshly built skyscrapers contributing to the recent evidence of downtown revival.

It can be demonstrated that the growing interest and success in product, structural, and community preservation and restoration, and the profitability of the nostalgia kick generally, have been made possible largely by the scientific and technological achievements in material provision and production, in more efficient and economic practices, and in the ability to create and sustain existing and new markets. Consequently, the accommodation of mechanization and technology has made possible the recapturing of our heritage. In other words, "simplified" life styles—like the causal look—are only achieved through an inordinately complex effort, and time, resource, and dollar expenditure; complexity is the mother of simplicity.

The need to adopt an "at the ready" stance for purposes of cushioning as well as effecting change has diminished the capacity to anticipate and predict. As we seek to create a climate in which modernization is always being redefined and manifested, and in which adaptation is valued and accepted as normative and endowed with a self-correcting capacity for remedying systemic dysfunctions, the stress shifts from end-state to process forecasting. The focus shifts from a specified end state, whether arrived at morally, ideologically, or analytically, to a process focus that relies on research and development, interaction, and adaptation. In a critical sense, end-state planning inhibits creative adaptation, tends to downplay or overlook the unexpected, and can discourage the inclination or prospect of massive change, despite the usual contrary claims. Although bonds and resolve may be reinforced and commitment secured as goals, values, and principles are strengthened, once end states are specified, the outcome becomes institutionalized—a yardstick against which changes are measured and a source of denial or resistance to subsequent knowledge or experience that may dictate alterations in the predetermined end state.

Modernization, however, extends beyond issues related to adaptations in plant, product, and practice. At a far more profound level, what is at stake is the modernization of the system itself. We see this in the fundamental changes that have occurred in the character and quality of human settlement, and in the massive changes that have developed in the nature and functioning of the marketplace. The demand for modernization reaches throughout the structural and systemic networks of our institutions, associations, and organizations. These intersect with our public and private spatial, social, and economic infrastructure and activities and transform the ways we organize our work, life, and play. The emerging human-settlement patterns and the new market constellation have outmoded the existing physical and social structures and the prevailing market mechanisms. The lag is observed most notably in the declining (and transforming) city and in the widening gap between our traditional governing forms and the population distribution, the residential and functional activity systems, and the support systems that are spread over space. It is these basic systemic structures and their principal components—a whole host of perceptions, conceptions, and relationships—which require examination and modernization.

Seldom, however, do we enter into this reexamination directly, no matter how much we recognize the need to do so or how conscious we are of workable reformulations. We tend to avoid dealing with modernization questions in a forthright manner because to do so would risk intensifying politically damaging conflicts. In a large, complex, and pluralistic society such as ours, we exist in a network of delicately balanced relationships and only reluctantly do we undertake their modification. We avoid seeking large changes at one moment in time, preferring to effect change more slowly, in imperceptible stages. We deliberately devise elaborate schemes and arrangements to do by indirection what we hesitate to do by direction. Thus with direct action deferred, we are allowed time to secure support and achieve sanction. In a critical sense, we are caught up in a desperate dilemma. On the one hand our survival depends on modernization, yet on the other hand modernization requires such heroic initiatives and expenditures that it threatens our way of life, existing political patterns, and entrenched interests. It requires political accommodations, personal adaptation, redistribution of resources, and numerous interventions that seek to alter conventional institutions and systems positively. In many instances these changes are likely to result in dislocation, instability, and disorder. How we should structure such a radical pursuit becomes a critical question, particularly since the burdens of modernization fall inequitably on the poor, the unskilled, and the lower middle class who are least able to pay the emotional and financial price. This hidden modernization tax on the economically disadvantaged is all the more dangerous since society as a whole tends to resist providing the programmatic and financial support required to offset the damage done in the process. The political arguments with regard to modernization consequently become complicated and confused, weaving back and forth between those approaches that focus on achieving modernization and those designed to cushion the side-effects of such change. Ends and means arguments become entangled in interminable debates on the relative merit of such issues as centralization and decentralization, professionalization and participation, and top-down and bottom-up approaches.

The cultural shock associated with intervention for modernization is often greater than the social consequences, which generally lend themselves to remedial actions. Nevertheless, related social and cultural conflicts surface in small and large connections. Modernization efforts may radically affect fundamental changes in life styles, in familial and group arrangements and support systems, in social and psychic relationships, and in historical and ethical assumptions. All too frequently, the very people most affected by the social consequences of modernization are without the personal, emotional, and financial resources needed to cope with them. Their capacity to cope is further undermined by the real or perceived assaults that their prevailing cultural system is forced to absorb from the modernization efforts.

These effects are observable in a variety of local settings in connection with such activities as urban renewal, urban redevelopment, city restoration, and community rehabilitation efforts; in connection with efforts to close the gap between contemporary patterns of life and outmoded institutions, governing units, infrastructure, and facilities; in the adaptation dictated by the changing roles and functions of the central city; in the massive adjustments dictated by the redistributions of population, political power, and the economy among regions of the nation; and in a host of other modernization processes. These effects are observed in entire underdeveloped continents—Asia, Latin America, and Africa— and in entire nations—most dramatically perhaps in Iran, which seems both to seek and resist the process of modernization. The consequences of modernization, and the effects of failing to modernize, can be seen in the private sector—for example in the auto industry, the steel industry, and the energy establishment. Wherever some attempt has been made to initiate the process, we see evidence of the inability of either the individual or the society to deal effectively with the by-products of modernization. Attempts at social amelioration have been modest at best.

One might argue that the especially heavy burdens on segments of the population least able to carry them, and the failure of the larger society to provide adequate forms of support, mean that more social damage than good results from change. But leaving things as they are is no longer a viable option, since survival in the face of diminishing resources, increased equity demands, and competition from aggressive public and private rivals have eliminated any reasonable prospect that modernization can be perceived as the greater of the available evils. This includes efforts at modernization through renewal, restoration, and rehabilitation that seek to reverse the patterns of obsolescence on terms that permit the city to survive within a rationalized metropolitan framework. Clearly modernization brings its own set of problems and conflicts that cannot be ignored, but these problems should be addressed as symptoms and consequences rather than as primary causes.

Long-held definitions and conventions, historical roles and functions, and generally accepted relationships have all been brought into question as a result of modernization processes. The instability in both personal and institutional behavior, and the widespread unease, anxiety, and apprehension are attributable in large part to fundamental changes in roles and relationships. The result is that the framework within which individuals and institutions identify and define themselves has been eroded and shaken.

We see this in many ways. What is recognized and accepted as normative reflects changes in how a "problem" or a "dysfunction" is defined. Thus a presumed problem or dysfunction, representing a widely held belief or moral conviction and frequently legislated into remedial programs, may come to be recognized and accepted as a newly emergent normative social and behavior pattern. A prime example is the matriarchal family, where men may be present only erratically, with or without marriage or divorce. Marriage and divorce constitute variables largely determined by the socioeconomic status of the individuals and by the prevalent practices of the individual's peer group. It has been presumed that such a family structure was related to poverty and was typically characteristic of the welfare recipient. The fact that single-parent heads-of-household exist in many segments of the population, and are statistically significant even among the affluent, suggests that they represent a normative rather than a dysfunctional behavior. That the behavior may have surfaced first among the poor is not surprising since this is a highly visible group, dependent on public assistance, frequently studied, and least able to compensate for the absence of an adult family partner. The lack of material resources may be the critical variable differentiating the more or less affluent families headed by a single parent. Problems of discipline and motivation among children of single-parent families on welfare might be attributed to the absence of two responsible adults, rather than to marital or welfare status.

Such societal changes and the reformulations they demand are bound to have a profound effect on legislative and executive programs. If assistance is viewed as supportive and compensatory, rather than remedial, aid is less likely to be viewed cynically, contemptuously, and punitively by both the provider and the beneficiary. If aid to agriculture and the farmer can be generally viewed as necessary compensation for the normative behavior of the marketplace, why cannot aid to the dependent single-parent family and others be justified on similar grounds?

Economic, social, and political changes have altered the role of women, shifted the traditional emphasis on family, and raised disturbing questions about the gratifications and benefits of parenthood. Children are now frequently considered a personal sacrifice and a societal burden. There is little traditional social and cultural support for having them. The effects of such changes on public and private policies, on institutional practices, and on required structural facilities and services are self-evident.

Similar reformulations are emerging in connection with the so-called drug culture. It is now recognized that drugs are used by significant numbers of the population, and though trafficking and the use of the most devastating substances are still looked upon negatively, general drug use is more and more accepted.

As behaviors are accepted as normative, there is uncertainty as to the appropriate subsystem to serve client groups. The establishment of new normative base lines has heightened the difficulty of matching the client and the behavior with the appropriate subsystem. The conventional subsystems are not customarily equipped administratively and conceptually to meet the new demands placed upon them. Sometimes, as a matter of fact, "dysfunctional" behaviors can be viewed as assets providing quality, character, and distinctiveness that should be preserved.

As a response to these modernization demands, agencies have sought to rationalize their purposes, to more clearly refine their functions, and to define their client group more narrowly. This has resulted in a massive game of musical chairs. The law-enforcement subsystem has excluded a whole set of clients by redefining crime and the criminal. As a result, a large proportion of their traditional workload has been taken over by the social-service system or the mental- or physical-health subsystems. Alcoholics and others who run the risk of primarily damaging themselves are often the victims of this "reshuffling." It is also evident in the extensive deinstitutionalization of the mentally ill, penal inmates, and the aged. In all of these situations, people are by fault or choice transferred from one subsystem to another—often without prior consultation or arrangement—and are left to their own devices. The narrowing of subsystem jurisdictions has created a dilemma in yet another connection. Whereas knowledge building is based on refining, specifying, and deepening each of the content areas, effective use of knowledge for service delivery is dependent on the capacity to combine subsystems in diverse ways. This dilemma is most sharply felt in the academy in connection with curriculum development and implementation-related research, which, on the one hand, depends on specialization to meet the particular demands of knowledge building and, on the other hand, seeks to prepare professionals to manage systems and deliver services cutting across the specializations.

Modernization also requires that the boundaries of geographic units appropriate to the new urban system be reformulated to facilitate problem solving and decision making. A growing dichotomy exists between those territorial units that approximate the spatial, market, and functional systems at the metropolitan and subregional levels and the formal governing units that are becoming anachronisms. Nationally, the regions of the country (the Northwest, the Middle West, the Southwest, the South, and the West) are likely to become the pivotal territorial units for debating, shaping, and formulating national and local policy and for organizing, applying, and disaggregating powers, functions, and responsibilities to, through, and among the state and local governing network.

Reconciling technology and humanism challenges the belief that modernization and technology are interchangeable and misses the essence of the meaning of modernization. Modernization in its highest and best sense offers an opportunity not only for introducing efficiency and technology and creating competitive capacity through the imaginative application of science and technology, but also for enhancing the quality of life. Humanistic goals and approaches cushion the harsh effects of technology. More important, however, the benefits of technology, the commitment to service delivery, and the provision of quality control are dependent on humanistic concerns and practices. Modernization augments rather than diminishes reliance on value judgments, on multiple choices, and on selection among alternatives, affirming the importance of participation and enhancing the decision-making process. Both the individual and the group instruments that strengthen the roles of citizen and consumer are frequently the catalytic agents in the modernization process. Humanistic concerns are of no less concern or importance than technological ones, if the interests of modernization are to be served and its potential benefits achieved.

Allocation and Equity

In the face of the increased pressure for access to society's goods and services, more appropriate allocation and distribution of the diminishing supply of available resources are critical needs. The two factors of modernization and allocation reinforce each other. The growth in the demand for the benefits promised by society is coming at the very time that the resources available to provide these benefits are being reduced. These worldwide phenomena are being played out in intricate ways. The "have not" countries that control particular resources utilized historically for the benefit of "have" countries are no longer willing to accept this pattern.

We lack adequate means to make critical allocations, whether of dollars or of power, among individuals and groups, among socioeconomic classes, or among levels of government. Occupational status and income are no longer universally accepted standards for determining one's degree of entitlement to dollars, services, and benefits. Further, the widely accepted historical assumption that one's legitimate aspirations include only the right of equal opportunity to achieve evenhanded access among individuals, groups, and institutions is being challenged. The traditional approach is being replaced by one that asserts that the individual's inherent right to the benefits of the system and to more equitable allocations of the dollars, goods, and services only indirectly relates to the issue of opportunity. In the human-services area, particularly with respect to health services and benefits, for example, all people expect decent health care irrespective of their occupational or socioeconomic status.

The redistribution of power is similarly being affected both by deliberate intent and as a by-product of activities undertaken for other, sometimes conflicting purposes that will inevitably create new patterns of ownership and control over time. We see this in connection with real estate, where new forms of ownership are diffusing the traditional approaches to real property and to its control. This is the case in the growth of condominiums and cooperatives in both residential and commercial and industrial property. We see a variation as well in connection with the large-scale shopping center where shared responsibility and destiny blur differences between owners and tenants.

The growing use of inclusionary zoning to serve selected socioeconomic groups and then modify and guarantee the risks is additional evidence of refashioned private-public relationships. The increased number of employees, consumers, labor-union, and community and minority group representatives on corporate boards is a further manifestation of a changing distribution of power and control. On the public side, the growing number of attempts to decentralize power, to provide for community control or other more modified forms of participation, represent additional evidences of the new balances of power. The most dramatic indicators of the changing character of the exercise of power, signaling future significant and substantial change, are the experimental, and to date halting, efforts at worker participation and worker self-management. These are early indications of new decision-making forms, and refashioned roles and relationships, between employer-employee, supervisor-worker, producer-consumer, and corporation-union. These changes tend to consolidate power in reconstituted forms and combinations. New alignments and loyalties appear not only among a growing number of multinational corporations but in privy cross-governmental arrangements that are concealed from the public and dilute national loyalties. These phenomena can also be observed in the connections and alignments that exist between multinational corporations and governments. Equally significant is the political connection between the foreign investor and the domestic corporation, with the consequent effect psychologically on the quality of citizenship that results from the relationships that emerge between the "foreign" employer and the "native" employees. This latter factor is comparable historically to the colonial experience, and contemporarily to the circumstances in the United States characteristic of its disadvantaged inner-cities, resulting from absentee ownership, disinvestment, and an external decision-making apparatus.

A consolidation of power, a fusion of public and private goals, the merger of public and private planning and programming activity, and the ascription of public and private functions are based on pragmatically determined decisions, operational criteria, and political and tactical judgments, rather than on deeply held philosophical positions. Thus, in those cities with sophisticated and successful urban programs, the public and private interests share and promote common goals, mesh their purposes, and arrive at negotiated understandings that in fact create conglomerate public-private superstructures dedicated to the modernization efforts. Public welfare and private welfare lose all distinction. This blending leaves little room for power to be redistributed; what is left to be distributed are functions and responsibilities among public and private activity centers.

There exists an underlying tension between the forces that are working to modernize the public, private, and nonprofit sectors, and the incessant demand for a reallocation and redistribution of power, goods, services, and resources. These are pervasive and universal. At one level the forces are in conflict, inconsistent and at cross-purposes, obstructing each other's goals. The tension is manifested by the conflict between technology and humanism, centralization and decentralization, macro and micro approaches, and control as against participation. These sharply drawn polarities are likely to harden, and the battle lines between the positions are bound to lead to a widening breach and to a series of probable confrontations, many already observable. It may be that the stage is being set for either a frontal assault or an accommodation in the interests of individual and societal survival. Creative and imaginative management and control measures can incorporate and reinforce an operational matrix that achieves the collateral purposes of modernization, allocation, and equity. Each purpose constitutes an entry strategy and supporting condition to the achievement of the other, and correspondingly each purpose is dependent on the successful coordinate achievements of the others. The purposes are interlocking, existing in a complex and reciprocal state of mutual dependence. One may philosophically or tactically stress one or another purpose as preferable, more valued, or—more important—useful, or appropriate on the premise that it represents the most defensible and productive intervening strategy; one might ascribe and argue that one or the other is more logically a cause rather than an effect or the reverse. Highly organized efforts on behalf of one or another goal have the advantage of making visible the benefits associated with that particular goal. In stressing the advantages, the opportunity exists to relate and develop coordinated and connected approaches among respective purposes.

The Management Structure

It is possible to perceive of the range of managerial devices and organizational forms as related and mutually supportive and reinforcing. Consequently, diverse goals and purposes need not be viewed as antagonistic, but rather as requiring simultaneous attention. Management and control approaches and mechanisms can constitute a network of interacting and mutually reinforcing components facilitating executive and central capacity, heightening organizational responsiveness, expanding consumer and beneficiary influence, more effectively connecting functional subsystems, improving access to and enhancing the quality of public and private service delivery, and reconciling humanistic and technological orientations and macro and micro approaches. For example, control and participation need not represent antagonistic alternatives, but rather should provide both the means and the ends for mutual achievement.

Thus, the devices that have been advanced to enhance executive control—such as quantitative and analytical measures, administrative consolidation, greater centralization, fiscal-management instruments, and system planning and programming—when they work as intended can also increase systemic effectiveness and produce substantial improvements in organizational responsiveness to consumers and beneficiaries. Similarly, improved executive control is made possible rather than thwarted by those measures that have sought either to expand consumer influence or control through such devices as the use of ombudsmen, outreach systems, the redistribution of decision-making power, decentralized administration, cash vouchers, performance contracts, advocacy planning, and community self-determination.

The above measures have created confidence in the system, and have expanded self and group expression in a way that has led to an increase in executive and central control. Whatever their relative merit for other purposes, the shifts in the terms of ownership represented by such trends as the cooperative and condominium movements, unified shopping centers, and the growth in institutional ownership made possible by the use of pension and retirement funds, have reinforced institutionalized and ergo executive capacity, along with broadening the participation base. The many forms of worker participation and self-management, ranging from public and private attempts at introducing MBO procedures to more elaborate involvement by workers in production and other critical management decisions are added illustrations of the ways in which top-down and bottom-up approaches intersect. The accepted theory is that central control and organizational goals are enhanced by increased worker participation. It is assumed that an increase in participation will result in improved quality control; and that an increase in worker morale will reduce absenteeism, improve the profit margin, eliminate product and service imperfections and inadequacies, and generally help create a climate in which top-down discipline and bottom-up satisfaction and pride are interchangeable and mutually reinforcing. This point of view would argue, for example, that the capacity to deliver a good or service is dependent not only on an identifiable central authority charged unmistakably with this responsibility, but on the character of the service-delivery network, the freedom of access to the services, the means by which the recipient-beneficiary derives the goods and services, and the opportunities to influence the services themselves and the form and quality of its delivery.

Increasingly, a critical challenge to private and public management is the need to administer over an extended spatial area and across geographic territories. This is abundantly clear in the public sector where human settlement patterns have extended activity centers far beyond the historical city boundaries into outlying metropolitan concentrations. These activity centers have come to comprise nucleated groupings that are each related to the other and that together with the central city constitute the new urbanized "metropolitan" or "regional city." This pattern is observable in every older central city in the Northeast and the Middle West, with counterpart urban and metropolitan developments in the enlarging Southwest, West, and Northwest regions. The urban metroplex is the overall result. Against this backdrop, a matrix of relationships exists between political and governmental structures on the one hand, and professional, administrative, and functional agencies and organizations on the other hand. We need only to take note of the growth of bureaucracy in government, generally the target of the popular attacks on "big government," to realize that in the public sector, a vertical organizational structure has come to dominate, in which each function— health, economic development, environment, etc.—has grown in power independent of general government and apart from other coordinate functions (see figure 1 and discussion in chapter 2). Each function has developed its own comprehensive approach to problem solving, in which related functions are drawn on in secondary relationships to it. Each pursues and solidifies its relationships across the range of governmental layers and engenders loyalties that are generally stronger than those toward the general government of which it is a part. Functional control is highly centralized and is facilitated by an elaborate administratively decentralized system. The functional (vertical) approach weakens executive and governmental control at the "top" and consumer, citizen, and beneficiary influence at the "bottom." Since these functional bureaucracies take on a semi-autonomous existence and a life of their own, they tend to be less responsive and to threaten both political centralization and decentralization. In effect, what has occurred is that the delivery of knowledge, goods, and services has been accomplished at the expense of corporate government and the general welfare. The price has included an increase in dependency, the exclusion of large numbers of the population from the decision-making process, and the alienation of that part of the population unable to compete for (or outpriced by) particular services and benefits. Domination by the functional activity systems, in which management capacity is exercised by such functional groups vertically across governing layers, has undermined executive and consumer control and influence. The executive- and consumer-beneficiary depend on a horizontal rather than a vertical capacity to achieve control at the top and the bottom. Such horizontal capacity depends on the restoration of governmental power across coordinate functions at each layer in the governing hierarchy, and where formal units are nested in a politically decentralized network. Top-down managerial mechanisms are intended to modify the increasingly independent and growing power of the professional, the bureaucrat, the functionary, and the administrative agency; to enhance the executive capacity to cut across functions horizontally; and to make possible the development of a unified plan and program drawing from the collection of functions and activities. The range of bottom-up approaches similarly seeks to restore the individual's preeminence over the multiple service delivery system by serving the individual holistically in order to overcome the tendency on the part of the functional network to treat the individual categorically and to place the users at the networks' mercy.

Management capacity and control are affected by the size and scale of the organizational and management units, the activities to be performed centrally, the assignment among the coordinate functions, and the geographic distribution of activities. If competition and negotiation between coordinate functional systems cease to be the means by which dollars and powers are allocated, the executive and the consumer will need to rely on analytical tools and evaluation measures so that control can be exercised intelligently and judiciously.

Balancing Public and Private Approaches

In the final analysis the capacity to deal with the issues of modernization, equitable and rational distribution, and management control will be dependent on the successful dovetailing of efforts across national boundaries. No country, no people, and no socioeconomic class is likely to continue placidly for any extended time to accept sharp distinctions and differences that result from inequitable allocations of their own goods, services, or resources; nor will the social and civil instability thereby created be long tolerated by the "achieving" societies.

The three pivotal issues are of coordinate importance. They are interconnected and reinforcing. If one goal is stressed to the exclusion of the others, the results may be destructive. As a tactic, one or another issue may emerge for political, social, or economic reasons as crucial or most relevant; or may be selected as part of a deliberate intervention strategy designed to mobilize the relevant constituencies. In any case, however, in time the remaining issues must inevitably be engaged and must be systematically related to and addressed.

The ability to effect the new functioning threshold requires that the transition be achieved with minimum disruption to society, and particularly to those population groups least able to cope with the effects of massive change. In addition, political sanction—expressed or tacit— needs to be secured to undertake the changes dictated by modernization. Frequently the inability to achieve sanction, or at least the difficulty in doing so, delays, distorts, or aborts modernization and other related efforts.

The range of strategies and approaches needed to deal with modernization, equity, and management and organizational control are indeed diverse. Despite the inadequacy of utilizing the electoral process in a country as complex and wide-ranging as the United States, the increased reliance on the referendum testifies to the intensity of the public concern. The substantial number of voter-initiated referenda, and the corresponding number of executive and legislative enactments imposing taxation and spending limitations, represent attempts to signal unmistakable messages, and to do by indirection what may have proved impossible to do by direction.

The assertion of the public will, as expressed in tax and spending limitations, is frequently a reaction against the politicians as a group, against political instrumentalities, and against the bureaucratic functionaries perceived to be the politicians' handmaidens. However, this antagonism by the public, directed at the political institutions, is not necessarily aimed at science and technology and at the professional instrumentalities associated with and responsible for delivering benefits and services. The public reaction may be against the quality of representation and the nature of the decision-making process. Imposing financial limitations and demanding increased economy and more defensible organizational systems and practices serve to enlarge the scientific and technological role and responsibilities at the expense of the political. The pro-efficiency constituency, which is challenging political authority, is being joined by the pro-equity constitutency, which is placing greater faith in the anonymous and evenhanded effects of systematic and analytical measures than in the undependable and uncertain behavior of their political adversaries. When the public uses the referendum to impose financial limits, the result is an increased rather than a diminished role for the professional and the technocrat. Changes in the nature and quality of relationships are made at the expense of the politician and of the political process. Thus what may be emerging is an uneasy coalition of the public and the professional technocrat pitted against the politician and the bureaucrat. Allocation mechanisms, innovative and creative institutional structures and practices, and other refashioned approaches strengthen the professional and further the case for systematic analysis. Consequently, we may see more popular control made possible by an expanded professional and technical role and a diminution in the influence of the politically elected representatives. As a matter of fact, the time may not be too far off when political campaigns are fought by professional adversaries representing distinctive positions. The dangers of this phenomenon may be greater than those of the circumstances that gave rise to it. Big government, which is

the popular target, is thought to be incomprehensible and unmanageable. The professional and the technocrat assume that rational,
systematic, and analytical approaches that are nonpartisan and amoral in
nature are able to meet and overcome the big-government challenge.

Both public- and private-oriented advocates have come to recognize
that simplistic reactions and solutions to big government will not resolve
the underlying source of the antagonism. The disadvantaged populations, for example, have discovered that the decentralization of power
(evidence the poverty program, the model-cities program, and the like)
does not remedy profound inequalities, and that maldistribution of
resources, goods, and services may require a centralized presence that
makes allocations and equitable redistributions along with, rather than in
place of, decentralized units. The decentralization of power will not
assure access to resources located outside the resource-hungry jurisdiction. This requires centralized authority and centralized allocating mechanisms. The principal argument for decentralization in this regard is that
it might or will create the political capacity and muscle leading to a larger,
more equitable distribution pattern.

Similarly, on the private side, the case for decentralization and
against a centralized presence and authority has been undermined by
federal and state programs that have provided private enterprise with
fresh and attractive opportunities for investment and potential profit and
the prospect of playing a major role in urban reconstruction. The governmental role is predicated less on political and descriptive considerations,
and more on systematic evidences and proofs of impact, leveraging
effects, and other quantifiable and analytical devices. Once again representative government is superseded by technical government.

With respect to federal policies and programs in connection with
urban reconstruction, centralized approaches have turned from broadly
based examinations susceptible to value judgment and political debate to
analytical, quantifiable, and measurable approaches as the basis for
decision making. Thus, democratic—and therefore imperfect, sometimes
trying, and occasionally abused—decision making is replaced by technical decision making. Public instruments and mechanisms use dollar
and other supports to equate and express public power technically rather
than politically. Is it any surprise that private-enterprise advocates have
switched their target? These programs have been important to private
enterprise. Government has clearly not offended them, even though
politics may have done so. Private enterprise has been quite willing to
accept land write-downs, tax abatements, and industrial revenue-bond
benefits. The public presence is definable, and its terms can be built into
the business calculation. Differences between the Urban Development
Assistance Grants (UDAG), for example, and the conventional urban-

renewal program lie in the economic-development orientation of the UDAG approach, and in UDAG's private-enterprise domination in lieu of the more broadly based political orientation that characterizes the conventional urban-renewal approach. The private sector, rather than the public sector, establishes the UDAG parameters. This is another evidence of what has earlier been suggested. In the United States, the public-private relationships are more developed in the public-related than in the private-related sectors, even though the private sector exerts powerful collateral influences. In Japan, by contrast, the public-private relationships seem to be more developed in the private- rather than public-related sectors. It may be that the public-private relationships are more advanced in a nation's least powerful sector.

The success of programs like UDAG and EDA (Economic Development Administration) has led to proposals to extend these principles to such devices as the creation of Free Trade and Free Enterprise Zones. The assumption is that if partial giveaway programs like UDAG, with their range of benefits and minimal risks, are successful, why not extend the giveaways, expand the benefits, and reduce the risks even further. Those who sell these approaches on the theory that they are an antidote to governmental intrusion overlook the fact that most public programs were created to remedy the abuses created by these very same special pleaders who now seek access to public money and power freed of the constraints imposed by public policy. This is a seductive and pseudo-intellectual appeal. It is predicated on creating, extending, and maximizing incentives while eliminating any presumed constraints. It is largely a behavior-modification approach. If you can regulate and manipulate incentives, you can control and determine behavior. This is a highly managed public-policy course, rather than a free and unfettered market approach, relying on technological rather than political orientations. It is as if the private sector advocates, after learning how people perceive of their position, have acquired the ability to cushion and modify their message by blunting anticipated reactions with a new rhetoric to achieve deliberate and profitable ends.

The increased reliance on the professional and the technocrat is likely to continue as the public debate switches to the relative impact and validity of alternate strategies, which are susceptible to systematic examination and evaluation. The newly developing administrative and management mechanisms that are altering and redefining producer and consumer roles, private and public relationships, and the very nature of decision making down to neighborhoods and blocks and to production lines, result in a symbiotic relationship between technology and humanism and a synthesis among the goals and purposes associated with these central themes.

CHAPTER 4

Devising an Urban Strategy

Preserving the architectural and planning heritage of the city is important and has value in its own right. However, while restoration efforts that have strong design and spatial orientations are frequently advanced as people-oriented programs on the premise that they are conceived of on a small, civilized, and humane scale, in an increasing number of instances they are in fact an expression of materialism. They value buildings over and above occupants, since the aesthetic values tend to be dependent on ever-escalating dollar opportunities. When such places are also situated in highly advantageous locations, as is the case in certain parts of the Near North Side of Chicago, the discriminatory pressures exerted by the segregating influence of the distinctive design, reinforced by the delimited yet expanding market demand, combine to further reinforce the effects of race and class as the great territorial differentiators. The displacement effects of this approach are as devastating as those of a total clearance project due to the financial, social, and cultural distances that result and that are reinforced over time. The retention and restoration of existing structures do not imbue the particular building or the revitalization effort with a humanitarian quality or an attractive set of values. Serving and satisfying people's needs are humane acts. Service and satisfaction are dependent on cost, income, financing, and market, whether in connection with restoration or new construction. Thus while saving buildings may be romantic, doing so does not on its face assure widespread satisfaction, particularly for those populations with limited resources. Buildings are saved because it is lucrative to do so, not necessarily because their survival serves a civic or aesthetic purpose.

Immediately following World War II the issue of whether urban restoration should be limited to housing or should encompass broadly based programs often erupted into national debate and local conflict. Differences arose over the quantity of housing to be included, particularly in connection with residential displacement projects, and whether housing must be undertaken only in conjunction with a more comprehensive community development plan and program.

The new housing constructed in the central cities with Federal Housing Administration (FHA) support tended to be limited to prime locations with strong market appeal. Federal support was possible only if the construction was on a site that gave evidence of sound investment and assured return. Reducing urban densities and replacing residential structures with the types of housing that would appeal to the residents the city sought to attract were viewed as program advantages. Consequently, it was not uncommon to propose a smaller number of units than had previously existed on the project site. Many of these private projects were constructed under the FHA Section 608 provisions—which sought to stimulate private housing construction through generous financial mortgage supports—that were to become scandal-ridden in many parts of the country.

By challenging the soundness of investment in nearly all parts of the central city, the FHA policy helped to increase the influence of the savings and loan associations as an alternative financing mechanism. In an earlier period the savings and loans had been neighborhood and community oriented; they were identified with and related to particular "client" groups. Now, by making financing available to areas and individuals that had been refused assistance by the FHA, they helped to fill a total financing vacuum.

Outside the central city the stress was on housing. There was an almost frenetic effort to add to the housing supply by making the most favorable terms available to every major actor in construction in the suburbs: the mortgagor, the builder, the supplier, and the consumer. The aid was not limited to the structure itself, but included supportive site improvements—principally through sewer and water grants and indirectly through massive transportation, drainage, and other federally supported programs. The aid facilitated not only residential construction, but also regional shopping, industrial, institutional, and other major developments. Private enterprise was literally redefined in the postwar decades. Public housing depended on 100 percent financing, private housing depended on 95 percent financing. Nearly all suburban activity was made possible by federal policy and administrative regulation, with only limited prior community and area-wide public consultation. Private developments were dealt with as discrete projects, rather than as elements of a more comprehensive and systematic strategy. The community and area-wide public planning that took place was at best anemic, despite the attempts by the federal government to strengthen metropolitan planning through the 701 program, the A-95 program, and other measures and enactments (see chapter 8 of this volume for an elaboration of this concept and approach). The metropolitan planning activities were peripheral and dependent on the very people they sought to influence and oversee; only rarely did they affect private or public decisions in any demonstrable way.

The two-pronged urban and housing policy was differentially applied within and outside the central city, an inconsistency that heightened social dissatisfaction and frustration. The federal housing aid made available to the suburban areas was largely responsible for facilitating the rapid flight of populations from the central city. Although pull rather than push factors may account for the population movement to the outlying areas, the fact remains that the city was left largely defenseless without corresponding financial housing aid, which might have served as an incentive to retain the populations. The housing aid that was available to the city was embedded in elaborate development programs. The flight to the suburbs was accelerated by highway and other major large-scale public works projects. Prevailing federal urban policy was a "houseless planning policy" for our central cities, and a "planless housing policy" for our suburbs. Thus, the people in the central cities, those least able to absorb the "costs" of planning, had the fewest housing choices and yet were saddled with the burden of improving the environment at the expense of their housing needs. Those in the suburban areas, who were relatively better able to absorb the "costs" of planning, were given generous housing assistance and relieved of any responsibility to ensure the quality of the environment.

This distorted two-pronged approach required major modification, particularly in the central city. Modernization of the urban environment proceeded under the assumption that the affected individuals had the personal and financial resources to deal with the collateral social problems that are an inevitable byproduct of modernization. Alternative opportunities and facilities were assumed to be within the capacity of the affected population, enabling them to make the accommodations dictated by modernization. All too frequently the reverse was the case. Public efforts to stem and reverse community decline and deterioration, and to cope with structural and spatial obsolescence, often brought deep-seated social and economic problems for both individuals and families to the surface. Public interventions intruded on the lives of many individuals and families who were coping adequately with their life situation and improving their circumstances by stages, reflecting available opportunities and capacities. For these people, modernization precipitated a series of critical events that confronted them with the need to make decisions that they were sometimes ill-equipped to face—it was as if the pace of change was outstripping their readiness rate, both psychologically and practically. Not all of these people were adversely affected; for some the changes and the support offered by available programs and agency staff offered stimulation toward self, structural, and spatial improvement.

However, a large number of the affected population were, at best, simply managing to sustain themselves at minimum levels of survival, to cope only marginally with the personal and material effects of change. Modernization exposed the dependency and fragility of this population and made visible the range and extent of their problems. Most of them had not benefited from society's material or other "advantages." These were people without promising prospects. As this by-passed population gained visibility, it became apparent that society was ill-equipped to meet the needs of the extremely disadvantaged. Modernization became the scapegoat for society's shortcomings. It was a natural response to become angry at the "messenger."

Planning for Social Change

A number of modifications in the public efforts at urban modernization resulted from these experiences. The pace of these modernization activities was slowed, at the expense of housing, on the theory that early approaches were "too much, too fast" and had been undertaken naively and simplistically without sufficient awareness of their ramifications. Other modifications included housing assistance programs, some of which were oriented toward the lender, others toward the builder and developer, and still others toward the consumer. In all cases, however, an attempt was made to add to the city's housing supply and to serve a broader spectrum of the population, particularly the low- and middle-income groups. Thus the city was given the means to compete more effectively with the suburbs for at least some of the mobile population.

The early experience led to substantial modifications and redirections in the form and nature of many kinds of public programs—in mental and physical health, job training, and related areas. Programs to deal with poverty and with environmental controls were also introduced. These activities sought to alleviate and ameliorate the personal and social effects of modernization, to support and sustain the quality of life, and to stimulate a process of self-improvement, without sacrificing the goal of improving the environment. Limited attempts were made, largely as a result of federal pressure, to establish a metropolitan framework reflecting the new forms of human settlement.

The dual concerns of social welfare and the environment have led to diverse and alternative urban strategies. Of fundamental concern are programs to "save our cities," in which land-use instruments have constituted the principal weapon. These programs are predicated on reinforcing commercial, industrial, and institutional activity and strengthening the tax base; retaining and attracting middle- and upper-income individuals and families; and fostering community stability. Commercial areas have been modernized and their sales and employment opportunities expanded. Markets have been restored. Integrated middle-income areas have been created (frequently the only such achievement in the city). Institutions have secured space for growth in more amenable surroundings, and communities have been given assurance and assistance that their character will be safeguarded. Paradoxically, though these programs are strikingly successful (although not universally), they are responsible for many of the difficulties that persist. Whereas the city was traditionally a fluid place where the restless could fulfill their aspirations, programs to "save our cities" have tended to rigidify its institutional forms and reduce opportunities for social mobility. Stability and mobility challenge reconciliation.

The principal theme of these local activities is the "spirit of city renewal." The major ingredient is *stability*—save our neighborhood, avoid panic. Mobility and community fluidity are considered almost treasonable acts against place and city. Stability, in turn, is in large part associated with ethnicity, single-family home ownership, and social and economic homogeneity. The attitude is almost agricultural and rural in conception. The idea, however, has great appeal, particularly to those who have only recently achieved a modicum of economic security and have only limited choices, and to whom investment in home and local institutions represents a dominant value. The drive to modernize the municipal plant and improve facilities and housing conditions in order to root people in the central city has come to characterize nearly all renewal activities.

The ingredients of direct confrontation and value conflict are thus side effects to the stabilization process. For accompanying this drive to save the central city is the concurrent national need to meet and solve the problems of our disadvantaged populations. The city is the place of residence of the largest concentration of such disadvantaged populations. The push for "open occupancy" and the "open city," the inclusion of nondiscrimination clauses in a vast number of federal programs, the scattering of public housing projects, and the rent supplement program all tend to sharpen the weapons of controversy by directly confronting the value system built into the city's current programmatic stance.

The controversy and conflict are unavoidably compounded by the fact that the neighborhoods and communities in which the slogans of stability are most firmly entrenched are those that provide the most realistic opportunities—geographically and financially—for the disadvantaged to scale the walls that exclude them.

An aspiring population, whether disadvantaged or in the stream of active self-improvement, is dependent on public programs that accept and encourage diverse communities and regard them as settings for individual and family economic growth. Public programs that are undertaken in relation to presumed yardsticks of absolute achievement obstruct the sequential process of urban change. The central theme of the urban system must be fluidity, in which change is achieved over time and in which public programs provide direct and indirect assistance to accelerate the process of change and accommodate it in both personal and institutional terms. Although legal questions arise, fluidity and mobility would be reinforced if differential land use controls could be introduced reflecting the role and the "state" of the community at particular and relative stages over time.

Traditional urban and land-use planning approaches have emphasized housing and the environment as critical variables, and these have been reflected and incorporated in major federal and state housing and urban renewal and redevelopment legislative enactments. The use of housing and the environment as intervening strategies has been brought into sharp question. Increasingly, intervention strategies are being tested by the degree to which they constitute a triggering device likely to set in motion a process of change. Housing and the environment do not fundamentally alter the life circumstance or generate changes in other life-sustaining or quality-of-life measures. On the other hand, income, jobs, and economic strategies enable individuals to act and build on their strengths, capabilities, and potential. Jobs or income strategies, for example, can demonstrably affect the total life circumstance and precipitate change on many levels. Housing and the environment represent a consequent state rather than a precipitating or triggering event. They may in fact serve to worsen or exacerbate the living circumstance in inverse relationship to need and income, absent subsidies or collateral strategies, by increasing costs and thereby working against the very programmatic direction that is intended. This recognition is evident in the changes in policies and programs of the Department of Housing and Urban Development, which have moved toward community and economic development strategies and away from a focus on housing.

For the professional planner and administrator, planning has constituted the means by which the urban plant can be restored and the ideal environment established; for the financier and developer, it has been the means to use land up to its highest value with maximum return; for the small property owner and neighborhood or community resident, the means to maintain the status quo and resist change; and for the municipal executive, the means to stem the tide of population out-migration and achieve a degree of stability. If planning is to serve as a facilitator of social change, as the means to reinforce the aspirations of an upwardly mobile population, more, rather than less, population movement and population redistribution throughout the urbanized area will be required.

Public programs are frequently categorized as "racially sympathetic," as in the case of community preservation projects; or as "racially antagonistic," as in the case of industrial projects that displace housing. The irony is that many of the so-called antagonistic projects may have far greater sympathetic consequences by way of the public works and private enterprise jobs that are generated and the direct dollar transfers and longer-term benefits that are achieved.

Today the inner city is commonly viewed as a challenge to sales and market ingenuity. A realistic approach that builds on the social structure of the community and seeks to capture its rhythm and style, would replace service provision with a plan and program that maximizes opportunities and creates an environment in which cultural values and human aspirations are realized.

We claim to view the inner-city community comprehensively, but in fact we view it reportorially. We merely enumerate and document the characteristics of its population and its physical setting. As a result, we do not have an adequate basis for plannning and programming, for identifying problems, setting objectives, and establishing priorities.

Our present approach consists largely of accepting a static description of the aggregate negative characteristics of the inner city's population and physical milieu as enumerated by various professional fields. Each field has added an adjective to the catalog of slum deficiencies. Thus a slum is defined and recognized as an area in which the housing is old, dilapidated, or deteriorating; where land uses are mixed; where there is excessive overcrowding; where tax returns are low; where the people are poor; where illegitimacy, delinquency, and unemployment rates are high; where educational achievements are low and school drop-out rates high; where tuberculosis rates, infant mortality rates, and other measures of poor health are high; where there is little organized community life;

and where low voter registration and civic participation suggest apathy and alienation.

The tendency has been to accept each and all of the characteristics defined by any given professional field as an inner-city area's universal condition. Therefore, the list continues to grow, and cultural deprivation, the matriarchal family, lack of motivation, poor housekeeping habits, irresponsibility, and lack of respect for law and order have become firmly established as characteristics of the black and low-income community without benefit of empirical verification.

To the extent that we recognize a community's dynamics we tend to limit ourselves to the interrelationships within its boundaries. The widely held view, for example, is that the black ghetto varies from the desired norm according to every standard and produces within and by itself recognizable "dysfunctions." This is not only a dilemma but a defense. We can continue to generate and launch activities and devise plans that tackle problems that may be statistical and anecdotal, certain that there is no way in which we can test their relevance or effectiveness. We have not looked at the black community as part of a total complex reacting and responding to forces and pressures within the larger environment, and extending beyond its borders. We have failed to see how it is affected by the arrangements and relationships it maintains with the larger society, and to what extent it is the creature of broad social processes. No community can be understood solely as the sum total of the personal characteristics of the individuals and families living within its confines.

As earlier suggested, we lack certainty as to whether our text is John Kenneth Galbraith's *Affluent Society* or Michael Harrington's *Other America*. Is our task to modernize the city, to reach the stage where our urban profile mirrors our material wealth, or to redistribute goods and services so that society's benefits are more equally allocated and shared?

The social welfare approach and the environmental approach seem to be looking at different pieces of the mosaic. Each has spawned its own family of associated programs. In general, social welfare approaches center on the individual, family, and group; environmental approaches center on the use, ordering, and distribution of space. Social welfare assumes that influencing attitudes and behavior is the most effective way to bring about change; environmentalists assume that change is best achieved by shaping and fashioning the relationship between living and working space. The social-welfare approach focuses on the development of capacities; the environmental approach focuses on the development and deployment of resources. Social welfare tends to endow human characteristics and human settlement with a romantic quality. The social-welfare literature stresses the "richness of human diversity" and the "charm of the ghetto," focusing its attention on personal, housing, and community dysfunctions. Environmental advocates tend to stress the system and its functioning, the use and ordering of activities and facilities in space, and the organization, administration, and management of these activities and their support institutions. Each approach has generated its own apostles, litany, and theology. Each has been responsible for supporting the enactment of separate streams of legislation, codes, and ordinances, and each has been identified with quite distinct programs, strategies, and goals. The changes since World War II in the public stance and approach to spatial and social dysfunction reflect the reciprocal influence of social welfare and environmental positions. With increasing frequency these approaches have been incorporated, and sometimes consolidated, in federal and local program enactments. Social welfare has welcomed and encouraged ties to the environment in recognition of their interdependence; and environmentalists have come to view space-related interventions as instruments of social change, with significant social impacts and consequences. In the future some amalgam between the two approaches can constitute the basis for arriving at and achieving an as yet undefinable "social planning" theory and conception. (See chapter 5 for a detailed discussion of the marketability issue.)

Federal Housing Programs

We can trace the social planning tendencies in the federal-related programs over the last fifty years. Public housing in the late 1930s, for example, was an outgrowth of the desire to explore a variety of creative means to deal with the Great Depression by generating socially desirable and constructive public works projects, which simultaneously created jobs and achieved social ends. In seeking to incorporate a slum-eradication component along with the public works and rehousing purposes, public housing included an "equivalent elimination" requirement. For every public housing unit proposed and constructed, a deteriorated unit needed to be removed from the housing supply, either through structural clearance, building, fire, or housing code enforcement, or other means and circumstances.

The quantity of slum clearance that could be achieved as a by-product of the provision of public housing was extremely limited. In addition, the private sector sought a role in clearance activities, arguing that modernization required the exercise of far-reaching public powers massively applied to the extensive slums that predominated in the inner city and, further, depended on the joint efforts of the public and private sectors.

The Housing Act of 1947 was the first broadly based, wide-ranging federal enactment dealing with city decay and redevelopment, the urban environment, and growth policy. It was an approach whose time had come. Legislative action in some states preceded federal actions. In Illinois, for example, comparable legislation was adopted in 1945, and later linked to the federal authorization. The national enactment, which had broad-based support in Congress across political parties, philosophies, and regions, was further legitimated by the distinction of its sponsors. In the Senate, prior to passage, the enactment had been called the Wagner-Ellender-Taft Bill when the Senate was in Democratic control, and the Taft-Ellender-Wagner Bill when the Republicans were in control. Senator Robert A. Taft of Ohio, referred to as "Mr. Republican" by the public and the media, was considered the principal national and senatorial Republican spokesman and held strong conservative political and economic positions. Senator Robert Wagner of New York was a nationally regarded liberal spokesman in the Senate and strongly identified with Roosevelt and the New Deal. Senator Allen Ellender of Louisiana was perceived as a major symbol of the South and of its distinctive brand of political conservatism.

The Housing Act of 1947 made it possible for a locality to seek to identify particular deteriorated areas within its corporate jurisdiction, areas usually located in the inner ring of the central city, as slum and blighted—and to set in motion a process leading ultimately to the total or near total demolition of the structures therein located and to the subsequent resale of the publicly cleared land to private developers (as well as to institutions and public agencies) for reuse and redevelopment.

A number of related purposes were intended to be served by this slum clearance and urban redevelopment process. The removal of slum and blight was perceived as an absolute value, on the theory that the deterioration constituted an intolerable environmental strain, and an unconscionable consignment of the resident population to life in shameful physical circumstances. The slum and blighted structures, besides often having multiple owners, frequently had clouded property titles and were often enmeshed in complex financial entanglements. The legislation provided that the power of eminent domain could be invoked (after public hearings, and other legal and statutory requirements had been met) on the premise that the public health, welfare, and safety were threatened. Given the physical, legal, and financial condition of the property, private assembly of land without eminent domain was thought impossible. Further, systematic land assembly through the use of eminent domain was critical if buildable packages of adequate size were to be assembled to achieve orderly planned redevelopment. Along with the clearance of structures, planned redevelopment was also required to help ready the area for reuse, including the reconstruction, construction, location, and relocation of necessary site improvements. Planned redevelopment necessitated modernizing the total environment, including street patterns, new or added public and open spaces, schools and parks, institutional spaces, and the like. A key function was to determine the type, character, and distribution of the proposed land uses, and to establish criteria and standards to guide and govern the subsequent resale of buildable land for development and construction.

A sharp distinction was drawn between the costs to the public of planning, administration, property acquisition, structure clearance, site improvements, and community facilities, etc., and the price at which the cleared, improved, and rebuildable land would be sold for private, institutional, or public development. The concept of fair reuse value was established to reflect the potential value of the land that was to be developed in accordance with the redevelopment plan. The fair reuse value was based on the equivalent cost of comparable land, similarly developed pursuant to like standards, and at competitive locations. Writing down the marginal public costs to modernize the environment and overcome structural and site deterioration and obsolescence would permit private redevelopers to proceed competitively. The substantial cost differential between the total public costs and the dollar proceeds derived from the land resale was shared in the early period of the slum clearance program on the basis of a formula by which the federal government bore up to two-thirds of the cost and the locality no less than one-third. Under certain circumstances this could be altered to a three-quarter/one-quarter federal-local split. The locality was authorized to meet its local share by absorbing the costs of site and public-works improvement, providing community facilities and other works in kind, as well as cash, which was often made possible by local public bond-issue referenda.

Except for the latter cost-sharing approach, which has undergone substantial changes over time, particularly under the influence of revenue sharing and block grants, the description and guiding principles of federally supported and locally undertaken public acquisition and private resale activities have generally continued, despite other program changes. The slum clearance program as originally conceived was oriented toward the elimination of concentrations of physically deteriorated structures and thereby provided the public with an opportunity to reshape the environment in collaboration with the private sector. Since redevelopment in the final analysis was to be privately undertaken, the selection of the redevelopment areas was heavily influenced by developers, institutions, and other prospective partners in the process. These actors were perceived by the media as assets, and their interest viewed as evidence of civic mindedness. The dependence on private development, and on the contractual commitment to an agreed-upon time schedule, underscored the reliance on a demonstrated market for the project upon its completion. Considerable pressure was always being exerted to document the fact that occupancy was assured.*

The result was that areas selected for redevelopment, while qualified and eligible under the law, were often not necessarily in the poorest condition. The rock-ribbed slums were often badly located, with poorer market prospects than the sites ultimately selected. The tendency was to pick areas with prime locations, areas whose improvement would likely serve and support ongoing activities such as central business districts, institutions, or other identifiable activity concentrations critically important to the locality. These activities usually required land area for expansion or compatible surroundings, or were dependent on the creation or reinforcement of consumer or user market sheds to survive. Ultimate market considerations thus became the critical criteria in the selection of redevelopment areas from those eligible. Reinforcing this consideration was the hope and promise that redevelopment would be the means to enhance the city's competitive advantage in retaining populations and attracting them to the inner city. This goal was built into the original legislative conception and became a part of the public argument on its behalf. Redevelopment was perceived as the means to preserve and strengthen and, where necessary, to help restore the central city and its downtown shopping, office, and recreation activities, and to solidify its institutional base. The redevelopment process would thereby safeguard and expand the city's existing and potential tax base and tax yield. Redevelopment frequently became the program device forging a local alliance between city hall, and Main and Wall streets. City hall delivered the people in support of the alliance and on behalf of inner-city redevelopment; Main Street delivered the local financial interests, the major retailers, the media, and the major institutions. It was not unusual for the mayor to fail as a result of the alliance, as he or she became vulnerable and was exposed to assaults from the outlying neighborhoods and communities, the small businessmen and small property owners, the ethnic populations, the aged, the poor, and the minorities who began to forge their own adversarial alliances.

Major changes in the nature of the program did not arise solely as a response to these political realignments. It became clear that the program's original conception was too environmentally oriented. The modernization of space and the enhancement of an area's market prospects could not by themselves cure what ailed the cities. There were some

---

*Sections 235 and 236 made possible highly attractive federal financing for private rental and sales housing, under specified conditions and to serve particular groups of the population.

spectacular achievements—generally of a monumental nature and usually focused in or around the downtown business district, a government or cultural center, or on a site with particularly advantageous vistas or other situational assets. The narrow focus imposed a sharp constraint on the scope of the slum project undertakings. The program tended to delimit the geographic areas from which redevelopment projects could be selected. This delimitation did not always coincide with a locality's strategy and priorities for dealing with city-wide recovery. The location of areas inevitably influenced the nature and character of redevelopment in a way that was often in conflict with broader city-wide strategies and goals. Conflicts usually centered around nonresidential and high-density residential redevelopment proposals.

The program during its early stages was only minimally concerned with the socioeconomic problems that surfaced or were generated during the course of the redevelopment undertaking. Frequently such problems were deliberately avoided. It was common practice for the decision makers and practitioners to argue that these problems were outside redevelopment concerns, deferring to those agencies and jurisdictions charged with social and service responsibilities. This stance was prevalent among the professional planning groups, most of whom were only beginning to confront social problems. The program was fixed by Congress with responsibility for relocation. Relocation was the one major opportunity provided by the early slum clearance program for confronting and dealing with the social problems associated with redevelopment. Relocation required that the program interface with the affected population as well as with the public and private service groups who traditionally served them. Although the redevelopment proposal made it necessary to examine and analyze social data to establish planning standards, these materials were developed on a professional and collegial basis, and usually without resident or political participation. Relocation in these early program stages was rarely a satisfactory experience. To the relocator, displacement is the means not the end, and therefore even when conscionably undertaken, it is perceived as an obstacle to be overcome so that the redevelopment can proceed. The relocator, either by direction or choice, limits himself to helping the individual or family move to a legally acceptable housing location off the redevelopment site.

Many people benefited from the relocation experience by an improvement in their housing and by the opportunity to move into communities that they might not previously have considered. While rehousing families in communities alien to them was frequently viewed as a program defect, relocation facilitated the distribution of minority populations and thereby helped overcome the rigid segregation that characterized the inner city.

On the other hand, the problems faced by displaced families were frequently wide-ranging and profound. The necessity to move often compounded existing problems and triggered new ones. It should have been possible to treat displacement as a creative and constructive opportunity to mobilize the service delivery network on behalf of the individual and family in connection with employment, training, health, and other support services.

The relocatees generally had limited financial means, were vulnerable to diverse pressures and forces, had few housing and community choices, and had a small number of support service systems to draw upon. Theoretically, relocation could have provided the relocatee with an advocate, with an agent and ombudsman to safeguard and advance his interests actively, rather than leaving him at the mercy of the marketplace. We can only speculate what the consequences of the creation of an aggressive and autonomous rehousing agency would have been. Rehousing might have been connected to the service delivery system and placed in the charge of service, rather than remaining a responsibility of the redevelopment practitioners. Housing for the disadvantaged is human services related, not development related. Many public housing and redevelopment problems are a direct result of this conceptual confusion. Rehousing can represent an affirmative opportunity. In the prevailing system the individuals affected by displacement have been within the charge of providers responsible to different client groups and utilizing conflicting performance criteria. All of us, including the relocatees, are customarily at the mercy of the marketplace. However, since these forces are anonymous and are exerted evenhandedly, they leave each to his own financial and personal devices in dealing with the effects and consequences of relocation. Displacement, on the other hand, is the result of deliberate public activity, and even when the most careful and generous assistance is provided, the individual and family rightly feel intruded upon and manipulated. The sponsoring public agency is targeted as the agency responsible for precipitating the displacement and creating the personal and housing crisis. Even when assistance is provided by the public agency, the need to relocate arouses more resentment than impersonal and often callous treatment in the marketplace.

Developing an Urban Public Policy

For all the reasons cited, national policies toward the modernization of the central city became the subject of extensive reexamination. Ways were sought to incorporate and reflect social considerations in the development of the plan and program more adequately and to expand the market and the range of beneficiaries of the modernization process.

In the early 1950s, presidential study groups were convened, congressional committees held hearings and conducted investigations, research and evaluation studies were undertaken, and articles and books were produced for popular and academic consumption, all seeking to strengthen the efforts directed toward reducing the problems of the city. On the whole, these extensive inquiries and reexaminations were constructively undertaken and were unbridled by the acrimony and sharp edge of criticism and cynicism that marked later periods of national inquiry and debate. In the mid-1950s, during the Eisenhower administration, the extensive national discussion resulted in a major new legislative enactment that reordered the approach adopted a decade earlier. Slum clearance was extended to include slum prevention and conservation and was ultimately encompassed under the urban renewal umbrella. The theory underlying the change was that the initial slum-clearance approaches were based on definitions that were too narrow, were limited in the activities and functions they brought into play and in the tools and mechanisms they relied upon, and were too restricted to the geography they affected. Approaches were too often directed at particular and limited locations, were serving too few people, and too often brought disproportionate benefit to the larger property and monied groups. Finally, it was asserted that public powers would be better utilized to prevent rather than to eradicate slums.

Slum clearance was generally a single-purpose program with a limited function. It sought to remedy environmental obsolescence by the elimination of slum structures and by the preparation of a spatial plan for reconstruction that would induce private developers to join in the effort to enhance the project site so that it became marketable and would attract people to remain or return to the central city. These activities were intended to preserve and strengthen the city's commercial as well as its tax base. As a result of spatial and environmental stress the activities generated by the slum-clearance program tended to focus on site and public improvements, such as streets, utilities, and sewers, and on community facilities, such as schools and parks. Slum-clearance programs supported educational and medical institutions, central business districts, and other uses deemed to be of public value. Consistent with the slum-clearance-program focus, project locations tended to be limited to the inner ring of the central city and were chosen to serve market-directed purposes.

Slum prevention and community conservation extended and broadened the scale and reach of public policy as it sought to deal realistically with the issue of modernizing the central city. Increasingly, these public policies were directed at improving the city's competitive position and reconciling the interests and functions of the central city and suburbs. The efforts at broadening the public capacity to cope with central-city modernization and restoration were occurring in the face of a dramatic movement of people and jobs out of the city, which exacerbated the city's obsolescence and further obstructed its ability to compete for residents, shopping, and jobs. Consequently, what was required by way of intervention went far beyond project-clearance activities. It was not only sites that needed restoration; whole communities required preservation and modernization.

Slum prevention and community conservation were outgrowths of the slum-clearance program. Initially, it was assumed that slum prevention and conservation purposes would be served by eliminating slum pockets in otherwise stable threatened community areas. Early on, it became clear that a range of factors needed to be brought into play to cope with the real or perceived threat and to reverse the process of community decline. These factors included building, housing, and fire code compliance; zoning ordinance enforcement; structural improvement; tenancy and ownership policies; financing programs and practices; craft union policies; market appeal and demand; assessment and taxing policies and practices; type, character, condition, and financial status of structures; socioeconomic characteristics of the current and prospective resident population; the vitality of community organization and institutions; individual and family attitudes and behavior; and a host of other critical factors that determine the community's future prospects and establish the capacity to stem and reverse community decline.

Conserving, preserving, and restoring older central city communities depended on overcoming the obsolescence of the spatial environment, with particular attention paid to traffic and circulation, parking, and the growth and expansion of space required by institutions, shopping areas, etc.

In addition, the conservation effort concerned itself with municipal housekeeping, law enforcement and personal and property safety, the adequacy and quality of schools, and the socioeconomic mix of the community-wide population, as well as the distribution and use of the major community facilities, including the schools, parks, and churches. These concerns influence resident attitudes and behavior, institutional decisions, the practices and policies of financing institutions, and owner attitudes with respect to undertaking structural improvements.

Structural conditions and obsolescence constituted another major factor in community conservation. Three concerns operated in dealing with the physical condition of structures and living units: the federal requirements; local codes, ordinances, and practices; and market considerations. The federal agency responsible for determining eligibility established criteria for redevelopment and conservation areas, and particularly for the clearance of structures and living units. These criteria reflected a desire to identify and classify the structures and living units that were a threat to human occupancy and to "the sound growth of the community." A further goal was to establish which of these structures were beyond the prospect of feasible retention through structural improvement at a reasonable cost. It was difficult, of course, to develop national criteria; defining the threat was a relative judgment, varying with local custom and perception, depending on the prevailing socioeconomic circumstance of the community at any given moment in time, and on the city and community program and project goals.

Identifying and determining which of the "slum" structures needed to be eliminated to stem community decline and reverse the downward slide and thereby set in motion a process of self-renewal was even more difficult than establishing, measuring, and classifying structural condition, since these activities were predicated on gauging individual attitudes and forecasting human behavior. The task was to determine which of the deteriorated structures could possibly be improved and thereby retained, and which could not. The final judgment depended not only on the actual condition of the structures and on the cost of correcting any deficiencies, but most importantly on the structural and community standards to be met. The scale and cost of the necessary and desired structural improvement were affected by the population to be served and the conditions they imposed as a prerequisite to their residency in the area. The feasibility of arranging and securing the necessary financing to undertake and complete the improvements, and the capacity of current or new residents to repay costs of the improvements, constituted other key factors.

Determining the extent of local housing, building, and fire code violations and compliance served a number of helpful purposes. It was a locally sanctioned measure for establishing structural and living unit standards and provided a useful comparison with federally imposed criteria in developing program recommendations. The degree of code compliance reflected owner and resident attitudes and behavior and helped to establish the prospects for launching a conservation program. Rigorous code enforcement also constituted an important tactic in triggering a more ambitious structural improvement program, by forcing the property owner to determine whether the costs of code compliance could be recaptured only by more extensive improvements. While utilizing codes and ordinances in connection with redevelopment and conservation programing was both useful and reinforcing, it did not, as hoped, act as a great housing leavener and a common national housing denominator. There was wide variation not only in the criteria and standards among codes and ordinances, but in the extent and quality of code enforcement among different cities and even within the same city.

In the final analysis, the standards and requirements imposed by the market shaped the criteria and constituted the basis for the clearance and conservation programs and activities. It was the market that mediated the issues and dichotomies discussed here, and it was the market that was relied on to resolve the dilemmas and conflicts as they arose. Codes and ordinances were used to provide assurances to property owners, tenants, investors, and financial institutions that minimum levels of maintenance could be expected. This was also a signal that the area preservation and improvement had the support of the official city, and that an attempt was being made to influence occupancy by imposing minimum standards. Most important, the enforcement codes and ordinances were utilized as the lever to trigger the restoration process, by activating the relevant and affected parties. The need to comply with the codes, and the costs thereby imposed, generally resulted in a comprehensive assessment of the property, the occupancy, the surrounding community, the alternative investment choices, the financial opportunities and constraints, and all of the other critical and wide-ranging factors. The cast of relevant actors was also wide ranging; it included the property owner and occupant, community residents, financers (banks, savings and loans, and mortgage companies), insurance companies (fire and theft), trade and craft unions, and city-wide and community leaders and business people.

Faced with the need to comply with the codes and ordinances, the property owner had one of three choices. He could walk away from the structure—that is, abandon it; he could comply with the codes; or he could exceed code requirements. Abandonment was not uncommon, and code enforcement and compliance were not the only reasons for it. Usually the abandoned property had been fully depreciated, had extensive maintenance problems, and was experiencing rising taxes and insurance and utility costs. The structures were losing tenants, and minimum levels of occupancy were becoming harder and harder to maintain. In addition, they were facing increasingly severe management problems along with a deterioration in the quality of owner-tenant relations. Frequently the buildings threatened with abandonment were among the better structures in the area, those with the highest prevailing costs due to the levels of maintenance the owner sought to sustain, and the reasonable return the owner was willing to accept. The housing occupants of these structures had relatively greater freedom to make residential choices and were therefore better able to move. The early moveouts consequently tended to be people with the financial and emotional resources to be upwardly mobile. Thus the owners, fearful or reluctant to operate a property that was allowed to deteriorate, and with limited prospects for attracting a comparable replacement group of tenants, simply walked away from the structure, exacerbating and reinforcing the process of housing abandonment and community decay.

Another course open to the property owner was to attempt to comply with the codes and to maintain a minimum structural standard. This generally was the prevailing course when the structure was located in an area or community that was essentially stable, when it was generally sound, and when the property owners were assured of a pool of new buyers and occupants of the same or higher socioeconomic class as the then-prevailing population. In these instances, code enforcement and compliance with the code constituted important tools in a preventive program—similar to a temperature and pulse reading in a medical checkup.

However, in areas and communities where the issue of the frequency and quality of code enforcement and compliance was of central and pressing concern, owners and others tended to be caught up in a more complex and imposing network of decisions. Faced with the need to comply with local codes, the owner confronted a moment of truth, particularly if the structure was part of a slum prevention or conservation program, or in an area that was at a restoration crossroads. In most instances it was the market that governed. All of the pressures operated in the market's behalf, and the evidences of probable and ultimate success were measured in market towns. The financing institutions tended to qualify their loans according to the quality of the proposed structural improvements, and on indications that individuals and families of relatively higher socioeconomic status would be retained or attracted. These practices were often subject to abuse, as in red-lining. It was sometimes claimed that there was insufficient evidence that potential income in improved structures justified the return on investment, or that more profitable alternative investment options existed elsewhere. The prevailing test was the relationship between the income capacity and social status of the existing and future residents, and improvement costs and financing—that is to say, whether rental and sales return would recapture the dollars invested. It was hoped that the initial intervention would trigger a continuing escalation of structural improvements and would broaden the area's market appeal by attracting people of even higher socioeconomic status. This goal was generally shared by all of the actors engaged in the redevelopment transactional system: owner, agents, mortgagors, insurance companies, retail businesses, professionals, and others who sought the financial advantage that derived from a continuing rise in the socioeconomic status of the area and its population. The media also reveled in both the newsworthiness of the restoration "happening" and, far more important to them, in the benefits of lucrative advertising and other growth and dollar opportunities. They deliberately set out to shape public attitudes and influence market behavior—through the news columns themselves in the wording of headlines and in the lead paragraphs, through the selection and slant of video features, and through the arrangement and content of both real estate and business sections of the newspaper.

The pressure to respond and conform to the marketplace also came from the federal government. It exerted these pressures in many ways. It oriented its lending policies, for example, to structural and occupancy standards that generally exceeded those required by local codes and ordinances. They were usually pegged at a level that helped shape and reinforce the tendency to serve relatively higher socioeconomic status groups. Frequently, as a matter of fact, as with the private lending institutions, the federal test of the adequacy of housing improvements and of loans was met almost exclusively by financial criteria. What better assurance of the soundness of an investment than a population with stable occupations and steady or rising incomes? Developed approaches that increased the exposure to risk by consciously and deliberately extending federal help to the tenant, the small property owner, the less desirable structure or area, or a needy target population were usually tagged as special and time-limited risk programs, and they constituted newsworthy events.

Except for rock-bottom slums and the area containing a preponderance of such structures, all areas and structures are salvageable at a cost. The city may, in its best interests, seek to recapture a particular salvageable area for industrial or other uses. However, for most older residential structures and communities the two key and qualifying factors are the cost of the "salvage" and the source of payment. Government had taken the initiative to modernize the community's spatial environment by selectively or totally clearing structures; arranging for or providing new or reorganized site and community facilities and discounting the costs to the point thought necessary to complete the restoration and modernization process; and introducing financing programs to lubricate the process. Each of these phases had been predicated on and oriented toward marketplace considerations. These had been initiated and undertaken on the premise that the public is best served by rising socioeconomic indicators. The behavior of tenants, owners, developers, and financial institutions was rewarded, and program success was judged by upwardly spiraling physical and spatial measures of achievement: land costs, tax rate and tax yield, tenant income and social status, etc.

It was clear, however, that there were alternative methods to salvage, preserve, and improve structures and areas without a total reliance on a spiraling socioeconomic market. Social criteria could be adopted to measure success, and other methods could lessen the dependence on higher income groups to help recapture modernization costs. Modifications in existing practices to accomplish some of these purposes were sought by such modest remedial measures as rent-supplement programs, the section 235 and 236 low-interest programs, and the like. These measures frequently constituted add-ons prompted to secure political or popular sanction. The measures might have been extended and expanded in scale, and more ambitious approaches could have been introduced that would have sought to create, consolidate, and sustain less affluent constituencies with different goals. More modest structural and spatial improvements, and a shift from producer to consumer subsidies, among other measures, could have made this a viable alternative strategy.

The prevailing measure of community improvements, however, was always defined by escalating investments and tested by the extent to which the activities succeeded in retaining the existing population and in attracting new populations with the same or higher socioeconomic status from other parts of the city and metropolitan area. The process was circular: modernization was essential to attract higher status populations, and the higher the status of the population the more pressure was likely to be exerted to raise the modernization standards, multiply structural and community improvements, and increase the quantity and quality of the investment. The market was, in fact, to be the judge. Once an area's locational advantages and the essential soundness of its structures were established, the market and modernization were the paramount considerations. The soundness of the structure was largely determined by whether the cost of improvements in the basic structural systems (heating, plumbing, and electrical), and in the building's market-related features (kitchens, bathrooms, public spaces, etc.), could be recovered. As a matter of fact, many buildings went through two stages of improvement. Improvements in the systems were often effected by owner-occupants to retain or attract tenants or to prevent the property from deteriorating into an unmarketable condition. The improvements effected in this initial stage of modernization were not viewed as dramatic achievements, or necessarily as a part of any widespread restoration program. While more recent preservation and restoration efforts often included modernizing the heating, electrical, and plumbing systems, they tended to focus on market-related elements.

The Complexities of Effecting Urban Change

These practices and their market orientation were not distortions of legislation (or public) intent. A prime motivation for the slum clearance and subsequent slum prevention enactments was the conviction that heroic and drastic measures were necessary to reverse the decline and decay of the central city. It was generally thought that what was at stake was the city itself. At the outset, the public, the professionals, the real estate and land development–related operatives, and the legislature assumed that the urban "crisis" could be contained and that activities should be limited to the "surgical removal of the cancerous" slum condition. Eradicating the slum would eliminate the threat and reverse the obsolescence resulting from the outmoded spatial environment that was the product of earlier stages of urban growth and ill-adapted to contemporary needs. Such an enterprise had the highest public priority; the alternative was an acceleration in urban decline and in an increased loss of people, productive activities, and tax yields.

In the central city a higher weight was assigned to this broader objective than to the housing needs of the population, their social dysfunctions, the services they lacked or might require, and to the possible consequences of the intervention. Since greater weight was assigned to "saving the city," it is not surprising that a program of "maximum" modernization and market strategy was adopted. Given the limited prior experience with intervention of this type, scope, and scale, the tendency was inevitably to extend the program reach by seeking to broaden the modernization efforts to the limits of financial and design capacity, and to encompass within the market to be served as high a socioeconomic status group as the modernization efforts could allow. This approach would not only involve the least margin of uncertainty during program development, but would also permit far more predictable and measurable results than would likely be achieved by less ambitious efforts and undertakings. In addition, from a very practical point of view, it could be expected that proposals would be advanced, particularly in the first group of projects, which sharply contrasted with the condition the intervention sought to remedy and correct—if open space was nonexistent, for example, a special effort to provide it would be made.

A whole range of such illustrations could be provided where deliberate attempts to correct a presumed environmental imperfection resulted in an overreaction to achieve compensatory benefits. The open space illustration constitutes a typical and widely used example, and it was cited in many of the early projects. There are also instances, again principally in the early projects, in which, in the desire to avoid the problems associated with the "overbuilt and teeming slum," replacement residential uses were proposed and constructed at densities more appropriate to suburban settings, in structures with unnecessarily low percentages of land coverage in relation to building height and bulk, and in surroundings in which more land was provided for open space, institutions, and community facilities than would be expected in a conventional urban setting. Along with the tendency to push the limits of modernization to reflect current technologies, and to meet contemporary (and even anticipate future) standards of environmental excellence, it was hoped that people of relatively higher socioeconomic status would be attracted. This latter desire in itself acted as a pressure, since it was assumed such people require a higher structural and environmental standard as a condition of their locational interest. This was all the more necessary if they were to be attracted to areas that customarily did not appeal to them personally; it was to overcome their natural reluctance and resistance, and even apprehension and fear.

The lack of experience with these issues, and therefore with the mix of actions required to affect the stated purposes, also resulted in a lack of precision with respect to the character and magnitude of the particular actions necessary to achieve the desired goals. Thus, for example, it was a common occurrence in the early project efforts—and it continues to be the case, though with less frequency, even today—that more or less area is cleared than is necessary, standards are established that are higher or lower than is necessary, and modernization takes place to a greater or lesser extent than is necessary in order to sustain or create new markets for the range of activities provided for in the plan. However, in the early stages of program development, "more" (clearance, modernization, standards, etc.) rather than "less," for the reasons discussed, tended to be the prevailing pattern. The appropriate actions at any given moment can only be justified by the reality at the point of intervention—by the structural, spatial, and related relevant circumstances, by the degree of political and public sanction, and by the prevailing attitudes and behavior of the critical actors and reactors—and all these factors are influenced by the anticipated consequences of the intervention. The capacity to predict is sharply limited in these regards, and therefore wisdom tends to be retrospective rather than prospective. More than this, a particular collection of plan activities and proposals might be necessary at the outset to generate a market interest and demand; and then, depending on subsequent market behavior, the initial mix of activities and proposals may need reordering. A strong subsequent market suggests that a more modest initial approach would have been adequate; a weak market, a more ambitious initial approach. The recognition that cumulative effects can alter the needed constellation of activities and proposals has been institutionalized in more current practice by an increased reliance on process rather than product and on more selective and staged intervention.

These modifications in an orientation based on a "maximum" strategy also resulted in the scaling down of the measures proposed for modernization, despite the intention to reach for the high status groups in the marketplace. A number of additional factors were responsible for these changes. Evidence began to build that if the initial interventions were at all successful, community conservation and restoration could be achieved by more modest modernization measures, and the high status approach to the market could be modified without damage to the conservation and restoration effort—and without sacrifice to the prospect of ultimately serving the elite market.

A strategy that set in motion a restoration and reconstruction process that effected change over time, even if it was imperceptible at any given moment, was more appropriate than a "maximum strategy." The increased reliance on and confidence in the ultimate efficacy of the process led to the recognition that this approach was less disruptive socially and, therefore, more acceptable politically. Since the social problems that exist within an affected area, and the emotional, financial, and other critical problems being experienced by the resident population, no longer surface in dramatic form, they are easily and frequently obscured and ignored by the public. On the other hand, the opportunity exists for the affected individuals and families, and the institutions and public operating on their behalf, to deal with these problems on a more manageable scale and in a more manageable form. It should also be observed that the more modified and measured approach to community conservation, preservation, and restoration is in large part a response to the social consequences of earlier, more ambitious efforts, and a reflection of the growing sensitivity to social needs and to the merit of relating spatial and social interventions.

The fact is, however, that no territory exists in a "steady state" over any extended period of time, nor can a set of circumstances be created on the assumption that it will constitute a "fixed point" that can be held firm. A community is changing constantly—spatially, structurally, demographically, socially, and economically. The changes that are occurring can be measured by absolute criteria, which establish whether the community or area is improving or declining, that is, criteria related to condition, investment, usage, etc. These measurements tend to be made and these judgments tend to be formed, by the public and by the major financial, social, and other institutions of society. However, people tend to make relative rather than absolute judgments, reflecting their income and their viable choices. They define structural and community improvement or decline in relation to their current living condition. Consequently, an area may be on the "decline" by absolute criteria with respect to structural condition, but an "improvement" when judged by an individual for whom the area represents an upwardly mobile stage in his or her self-advancement. Such relative judgments and perceptions have

transformed the character of slum clearance and slum prevention programs. Simplistic approaches related to and limited to condition criteria
or to facility provision, or to other comprehensible and measurable
factors, while they may constitute reassuring and definable indexes, fail
to reflect the reach and range of the mission. For if what is at stake is in fact
the city, then the obligation that is imposed is to encompass the urbanization process within one's vision, and to capture and reflect its
sweep and scope.

The complications of the task are evident in so many ways that they
often defy attempts at straightforward definition or the setting of precise
dimensions. For example, the physical condition of structures and of an
area have been and continue to be a basic component in establishing
eligibility under the law and are a major element in fashioning plan
proposals. Yet experience has demonstrated that areas with structures in
relatively more deteriorated condition are less likely to be the targets of
public action if they embody relatively higher orders of social organization than does a less deteriorated area. The presence of social organization is often a sufficient basis to avoid targeting the area for public
action, even though evenhandedness and structural condition would
warrant its selection for public action. The importance of social organization as a deterrent is dramatized in those few instances where such
areas have been targeted. The clamor and the intensity of the community
reaction have stood as a signal to avoid such places wherever possible.
These cases have generally involved ethnic areas of low to middle socioeconomic status, as on the West Side of Chicago, or the West End in
Boston.

Distinctive areas, which exist in every city, provide added examples
of the increasing complexity of the tasks. These distinctive areas are
generally privately developed, without conscious public intervention,
and are frequently perceived as without lasting character. They are areas
that were constructed as part of a unified development whose appeal
rests on their spatial arrangement and their structural relationships, and
on the total effect achieved by their site plan. Not uncommonly, the
individual buildings and other environmental components are without
particular architectural distinction. Almost without exception these areas
have managed to survive far beyond the life of their surroundings, have
withstood the deteriorating effects and pressures from their adjacent
areas, and over time have constituted the rallying event and catalytic
element around which widespread community restoration efforts are
undertaken. These areas have not only maintained a special market
appeal in contrast to other places, but provide the basis for generating
large-scale market demands. Isolating and defining those factors and
characteristics that account for the distinction and durability of these

areas are of particular interest. With such knowledge, the quality of conscious and deliberate public planning interventions could be enhanced. Guidance and insight, lacking all too long, would be provided to strengthen the spatial and environmental relationships in community and urban restoration. The factors that might be explored include the role and relative weighting of isolation, closure, and human scale, and other sensitive considerations that relate spatial, environmental, behavioral, and social characteristics. An improved understanding of these relationships would be expected to influence the character of subsequent public interventions.

CHAPTER 5

Marketability: The Major Determinant in Clearance and Restoration

The changing attitudes and behaviors toward land clearance are a sensitive barometer for tracking the development of an urban strategy and a useful means of illustrating the narrowing gap between planning and action.

Each urban progam enacted during the New Deal and after World War II constitutes a phase in a continuous process directed at enhancing and sharpening the public capacity to adapt to the changing needs of society and the ever-rising expectations of its citizens. All too frequently we view each legislative enactment as a culmination, and then in the face of disappointment and frustration charge forward with new enactments, advanced as representing fresh—and again culminating—programmatic panaceas. No program at any point in time warrants blind attachment or unbridled indictment. Each should be viewed as a stage in developing insight and skill, reflecting the knowledge and sanction that are available at any given moment. Each program solves some problems and creates new ones—and it is the net effect that must, therefore, be assessed.

A series of long-standing problems, largely social in nature, have beset restoration efforts. Restoration is usually pursued on the premise that society, the family, and the individual have the demonstrated capacity to deal with all of the attendant social problems associated with the undertaking. Restoration planning is a by-product of affluence, with strong environmental, structural, and spatial implications. These efforts frequently tend to ignore or minimize the fact that aspiring groups are forced to rely on available and graduated choices. Situational improvements for the socially disadvantaged are likely to occur by increments over time. Consequently, the supportive role of urban restoration activities is limited. If a "social cost factor" were assigned the same legitimacy and status as a building and land cost factor, this limitation might be remedied. The "social cost factor" would be introduced in those instances where the individual or family is burdened by social and emotional disabilities and has neither the resources nor the opportunity to find satisfactory alternatives, and where society has failed to provide compensatory payments as a condition for restoration.

A related consideration is the need to explore the experimental use of the benefit assessment (as is the case in Great Britain), employed where public actions on fortuitously located properties result in private accretions in land value. The measured private gain would be captured and retained by the public or distributed in some equitable fashion, at least to those disadvantageously affected by the public actions.

Planning for Clearance and Restoration

An examination of the evolving role of clearance as a critical component in urban restoration efforts is a useful means of tracking changes in prevailing planning practice and in the strategies that have characterized the nature and quality of intervention. The shifting role of clearance reflects at any given moment what is achievable, marketable, and attitudinally digestible and acceptable. It is useful to think about these factors in terms of their limitations, that is, the constraints and the challenges they impose. The operable range within which political (and popular) sanction is likely to be achieved needs to be established; for example, what are the required terms and conditions that need to be met prior to securing sanction?

The extent of clearance is determined not only by what is possible politically, but by what is required to serve the market. The prevalent attitudes and their influence on individual, family, and group behavior are largely responsible for defining and determining the extent of land clearance. The assumptions about clearance that prevailed in the early history of urban restoration had widespread political sanction, or at least sufficient vocal and visible public support. The emphasis was on the physical condition of buildings and on the deterioration and obsolescence of areas and communities. The objectives in the early stages were the clearance of slums and the elimination of slum structures. The underlying attitude was that areas that had been built-up in earlier eras had outlived their usefulness and needed to be replaced in accord with modern design and community planning principles if they were to be brought into the twentieth century. The deteriorated and decaying structures were assumed to be unfit for acceptable human habitation. The humane approach was to assist the residents in relocating to "decent, safe, and sanitary housing within their means and in easy access to their work" (the exact language in the federal statute). The physical decline and spatial disorganization of the area were further assumed to reflect social disorganization as well.

But with the growing power of grass-roots and inner-city community organizations, the mobilization of community and city-wide minority organizations and the increases in minority representation, combined with the formation and consolidation of small property owner, taxpayer, and outlying community groups, the political attitudes towards clearance programs changes drastically. The capacity of these groups to flex their muscles altered the base for determining what and where clearance was achievable. There was no longer a prima facie assumption that clearance was approvable—desirable or not. Spatial disorganization and social disorganization no longer seemed to go hand in hand. Many of the designated slum areas began to give evidence of a social and political organization already in place, even if not heretofore visible or acknowledged. Yet the residents recognized that they clearly lacked the means to make alternative arrangements. Neither they nor the society acting on their behalf were ready or equipped to meet the emotional, social, and material needs that were created or exacerbated by the proposed displacement. For these populations, environmental and spatial improvements were far less important than economic assistance and supportive services and benefits. In addition, the displacement was likely to remove their community and family support system and aggravate the hardships brought on by their economic circumstances. The defects and inequities of such drastic surgery were becoming all too apparent. An urban restoration strategy based on extensive land clearance, which hoped to achieve environmental excellence and improved housing, was both imperfect and even damaging and counterproductive.

Housing for the disadvantaged and upwardly mobile is better perceived and dealt with as a consequence than as a precipitating event. Unless the target population has resources or is provided income equivalents by way of subsidies or other compensatory devices, housing will not trigger a process of continuous and self-improvement, as is the case, for example, with jobs, economic development, education, and other "pump-priming and generating" activities. A rise in housing quality without a commensurate rise in income or income equivalents deprives lower-income groups of any access to the improvement. If housing is to be relied upon as a strategy, the supply must be increased at a rate that accelerates the filtering-down process, even at the risk of increased abandonment of the inner city.

But it was not only the displaced families and communities that were questioning the clearance programs. Public doubts were growing. Those at the receiving end of the clearance process—not surprisingly they tended to be lower-middle-class residents of blue collar and ethnic areas—had some misgivings of their own. The institutions, associations, and organizations identified with these receiving areas—such as the Catholic church and the craft unions clearly motivated by the threat of the movement of the displaced populations into their communities—entered the fray, using class and minority rhetoric to oppose the clearance activities.

There was obviously a need to reexamine and reevaluate the initial premises. The assumption that total clearance was required to overcome built-in and environmental obsolescence, and to modernize the older inner-city areas, was open to question. The assumption that total clearance was the only viable recourse, if the marketability of the target areas was to be restored and people with economic viability retained and attracted, could be seriously challenged. New political alignments and realities, the sharp shifts in market behavior, and the changes in the popular attitudes toward particular areas that had been either "written off" or assumed to be on a tobogganing decline brought a significant modification in approach.

Clearance was no longer the sole strategy. The initial assumption at the time urban development was introduced had been that intervention should be limited to the hard-core slum areas, where clearance presumably constituted the only defensible course of action. This stance was substantially modified to include areas and communities where slum prevention was the more appropriate objective. This new approach received further encouragement from a changing market demand and newly developed and available financial support mechanisms that made structural and community improvements possible that were heretofore not achievable. The improved market and financial prospects were both generated and reinforced by new social groupings and concentrations in a limited number of selected sections of the older inner city where urban regeneration and restoration were taking place.

The amount of clearance required in a particular community or area was in large part dependent on the market the public and private sponsors sought to serve. Clearance was not solely determined by a set of universally applied criteria or a prescribed definition. What was "necessary" could change over time, depending on the stages in the restoration process itself and the community's experience and degree of sophistication. In the restoration effort it was the market that determined the appropriate level of deferred maintenance, major rehabilitation, or redevelopment.

Alternative financing packages to facilitate restoration largely determine the socioeconomic character of the market and the social goals that are likely to be attained. Restoration is not an absolute public good; it exacts a social price with consequences and penalties that are not always easily dealt with or remedied.

Ambivalence in public intervention policy created a constant tension between the inclination and pressure to trigger the market by elaborate public and private structural and community improvements and favorable financial arrangements and, alternately, to constrain the market and its socioeconomic excesses. The associated conflict was frequently sharply felt in older, inner-city areas situated in potentially attractive and strategic locations where structures were essentially sound but neglected and deteriorating and there was substantial overcrowding of both buildings and community. Generally, there was more obsolescence here than decay; it reflected the lack of current market demand by people with the financial resources to stem the decline. These structures and areas were generally peopled by poor, aged, and otherwise dependent populations with limited options. The physical condition of these structures and areas, the inadequate resources of the residents, and the lack of financial incentive by owners who failed to see any prospect of creating a market demand, led to the "inevitable" case for land clearance as critical and necessary.

It had also been impossible, given the cost of land and buildings and the inflated rental income created by overoccupancy (which was the result of structural conversion and conversion by use), to overcome and reduce these costs to a level that would permit adequate maintenance and housing code compliance and generate sufficient dollars for structural improvement. The test was whether the location of the community and the structure, and the new structural improvements, would attract a market able to pay the rental or sales prices and justify the property and improvement costs, and whether the financing terms available to the property owner and investor and the buyer or renter would be sufficient to lubricate the transaction, with the help of consumer or producer subsidy programs.

Clearly the market for particular structural types with amenable locations and other magnetic qualities played a major and influential role in bringing about a reexamination of the clearance strategy. A precipitating event was the increased reliance on code enforcement to stem residential and community decline, by providing both penalties and incentives for urban and community restoration. The enforcement of codes frequently resulted in the property owner's being forced to make expenditures to achieve code compliance which he could not recapture by increased rents or sales prices, since these expenditures did not create or attract an expanding market. Not uncommonly, therefore, rigorous code enforcement reduced or eliminated the margin of exploitation. The property owner in an increasing number of cases—depending on the type of structure and its condition, the location of the community and its relationship to the central area, and its inherent and potential amenities and attractions—considered structural and site improvements (beyond the code) to enlarge the market and thereby recapture his total dollars. This brought into question assumptions about the merit of clearance and about appropriate and necessary environmental and restoration strategies.

A growing number of tools and mechanisms were created and fashioned which accommodated and reinforced the sharply altered restoration policies and practices. In essence, they were predicated on the premise that since public dollars and power could be used for land clearance and redevelopment, it should also be legal and acceptable to use public dollars and power to reduce costs when less extreme measures short of clearance were appropriate. The rationale was that subsidies or other forms of assistance could be used to reduce costs as well as to stimulate and support restoration efforts and attract investment.

It is market factors and market-related phenomena that constitute the predominant factors influencing and determining the changing course of urban restoration activity over time. The three marketing factors that influence restoration undertakings are the physical structure, the community, and the costs and available financing. Packaging the restoration effort in a highly marketable form is consequently both an art and a science. Too elaborate a restoration will result in living and spatial patterns beyond the economic capacity of current and prospective groups of residents. On the other hand, too modest a restoration effort will fail to sustain or attract a resident population with the income capacity to manage and meet the costs of the effort. While it is possible to meet social goals in the restoration effort and accommodate the desire, for example, to serve a less affluent population by scaling down and limiting its extent, two observations in this regard are worth mentioning. First, while the effort can be modified at some risk to the success of the program, there is a level of restoration that needs to be achieved in order to attract a sufficient number of people with the economic ability to sustain the effort. Second, despite sincere efforts at modifying restoration activities to broaden the spectrum of service to diverse and lower-income populations, the appeal of the area may grow over time and attract more affluent populations without deliberate effort. These market-related factors are critical in determining the lower and upper limits of intervention activity at any given moment. This is particularly true with respect to the extent and distribution of land clearance, the quality of structural improvements, and the resulting rental and sales pricing structure. The costing and pricing structure is obviously dependent on the available alternative financing mechanisms, including interest rates, loan terms, and the like. Market potential is also affected by the location and size of the restoration area; the presence (or absence) of institutional or other anchors that help reassure, legitimate, generate a demand, and facilitate the restoration effort; and the character and condition of the adjacent communities. The size of the area is particularly important; it must be large enough to command and dominate both its immediate environment and its surroundings. In addition, the market is affected by the types of structures that predominate in the restoration area. Improvements in certain types of structures—for example, historical, architectural, or other distinctive attractions—have a broader appeal than others.

Marketability is a sensitive barometer, subject to cumulative influences and experiences. The interventions and activities required at any given time—for example, at the outset of an urban restoration effort—and the extent to which the public sector must be relied upon to trigger the undertaking vary at different stages in the restoration. More extensive intervention and activity may be required if the restoration is not proceeding as intended; or the effort may be modified or reduced if the restoration has ignited an explosive market. Regrettably, most urban restoration programs do not remain flexible enough to manipulate the tensions between triggering and constraining the market and forge a conceptual systhesis between environmental and social space.

Public attitudes and behavior (as distinct from issues of achievability, sanction, and market demand) create and alter the market and are simultaneously a product of the marketplace as well. Attitudes and behavior reflect changes in spatial, physical, and social fashions and in the way in which particular communities, areas, and locations are perceived. The changing attitudes toward density, older structures, mixed land use, abutting retail and commercial areas, through streets and narrow lots and structures, and walk-up buildings have challenged and upset the traditional standards upon which market behavior and planning principles were predicated and implemented. Such changes in attitudes and behavior toward traditional spatial and social patterns are apparent among nearly all population groups, but most dramatically among the young, the unmarried, the couples who are childless, and people with nonconforming lifestyles. In the major cities these latter populations constitute sufficiently large and identifiable social groups to influence or dominate particular market areas and those that are adjacent. Attitudes and behavior influence restoration prospects demonstrably. The receptivity toward social heterogeneity and toward racial, class, and ethnic differences exerts a substantial effect on market behavior, and therefore on the scale, character, and quality of the urban restoration efforts. The amount, extent, and type of intervention that are required or acceptable will vary with changes in attitudes, behaviors, and fashions.

The perceptions and realities of race and class determine community and market tolerance thresholds, and accordingly establish the scale and character of urban restoration.

It is clear, then, that three factors continue to be in a constant state of interaction, conflict, and accommodation: (1) the *physical* and *environmental* state and general health of an area, including the condition of structures and their repairability; the degree of community vitality, including the diversity of its retail establishments and the presence and vigor of its community institutions and organizations; and the extent of political and public sanction and commitment to community preservation and restoration; (2) the *market* position, appeal and potential of the area based on its location, the type and quality of its structures, the degree of improvability, and the range of perceived and real "magnetic qualities"; and (3) the *attitudes* toward the area particularly with regard to race and class considerations, and the social and spatial circumstances that are likely to attract people with choice to live and to invest dollars in that particular community.

Urban Rehabilitation in Chicago

The South Side

Some concrete examples of efforts at urban rehabilitation should help to clarify the ways in which the complex forces at work in massive social programs operate. I played a central planning role in many of the projects referred to here, and was able to view them at first hand.

In Chicago, the earliest post–World War II redevelopment activities centered on the Near South Side and entailed total land clearance. Here, as in many other early projects, the activities were undertaken at the instigation of and/or with the support of major institutions. The proposed redevelopment included sites for these institutions (principally the Illinois Institute of Technology, Michael Reese Hospital, and Mercy Hospital), for housing (principally the New York Life Insurance Company Lake Meadows project, housing on the Illinois Institute of Technology campus, and Prairie Shores, connected with Michael Reese Hospital), and for related facilities. These institutions generated not only a land demand, but also a substantial market demand for professional and skilled workers. The project areas had been classified as predominantly blighted. The institutional site plans and their facilities were perceived as obsolete. The areas surrounding the institutions were generally considered to be incompatible with the institutions and a threat to and a drain on the city. These major South Side projects, and a series of smaller-scale projects, including a few in which industrial or retail shopping development was the planned reuse, are among a relatively limited number of total clearance projects that were undertaken pursuant to the slum-clearance legislation in the roughly ten to fifteen years following the war. The intention of these projects was not only to make needed land available for institutions, housing, industry, and other purposes, but, most important, literally to eradicate and replace a total environment.

The Hyde Park–Kenwood project, which involved the community surrounding the University of Chicago, was the first major project initiated in Chicago to take advantage of the slum prevention and conservation modifications in the slum-clearance conception and legislation. The purposes and public policies of the legislative enactments were substantially different from the earlier slum clearance approaches. Rather than rebuilding the inner city by eradicating it and substituting a totally new environment, the new approach sought to preserve existing communities, stem the physical decline and the population flight, and prevent further slum creation by relying on a whole host of measures, including the selective (rather than total) use of land clearance, supplemented by other existing and newly created tools and devices. The hope was that these measures would preserve the basic character of the communities, encourage current residents to remain, and appeal to new residents by improving the housing stock and stimulating private investment for rehabilitation and new construction. A further aim was to modernize the community facilities and the public works infrastructure, make land available for schools, parks, and major institutions, and strengthen the tax base. In principle, these objectives were to be achieved with a minimum of population displacement and dispersal as a result of the removal of structures through land clearance. In essence, public attention was redirected toward slum prevention through preservation and conservation. The scale of the community universe was enlarged to achieve all this; a narrow project approach gave way to perceiving and "treating" a total community. Clearance in this context was ostensibly limited in scope to the degree required to support and sustain the community effort on a tailored-to-need basis, and it was justified and made defensible by its demonstrated relevance on a case basis. Central to this new conceptual approach was the spirit of community renewal. That is to say, whereas earlier unitary slum-clearance projects communicated the strong suggestion of being externally imposed and in the city's longer-range interest even if at the expense of the immediate area, the conservation-preservation-restoration efforts implied strong community-based support and reinforcement. Such support sometimes included responsibility for the program initiation, but it nearly always depended on continued community sanction.

The fact that the Hyde Park–Kenwood project was the first large-scale project of its kind brought the advantage of special enthusiasm and momentum. But being first carried with it a number of obvious disadvantages as well. There was no proven road map to go by. Never before had an attempt been made to use public intervention to stem an area's steady decline, its loss of populations, its growing number of residential and retail vacancies, and its other evidences of continuing deterioration. Guidelines were lacking; no useful literature existed; no prior relevant experience could assist in determining the extent and scale of needed action, the required instruments, and the most appropriate strategies to secure sanction, preserve and extend the market demand, and creatively and positively shape attitudes and behavior. The absence of the necessary knowledge and prior national experience, and the lack of certainty as to the appropriate measures, actions, and strategies must be seen in context. The dilemma was twofold: to stem the deterioration and overcome the obsolescence of both structures and the environment. In many respects the obsolescence rate was greater than the degree of deterioration. Additionally, Hyde Park–Kenwood was surrounded by decaying areas with increasing quantities of vacant and abandoned buildings and land. It was an island isolated in a decaying and declining southeast sector of the city. It not only faced the challenge of pioneering in urban restoration, but sought to do so by remaining an interracial community of high standards, at a time when the private lending institutions refused to invest in the inner city. As we have alread noted, FHA had come close to writing off the older central city, and its support tended to be limited to prime locations with strong market appeal.

The shortage, if not absence, of private investment and federal mortgage support, along with the steady decline in the surrounding areas, particularly in the communities to the north and south, underscored the fear and apprehension that the spreading decay would engulf Hyde Park–Kenwood. The Hyde Park–Kenwood efforts consequently were aimed at preserving and restoring the community as a defensible enclave. In the face of crime and other perceived and real anxieties, it is not surprising that a garrison attitude had developed in many of the area residents and institutions.

Further, the Hyde Park–Kenwood restoration effort sought to avoid the antiseptic quality of many prior slum-clearance and redevelopment projects. Earlier project activities, as a reaction to the overbuilt and overcrowded slums they displaced, tended to plan phallic structures in oceans of green space, symbolizing not only a dramatic and symbolic contrast but a rebirth. Even when the gross density was high, the land coverage tended to be low. The new structures neither recaptured nor created an urban feel, nor did they match the presumed spatial attractions of the suburbs. The Hyde Park effort sought to retain its urban quality and preserve its basic spatial character, and thus avoid antiseptic and meadowland effects. Land clearance was therefore limited to eliminating the pockets of slum structures and to providing space for new or expanded community support facilities and local institutions. The scale, scope, and location of such clearance activities were highly selective and restricted to structures and sites presumed to be essential to these restoration purposes.

Consonant with these intentions and with the spirit of preserving and reinforcing the existing community rather than replacing it, the central goal was to stem and reverse the decline and to create the circumstances that would set in motion a self-renewing process of continuous community improvement. The aim was to achieve this self-renewal through the on-aging actions, behaviors, and interactions of individuals, families, groups, institutions, establishments, tenants, property owners, public and private agencies, and all other public and marketplace actors, agents, and constituencies. The effort sought to reestablish and systematize those conventional and constructive relationships on which community preservation and survival depend. Public intervention was firmly limited to those actions and activities deemed necessary to set in motion the remedial and restorative process.

It was recognized, however, that if the scale of the public intervention were inadequate to the purposes, it would fail not only to set in motion the desired process of restoration, but to stem, let alone reverse, the decline. Limiting the scale and the type of interventions would be an important way of assuring that the remedial and restorative process would take place through normative public and marketplace interactions, activities, and behavior, rather than through arbitrary or artificially contrived sterile and massive public interventions. Thus the residents and their political, social, and economic institutions and support systems would become the responsible intervening agents. The social and spatial environment would be put in place over time, weathered by need and experience. This approach led to the conscious and deliberate decision that these community purposes would not be well served by a detailed and comprehensive redevelopment plan imposed on the community as a blueprint for determining the form and character of future growth and change. The key was to trigger a process based on thoughtful diagnosis, rather than to impose a corrective remedy in prescribed and predetermined dosages.

Unfortunately, there was no absolute certainty as to the measures necessary to achieve the purposes of this missionary and pioneering effort. Hindsight does clearly suggest that the extent and character of the clearance and the interventions in Hyde Park–Kenwood might have been modified to advantage. Knowledge and experience have been accumulated, in both the Hyde Park–Kenwood and other restoration efforts, that were not available at the outset of the undertaking, regarding appropriate scales of intervention. Yet the continuing capacity of the Hyde Park–Kenwood area to retain and attract new residents and to withstand the external pressures resulting from the continuing decay in the surrounding areas does argue that the extent of the initial interventions were not too far off their mark.

The amount of appropriate intervention is, in large part, whatever degree it takes to hold existing residents and to attract new residents with economic choice. Such a judgment was difficult to make in the Hyde Park–Kenwood area because of its location and the condition of its surroundings, the quality of the area itself, and the social, cultural, racial, and economic mix that has existed and continues to exist.

Limiting the amount of intervention bought time for the market to expand and for the area to accommodate in stages, as needed, to the scale, style, and evolving demands of the changing community. It was also of considerable importance to avoid creating settings that would aggravate cultural clashes from both within and without the community. Further, the time that was being bought would permit not only the expansion of the Hyde Park–Kenwood market, but also the restoration of the greater southeast Chicago sector on which the long-term future of the community depended.

Retail areas presented a special problem. The geographic scale of the community limited the number of individuals and families on whom the retail establishments depended. The retail market shed was severely constrained. Clearly this made it impossible for many retail and entertainment-related activities to locate or survive in the community in the absence of a sufficiently large universe to draw upon. The community itself, despite a relative high per capita spendable income capacity, did not have the density of other North Side lakefront communities; as a matter of fact, its relatively low density was among its attractions. But the population could not support elaborate retail, entertainment, and related facilities. Nor could the limited population and resources in the immediately surrounding areas add appreciably to the community potential. The distance to the community facilities that did exist, and to the downtown, gave the community no competitive edge or monopolistic advantage. The existence of cultural differences, both within the community and between it and the surrounding communities, created anxiety and fear that an oversupply of retail and related facilities would exacerbate such differences and serve as a magnet precipitating possible conflict until the market shed was large enough to sustain retail and related activities geared to particular social and cultural groupings.

It might be argued that the excess retail space could have been converted to housing, particularly since some of the retail use structures already included residential units above the shops. But this usage was not then fashionable and, in the period of the Hyde Park–Kenwood Renewal Project, was potentially unmarketable. The argument for such conversions is that they can attract a more affluent population by the creation of elegant restorations, or that the more affluent will generate elegant rehabilitations. Given the moment in time and the location, residential conversion of retail stores would probably have served the less advantaged. It was unlikely that the community could have risked pioneering in this regard since it is probable that such provisions would have been perceived as a further symptom of decline and of structural abuse and misuse—comparable to the abuses associated with conversions and other deleterious practices in residential buildings.

As has been suggested, the central goal of the Hyde Park–Kenwood project was the strengthening, reinforcement, and expansion of the market base, both within and without the community, by increasing the middle-class population and by seeking cultural accommodations and reconciliations. Universally, the battle over control of the marketplace—the street—determines the destiny of any area. It is highly unlikely that an active retail and entertainment strip could have been sustained, given the sharp economic and cultural differences that existed in the community and in the larger south sector. A stable, residential community attractive to individuals and families with locational choice was the principal objective. The price of stability was clearly less diversity.

Permitting the community and the marketplace to shape the spatial and social character of the community ideally requires more flexibility in the quality of the restoration instruments, procedures, and practices than was available at the outset of the Hyde Park–Kenwood program, or is available even today. In developing an approach that stresses restoration and seeks to see change conditioned by experience and by a weathering process, it is useful to reexamine, reorder, and restructure the intervention strategies at regular intervals to reflect the changing market and circumstances. Only then is it possible to adapt and conform to the cumulative experience, prospect, and potential at each such critical interval. The right mix, or equation, of interactions and interrelationships at the initiation of a program may not be the right mix at a subsequent stage. There is obvious merit to making accommodations and redirecting efforts as prior actions take effect and are influenced by new and changing prospects. For example, it may be discovered that less or more clearance is required to achieve the market results than assumed at the outset of the program. Fashions may change, creating a demand for certain kinds of units or structures in different locations than had been the case at an earlier stage. In the face of uncertainty as to both program consequences and potential market demand, a community's threshold for tolerating dysfunction or risk comes to the fore, and the extent of its willingness to rely on normative forces and future positive demand rather than on immediate aggressive intervention becomes an issue.

In Hyde Park–Kenwood, the absence of a national experience with selective clearance, and with custom-made programs that depended on urban restoration in stages, combined with the uncertainty of the potential market, created anxieties about the project's prospects for success. The community and the program planners opted for more rather than less clearance, and in locations that might now warrant second thoughts. In the light of subsequent experience, it is obvious that more pinpointed clearance might have been proposed for the peripheral areas. In the case of the large, overcrowded, and overused apartment buildings containing efficiency, studio, and other small units, more extensive clearance would have been desirable, particularly if other locations had been made available to the population in the clearance area. In retrospect, we can see that less clearance was probably required to achieve the program purposes in family units and in the interior of the area.

The success of the Hyde Park–Kenwood effort in retaining and attracting populations had political implications and significance for the black community. The presence of middle-class populations made it possible to keep alive and sustain an independent movement on the South Side and furnish a rallying point and support for a black political force in the city.

The Hyde Park–Kenwood community effort had its counterpart in the experiences of other universities coming to grips with the problems of their surrounding communities—Columbia University, the University of Toronto, the University of Pennsylvania, and others. University purposes are varied and diverse, but there are commonalities, too: seeking a compatible and amenable environment, providing safety and security, preserving or creating a student and faculty housing stock, securing land for expansion, attracting a usable labor pool, and the like.

In 1979, approximately twenty-five years after the initiation of the restoration effort in the Hyde Park–Kenwood community, the National Opinion Research Center (NORC) undertook a survey and found that the community continues to be integrated racially (60 percent white, 40 percent nonwhite) and economically (36 percent with incomes over $20,000, 21 percent over $30,000, and a third each under $10,000 and between $10–20,000). In addition, 86 percent of the residents were found to be generally satisfied with their community.

The problems that plague the community are both internal to the community—localized to its geographical sector—and external to the community and sector and essentially beyond their control. The internal problems have been touched upon and are generally market-related, tied to the size and capacity of the base on which the community draws for a variety of supports. These problems are likely to continue to beset the community until the urban restoration process is set in motion and extended to the entire southeast sector of the metropolitan area. Cyclical succession and restoration are common characteristics of urban change. The revitalization of the north sectors of the city will inevitably reach fruition. As maturation is achieved, new sectors will begin to attract populations and take root, building linkages and extensions to the developed sectors and drawing on and adding to those community islands that were able to sustain themselves during the transition period. In Chicago we see the evidences of this cyclical change and the beginning of a restoration process that builds on and extends the Near South Side redevelopments (Illinois Institute of Technology, Michael Reese Hospital, the New York Life Lake Meadows projects), the Hyde Park–Kenwood community effort, and the South Loop development. We can anticipate that the reach of these revitalization efforts will extend south and southeastward through the Chicago communities of Woodlawn and South Shore, will include the underdeveloped Lake Calumet area and the adjacent Roseland community to the city line, and merge into the south suburban sector, the least developed part of Cook County. The critical issue for the inner-city communities on the South Side of the city, as evidenced by Hyde Park–Kenwood, is to hold the line and buy the time that will be necessary for the islands of revitalization to merge and consolidate, and the restoration universe and accompanying market to expand.

The external pressures on inner-city communities are far more difficult to contend with. While the effects of rising interest rates and of problems in the economy are felt universally, they impact on these communities most severely, much earlier, and for more extended periods. These communities are highly vulnerable; economic dislocations are reflected in a damaging slowdown in the purchase and sale of housing, and in a reduction in the local purchasing power. The increases in crime, particularly robberies, which are the result of rises in unemployment and reductions in human services, make the more affluent populations the target of poorer adjacent populations.

These inner-city communities are also least able to withstand the consequences of, and effects of, the accommodations to changes in historical practices and patterns. For example, the increasing reliance on the automobile has exacerbated community problems in the face of outmoded traffic patterns and, more critically, the lack of adequate on-street parking or available land for off-street parking spaces. The use of the automobile and the growth of shopping centers have threatened and undermined traditional urban commercial development except in the densest areas where vast populations have substantial purchasing power. Further, the general obsolescence and lack of economic function of the community-based transient and residential hotel, except for those serving high-income markets, are a particularly burdensome problem. These hotels, created at almost a single moment in time, represent a massive land use threat to the communities engaged in restoration efforts. Similarly, the shift to chain-store operations, to larger-size establishments, and to different retail practices by supermarkets, drugstores, bakeries, and other retail outlets, has resulted in a growing number of building vacancies in these communities and the severe loss of services. The structural and land spaces that exist are inadequate to meet the new spatial and building requirements that have been imposed to accommodate these uses. Consequently, the intervention that, for example, reduced retail space reflected widespread shifts in shopping patterns and behavior and an affirmative attempt to accommodate to the changes in occupancy and to deal with the damaging uses and existing and potential vacancies in retail space. In Chicago, for instance, 4,500 stores were lost in the period between 1970 and 1980.

All of these factors together account for the desire in the Hyde Park–Kenwood program to reduce vulnerability by limiting the variables, risks, and uncertainties. Other urban restoration efforts facing similar circumstances in comparable locations have had like experiences. Given the presence of the university and other institutions, the close proximity to the central area, and the lakefront location, it appeared that the most promising competitive market prospect for the area was to stress its advantages as a close-in, stable, family-based community area. Doing so, even at the risk of reducing the attraction for some individuals and childless couples, including students, seemed desirable because of the inherently strong family-oriented character of the community and the greater probability of program success that this approach provided. This orientation also posed less risk and conflict. The income and market demand to sustain an active and diverse regional retail and entertainment base no longer existed.

The tenuous state of the community accounted for the strong desire to moderate possible cultural and economic conflict rather than to place added burdens on the program by seeking to increase the street-oriented population. An increase in this population and in the activities to attract them, while advantageous and magnetic in many respects, would probably have accelerated the exodus of middle-class families and weakened the family base—the single most reliable community component. The relatively small scale of the Hyde Park–Kenwood island in the midst of a rapidly declining South Side area required that the sharp socioeconomic differences be moderated and overcome. It is highly questionable whether the area, given its vulnerability, could have survived the increased tension that might have resulted from heightened racial, social, and economic differences. These tensions and pressures had begun to affect the community adversely at the outset of the program, and had accounted in large part for the initiation of the restoration efforts. It might be argued that the program's failure to go far enough in the direction of insulating the community as a family area was a weakness. However, more extensive measures were constrained by the social and political realities within and without the community, as well as by the temper and attitude of both the community and the drafters of the restoration effort.

The central aim was to do what was considered minimally essential to sustain and preserve the community and to maintain and build linkages across the social-spatial-economic spectrum. The community sought the capacity to deal with perceived and real social and spatial threats, conflict, and change, and thereby avoid the fate of the communities immediately to the north and south that were being abandoned by stages. The aim was to enhance the relatively stable and socially integrated family character of the community, and thereby create—and over time extend— the community's margin of tolerance to risk and to social and spatial change.

The Lincoln Park Area

By contrast restoration efforts on the North Side were characterized by a much greater willingness to tolerate the risks and to accept the byproducts of restoration and transition.

These differences became clear in the North Side Lincoln Park community area urban restoration. The Lincoln Park area had already experienced the beginnings of highly successful restoration under private auspices. The North Side, of which the Lincoln Park community was a part, had never experienced the degree of population exodus, abandonment, and vacancies that had characterized the South Side. Racial and economic diversity was far less extensive and the disparities less sharply drawn than in the Hyde Park–Kenwood community. The deterioration and structural and spatial decline in the Lincoln Park community were far less severe and extensive than in Hyde Park–Kenwood, and the clearance proposals, therefore, were far more selective, scattered, and limited. The restoration in Lincoln Park began and took root at a much earlier stage in the area's deterioration and decline. In addition, until later stages extended the boundaries of the restoration and touched on low-income and racial areas—as in the case of the Cabrini-Green Public Housing Project— the initial Lincoln Park effort did not face problems of racial and cultural conflict to the degree experienced on the South Side. The Lincoln Park urban restoration effort was able to rely far more on private rather than public activities and intervention than was the Hyde Park project. The densities in preserved and restored buildings were substantially higher and could sustain a larger and more varied retail and entertainment base. It was far less vulnerable and was able to attract a large number of singles, childless couples, and nonconforming members of the population and to build a base around an emergent set of new social groups. It was further buttressed by the creation of a virtual "white city," which drew the affluent and banded them together into the north sector.

In time the area developed its own regional shopping and other facilities in a dense compact segment with an elastic and expanding outer boundary. It was thus able to accommodate a limited though significant number of in-migrants who were abandoning the rest of the city, not for the suburbs but for a city residence adjacent to and near the spectacular and extravagant lakefront setting. The new slogan became "Bring me your huddled elite." This huddle effect has created its own island, which has been less vulnerable to, and therefore better able to tolerate, by-product socioeconomic pressures. Relatively free of cultural and political conflict and resistance, the area was able to draw on a growing body of local and national experience. The substantial community market base that the restoration effort sought to preserve, reinforced by the north-ward, and to a lesser extent northwestward, market expansion made it possible to introduce and apply restoration techniques and devices with far greater skill and success than had been the case in earlier community efforts.

In essence, the Lincoln Park area was less severely deteriorated, more strategically located, with a high percentage of relatively affluent residents with a greater spendable income, and subject to far fewer (near absent) race and class pressures than had been the case heretofore in connection with publicly supported urban restoration programs. Further, the community was not dominated by one institution, as was Hyde Park–Kenwood, with all the financial, social, and political implications that thereby result, but rather included within or nearby a whole array of hospital-health centers, educational, and other institutions, which were continuing to expand. The Lincoln Park effort relied in greater measure on private resources, in contrast to Hyde Park–Kenwood, which depended far more on public and institutional intervention that was harder to sustain over an extended period of time.

In Lincoln Park the restoration effort could concentrate its focus on revitalization and on accommodating an expanding market. This has not been possible in most other restoration programs, which have had to deal with by-product social and economic problems and conflict, compensatory arrangements for coping with dependency and deprivation, and the provision of human services. Today the threat posed by the massive public housing project to the west of the Lincoln Park area, Cabrini-Green, is blocking the path to Lincoln Park's successful expansion. The community—and the city—are finding it difficult, if not impossible, to neutralize the threatening effects of the project, as they seek magically to remove, convert, or contain it. The community was far more successful in its callous displacement of Spanish-speaking and elderly low-income populations as marketplace demands pushed development westward and as more affluent populations took possession of the existing housing stock in Lincoln Park. Socioeconomic disabilities, particularly when the affected populations are a relatively small minority without political power residing in structures beyond the reach of the market, constitute an everlasting threat to elite-oriented urban restoration efforts.

Uptown

A key issue in most planning, development, and urban restoration is, more frequently than not, whether to build walls or bridges. Initially, such a determination constituted a spatial dilemma and distinction, but it has come to have social, economic, and political connotations and implications in which the spatial element constitutes the means to effect or obstruct the socioeconomic purpose.

We see these effects in the Uptown area project in Chicago, which sought to restore a community with a significant number of elderly, largely dependent, Appalachian whites and American Indians. A substantial number of buildings contain efficiency and other small units, either as originally designed or as a result of conversions. These structures have difficulty competing for single persons and childless couples with economic choice who are being attracted to Lincoln Park and adjacent communities that have newer and more attractive rehabilitated units. The Uptown structures have been declining steadily, and the area has been marked by a substantial number of fires, which, fortunately, are increasingly coming under control. Certain streets in the area have taken on a run-down appearance, and some approximate a skid row. At the time of the author's involvement, public instruments were not available to undertake a meaningful restoration program that served the less advantaged and those with limited economic choice—and in large part this is still the case today. The Uptown area is some distance north of the Lincoln Park community with its major rehabilitation activities. In Uptown the improvement costs required for the restoration substantially exceeded the income then produced, especially since property owners were treating their existing investments as wasting assets. No incentive existed to revitalize the community, and the scale of the dysfunctions defied modest administrative or financial remedy. The use of public funds to acquire structures that were generally sound and to resell them at a written-down cost low enough to allow expenditure for improvement and modernization, including deconversion if necessary, and at rental or sales prices within the reach of existing residents was not possible within existing legislative enactment or administrative regulation. Ironically, it *was* possible with the use of public funds to take more extreme actions, such as acquiring and tearing a building down and reselling the vacant land at a substantially reduced price.

Despite the support for restoration by major insurance companies and institutions located in the Uptown area, legislative and political interest was lacking, largely because of the limited number of public tools available to deal with the circumstances existing there, the extent of public intervention needed, and the amount of public money required. Recently, with the expansion of the North Side market and the growing lakefront investment advantages, particularly at the eastern end of the community, restoration has begun to take hold in Uptown, but only at the expense of the existing residents, especially the less affluent and more dependent. Restoration will continue to be a marketplace device limited in use to those with substantial economic choice, unless the principle of using housing subsidies as income surrogates to help write down the inflated costs of existing housing is introduced and adopted. This approach was proposed in the initial Uptown restoration plan.

The Near West Side

One of the most successful applications of restoration has been on the Near West Side of Chicago, a longtime Italian ethnic area in which Spanish-speaking and black populations had begun to locate. The area is adjacent to a large-scale medical center that includes a number of major hospitals, the University of Illinois School of Medicine, and a number of medically related county and state buildings. In many respects, the area is relatively secluded, with limited access and a protective degree of isolation. The revitalization program provided the occasion for a microscale restoration, largely relying on a limited and selective quantity of clearance and the retention of most of the area's distinctive features and characteristics. The area typified an almost European use of small spaces. The program incorporated mechanisms and techniques to make it possible for the existing residents to benefit from the restoration; but it also provided the means by which move-in populations could be accommodated in modestly priced rental and sales units. The site plans and replacement uses were designed on a human scale. Many were deliberately created to reinforce the area's ethnic distinction. In 1980, twenty years after the beginning of the restoration effort, about two-thirds of the original residents were continuing to live on the Near West Side.

However, the original intention to keep the community intact was modified and distorted by the intrusion of the University of Illinois Circle Campus, which was imposed on the community after the Near West restoration plan had been agreed upon. The campus reduced the community land area as well as parts of its housing stock—disrupting its holistic quality—displaced many of the residents, and removed critical spatial segments. The location of the Circle Campus did certainly assure a ready market for the Near West Side area and its housing, and created the prospect for an interesting academic and ethnic mix, but it did so by sacrificing the initial and long-range goal of preserving and restoring the community as it had developed historically and distinctively. The intent had been to retain the bulk of the residents in improved existing housing or in new housing proposed for construction in the community within their means. The loss of land areas to the University of Illinois made this impossible. For these reasons (and in the conviction that satisfactory alternatives—and arguably better sites—existed for the campus location), the author, as the Near West Side planning consultant, along with many others, expressed strong opposition to the use of the Near West Side for the Circle Campus.

Woodlawn

The Woodlawn program in Chicago was of a different order of community restoration. It represented a first effort at the urban reconstruction of a community that had experienced near-total abandonment and a program carried out in partnership with a community organization.

As distinguished from the approaches described earlier, which were based on either community replacement or community preservation or revitalization, the Woodlawn restoration was based on community reconstruction reflecting both the changing growth patterns in the metropolitan area and the consequent changes and adjustments in the inner-city communities of the older central cities. The Woodlawn program relied on participatory involvement, on the influence of, if not the control by, the community organization, and on the potential impact of community economic development corporations. Community participation and control were exercised not to reinforce but to overcome existing practices, policies, and external domination. This approach, largely pioneered in Woodlawn, sought to alter the decision-making process by assigning shared responsibility, and, in some cases, control, to the community groups, and modifying and shifting both professional and political power by putting knowledge and technology in the service of the community residents and program beneficiaries. The community itself turned away from the initial opposition and hostility that had helped to mobilize the residents and turned instead to creating positive programs and developing the leadership necessary to implement them. The emphasis on protest and on political strategies was expanded and redirected to stress community and economic development and service systems and programs. The goal shifted from provoking conflict to moderating and resolving it. The planning attempted to achieve and reconcile social and spatial purposes as part of the urban reconstruction process and to reexamine both professional-citizen relationships and professional and non-professional roles and functions.

Community decision-making efforts were directed at institution and community building, achieving representation and local decision-making through local political community organizations and economic development corporations in preference to appointmented and elected officials, the universally preferred city hall options. In this regard, city hall prefers to extend community services by the decentralization of city departmental and agency activity, with control located outside of the community. A variation in the external provision and control of services is the institutional sponsorship of services, usually by a university or hospital. This latter alternative, however, is often rejected by the community as another exploitive presence and influence. On the other hand, the preferred community approach is localized influence or control, on the premise that service provision is an additional opportunity for local institution and community building.

The Woodlawn urban reconstruction effort included major socioeconomic, as well as the customary spatial, goals. The social goals included supportive services for the dependent adult population, jobs for the young adults, and education for the young. Service provision was conceived as integral to the urban reconstruction. There were several guiding principles: people were to be served by agencies and organizations on an undifferentiated basis independent of income and the character and provision of the service were to be separated from the source or method of payment; people were to be treated holistically and the functions disaggregated, organized, and administered as a response to the individual's consolidated and integrated needs; and functions were to be linked and connected within an interdependent unitary network. Further, the community sought to decentralize city-wide political power and to centralize community power over the collection of decentralized administrative agencies and institutions. In addition, the Woodlawn restoration effort sought to convert beneficiaries into consumers wherever possible and to rely for service delivery on community rather than city or state agencies. Among other goals, the community sought to assume responsibility for evaluation and research as a means of extending community influences and achieving accountability.

Some Programs Outside Chicago

In addition to the Woodlawn program and the other Chicago programs earlier referred to, I was involved in similar programs in other parts of the country—in Des Moines, Milwaukee, New York City, St. Paul, and Baltimore, as well as in a substantial number of smaller cities, principally in Iowa, Illinois, Indiana, Wisconsin, Ohio, and Michigan. One of the least successful of these projects was the University-Euclid project in Cleveland. The area of the project included Case-Western Reserve University, University and Cleveland hospitals, the city's major cultural area, an industrial belt, and the Hough area—the city's largest low-income black community. In the Cleveland project, the only involved and influential participants were the institutions operating through their chosen instrument, the University Circle Development Foundation. The institutions in the University Circle area were of prime and priority interest to the city. To note that there was an almost total absence of a signficiant resident or community organizational involvement is only a partial overstatement. There was, at most, limited participation by local institutions and churches. Major clearance and related decisions were made by the city with the assistance and influence of the principal institutions. In my capacity as planning consultant I regrettably accepted the local decision-making process. I worked with the actors and constituencies legitimated by the city, rather than rejecting the approach and more aggressively seeking out and strengthening resident and community groups. The failure of the program to take hold is evidence of the inadequacy of the course of action that the city adopted and pursued and that was confirmed by professionals on the project.

In many respects, clearance was the major variable in all of the above projects. It was the component and activity that coalesced the political, market, and attitudinal factors. Total or partial and selective clearance to eradicate slum, deteriorated, blighted, or incompatible uses was an important goal in its own right in the effort to replace, preserve, or restore an existing community. There were a series of other project undertakings where proof of eligible condition was essential to make the site and project area available. However, in these cases the clearance activities were not a central objective but only a procedural necessity to achieve new redevelopment purposes. This was generally the case in connection with economic and industrial development to serve city and metropolitan goals, or where highly attractive and commanding locations were perceived to be underutilized.

Economic and industrial development projects frequently entailed major public works and flood control measures, as in Waterloo, Iowa, where the project undertaking made it possible for John Deere, the major industrial establishment in the area, to remain and expand—and thereby to stabilize the city's economy. Along with this and other major undertakings, such projects often took on more modest forms, as in Evansville, Youngstown, and Sioux City, among others. Other classes of projects focused on institutional preservation and expansion (Youngstown University, Marquette University, University of Wisconsin at Milwaukee, Morningside College in Sioux City, Knox College, Iowa Methodist Hospital, among others); and central business district revitalization (St. Paul, Cedar Rapids, Sioux City, Waterloo, Ann Arbor, Des Moines, among others). In addition, planning, policy, and analytical reports were often prepared that sought to establish a framework for urban restoration— including, for example, a Hartford social analysis and a development framework for southeastern Michigan (the Detroit metropolitan area)—and organizational studies to create administrative capacity— Wayne County, Baltimore, Syracuse, etc.

Conclusions

A number of conclusions can be drawn from the life cycles of the projects discussed here. It is clear, first of all, that the extent to which sanction is achieved, market demand sustained, and prevailing attitudes and behavior accurately assessed will influence the extent of land clearance activity. Thus the wide public perception that the "pro-people" stance is anti-clearance has caused programs to tend to be decentralized, piecemeal, and episodic. The "right environment" is being redefined. It is no longer perceived on a grand scale to be achieved in one grand moment. The absolute valildity of particular spatial relationships has been replaced by the presumed advantage of relative change achieved by stages over time. The social by-products of change are assigned the same importance as the change itself, and both are considered to have equal impact.

In the final analysis what distinguishes a so-called slum area from an ostensibly distinctive old and "romanticized" area are public attitudes and individual and market behavior. Social organization and stability are not confined to ethnic or more affluent areas. The static sociological principles and criteria that were once largely responsible for defining neighborhoods and communities have limited value and applicability. Thus, the long-held belief that homogeneity, familiarity, and predictability are essential preconditions to preservation, restoration, and marketability has been substantially modified in the face of a growing counterexperience. We are observing an increased acceptance of the theory that urban places are best left alone, that the wiser course is to rely on natural events and market forces, and that the "urban corpus" has the

regenerative capacity for amenable, defensible, and long-lasting revitalization and restoration. With respect to urban restoration, a strongly
held view is that crisis intervention, marginal and supportive activities,
and limited and narrowly contained scrimmages and brushfire actions
may be preferable to large-scale interventions. More ambitious approaches are supported and justified in connection with broadly based
policies and positions that establish the operating framework and facilitate systemic performance: more favorable interest rates, interstate transport and distribution, defense-related decisions, and benefit-transfer
programs. Advocates of this approach argue that after individual, institutional, and systemic relationships are established, particular practices
and prescriptions should be left to the interaction among the actors and
participants. What they aim to encourage are custom-designed and
individually tailored approaches based on measured and careful diagnosis that culminate in a program that allows for individual freedom of
action.

In the face of the near universal resistance to clearance that is the
outgrowth of a host of political, social, and behavioral objections, we are
at a stage now where the case for clearance needs to be strongly made and
defended. Excessive reliance on land clearance exacerbated the housing
shortage for certain socioeconomic groups within the inner city, pushing
them to reach out territorially to nearby and close-in, lower-middle-class
areas. This very process accelerated the dispersal of the "ghetto population," and did so with the aid and assistance of the public authorities
responsible for the land clearance intervention. In restoration programs
less reliant on land clearance, the by-products of displacement are equally
severe, and they are rarely mitigated by the assistance and moderating
effects of a proscribed rehousing effort. The poor and minorities can
consequently be deliberately excluded and contained by reliances on the
marketplace. Such has generally been the case, except for those subsidy
programs that have provided housing for a small number of individuals
and families in existing, rehabilitated, or new structures.

An escalation of urban restoration efforts could accelerate the population movement and, in time, reverse the historical direction of the flow
by increasing the number of poor and minorities outside of the central
city, at the same time as the number of advantaged—both whites and
minorities—in the central city increases. This is not an improbability,
since the flow would reinforce the historical process of succession and
segregation.

The increased stress on social space in determining urban form has
inevitably resulted in a greater emphasis on participation as a sanctioning
device. This has, to some extent, moderated the power of the providers
and the professionals, who have long dominated the decision-making

process. The search for workable interventions in order to sustain and create an effective market demand and achieve the political sanction necessary to initiate and undertake restoration efforts has forced more thoughtful, disciplined, and defensible approaches. A crisper articulation of the restoration challenge moves the effort toward a more satisfactory and affirmative result.

The by-product of preserving, retaining, and improving existing structures and facilities was a tilt toward tolerating outmoded public facilities and infrastructure, and a mentality that suggested "older is better." This mind set and value system can have, and have had, unfortunate effects on the competitive position of the older city vis-à-vis the metropolitan area, and the competitive position of the older regions of the country (the Northeast and the Middle West) vis-à-vis the newer regions in the South, Southwest, and West, since new growth, while less romantic, may be more efficient and competitive.

The great architect Louis Sullivan stated that the study of architecture was appropriately the study of the social conditions that produced it. Similarly, urbanized places in the United States are a reflection of the social, political, and economic conditions that produced them. It is the interaction among these forces that motivates us to intervene to affect attitudes and behavior, create the market demand, and secure sanction that will enable us to shape these forces consciously and deliberately, and thereby enhance the quality of life.

CHAPTER 6

Functional Networks and Dual Governance

U **Functioning Bureaucratic Systems**

rban restoration efforts reflect not only the complex interplay between what is possible politically and the exigencies of the marketplace, but also the special quirks and capacities of functioning bureaucratic systems. Extensive bureaucratic organizations exist in connection with each major professional and administrative function: health, mental health, economic development, education, and social services, among others. Executive authority and the power of government are undermined by the multiplication of functional bureaucracies and the range and diversity of their activities. Power and authority are concentrated functionally and located vertically across the diverse tiers and layers of the governing hierarchy. The administrative decentralization of these functional bureaucracies through the creation of geographically distributed instrumentalities has duplicated and threatened the historical system of governance in the United States by diluting the influence of the electorate and the integrity of the network of federal, state, and local governmental units. The expansion of the functional bureaucracies constitutes a challenge to management capacity and undermines executive control by the imposition of agency and professional control.

The tilt away from the horizontal toward the vertical and administrative bias replaces the politician and elected official with the appointee and the functionary; the citizen with the consumer and beneficiary; and a holistic approach to government and to services with prescribed benefit packages delivered on a proliferated basis. In consequence, benefits are determined and dictated by the producers rather than by the users of goods, services, and resources.

These phenomena are the result of an increase in the knowledge base, the universal desire for access to its benefits, the pressure for an equitable method of distribution and allocation, and the reliance on large-scale organization to achieve these purposes. Top-down and bottom-up depictions of the process are simply different expressions of the effects and consequences of this set of factors. Remedial measures and solutions will likely depend on simultaneous and related interventions to treat corresponding and complementary causes and symptoms.

Top down, the executive is seeking the capacity to rationalize and connect the proliferated and diffuse semiautonomous functional bureaucracies in order to administer and oversee the complex governmental network and thereby achieve social, economic, and political goals and purposes. Bottom up, the beneficiary and the consumer are seeking to cut across the spectrum of functionally oriented public, private, and voluntary service delivery agencies in order to achieve easy access and connect the associated range of services and join them holistically in appropriate combinations. The aim in both is to achieve a horizontal capacity across diverse functions by blunting and overcoming the powerful vertical tilt and provider orientation of the system and thereby reduce the power of, and the dependency on, the professional, the agency, and the functionary. The aim is to restore the supremacy of the electorate and the elected representative in the decision-making process. The executive and the beneficiary seek a reformulation without diminishing the incentive of the professional, the agency, and the functionary to expand the knowledge base, or the ability of these actors or of the system to deliver and make available the presumed benefits associated with functional and professional bureaucracies.

In the face of these observations it is not coincidental that at the point of the actual delivery of services, that is, at the lowest layer in the hierarchical system, microgovernance and service delivery are conterminus, interchangeable, and frequently equivalent. We see this most dramatically in efforts at community self-determination in connection with schools, zoning, economic development, and the like. For the citizen at large, the delivery of a service constitutes the most meaningful public and professional presence. Decentralized service delivery on the neighborhood or community firing line is the ultimate extension and manifestation of the large-scale centralized bureaucracy; and the large-scale centralized bureaucracy justifies its existence by the services that ultimately are made available and delivered to beneficiaries and recipients.

Large-scale macro-organization and "big government" and small-scale micro-organization, even down to the city neighborhood and outlying suburb, are both essential components and are critical to serving their reciprocal interests. Thus, top-down and bottom-up perspectives are mutually reinforcing and require attention as mirror images rather than as antagonistic forces. Administrative and political centralization and decentralization need to be related spatially, consonant with the emergent human settlement patterns and activities that extend from the neighborhood and community to the region and nation.

The jurisdictions and boundaries of local governments no longer coincide with the complex and nucleated human settlement concentrations and patterns. This lag in governmental accommodation, together with the absence of appropriate and relevant decentralized administrative and political mechanisms, compounds the problems of creating management capacity horizontally, and complicates the tasks faced by executives in overseeing their political domain. The result is a significant increase in the alienation, frustration, and disaffection experienced by the beneficiaries and recipients seeking to gain access to and "work" the vertically oriented service delivery maze. The beneficiaries of the service are forced to manipulate and gain access to it through their own devices and resources. Frustration with the service delivery system is no longer solely the concern of the disadvantaged, but is increasingly being universally experienced irrespective of socioeconomic class. The situation is exacerbated in most older cities that are either too large or too small to address the problems that confront them.

Establishing a Metropolitan Area Capacity

Efforts to date have largely sought to establish a metropolitan area capacity through any one of a number of means. Many localities have legislated metropolitan government. The efforts made in Toronto, Dade County (Miami), Winnipeg, Manitoba, the Indianapolis Unigov variation, and the city-county accommodations in Nashville–Davidson County, Atlanta–Fulton County, and Baltimore–Baltimore County are examples of attempts at creating formal arrangements. These variations have included outright city-county mergers or consolidation, city-county separations and extensions, and other related federated mechanisms. A number of proposals by such groups as the Committee on Economic Development, the Urban Institute, and others have been advanced to create local metropolitan federal systems. Suggestions have been advanced that would give large metropolitan areas separate county status. A widely used mechanism is the special use district tied to a specific function. This device has been utilized, for example, with respect to such important functions as sanitation, drainage, water, and recreation. It has been introduced in connection with activities that cut across multiple local jurisdictions and those that receive widespread support and sanction. The responsibilities of the special use district have been narrowly defined and limited to the specified activity. Recently, however, the device has been introduced to create a metropolitan capacity to do by indirection what cannot be done by direction. An agency or authority is created in connection with a particular function and then endowed with broad powers approaching the scale of a metropolitan government with all of the attendant beauty marks and scars. The most notable examples involve metropolitan and regional mass transit.

Increasingly, localities have also created voluntary associations among willing governmental partners, either around a particular "nonpartisan and objective" function, such as drainage or water, or around broadbased processes and activities, such as planning or economic development.

The most extensive attempt to create metropolitan presence and capacity has been the introduction and use of the "urban county" concept and approach. The federal government has played a major role in this regard. The urban county may come to represent the principal American alternative to metropolitan government, in which highly urbanized units begin to exercise extensive latent powers for noncentral city areas with respect to a range of functions that in time are exercised for the central city itself. Involvement in central city affairs, particularly in older areas, is likely to expand, especially in the face of the losses in central city population and activity and the corresponding growth in outside areas. The urban county itself could well become the new and enlarged central city.

All of the arrangements discussed above are largely bottom up in origin, formulation, and undertaking, and generally depend on voluntary local initiative or sanction. There are two top-down forces at work, which may, over time, constitute the more prevalent, pervasive, and powerful metropolitan de facto, if not de jure, governmental presence. These two forces are represented by the policies and practices of the federal and the state governments.

We already see this metropolitan influence in a wide-ranging number of federal actions that will likely continue, even under the new Reagan federalism. As a condition precedent to federal aid, a local agency must be designated to certify that a local proposal requiring federal assistance is in conformance with the growth plans for the applicable metropolitan area. Although under active reexamination by the Reagan administration, this provision is applied universally in connection with the Office of Management and Budget-A95 requirement for nearly all developmentally related activities. More specifically, comparable impositions have been introduced for health and medically related activities, which require comprehensive health agency sign-offs; for age-related activities, which require area agency and state agency sign-offs; for transportation-related proposals, which require a sign-off by a designated Metropolitan Planning Organization (MPO); and for other activities as well.

The federal metropolitan presence is also a consequence of growing federal efforts to increase local effectiveness and capacity. Federal departments and agencies have brought their respective regional boundaries and jurisdictions into conformity, a first step in creating a consistent subfederal network. Many have sought systematically to transfer an increasing number of central functions to the regions and to decentralize power. A federal regional council (FRC) with a full-time staff director exists in each region, and there is a rotating chairmanship among the federal regional directors who are members of the council. The FRC is the creature of the White House, representing the politically appointed heads of departments and agencies rather than the career professionals and bureaucrats. The FRC is closely related to the OMB. In many respects it is the White House presence within the regions. To date, it has modestly limited its activities to coordinating and negotiating among participating federal agencies and arranging settlements with states and localities. It has sought to enhance federal-state and federal-local relationships and to reach out increasingly for public-private partnership arrangements. However, it is within the realm of possibility that the FRC will ultimately act as a full-scale regional White House, with an appointed regional chairman or even vice-president and a cabinet consisting of regional departmental secretaries. This enlarged structure might be provided with a substantial political and professional staff and assigned functions and powers to cut across, connect, and supersede departmental and agency jurisdictions where and when necessary, thus overcoming arbitrary and de jure local political and governmental jurisdictions. One could even imagine the creation of an advisory board to the FRC and, in time, even an elected minilegislature. We can already observe some evidence of federal concern with programmatic constituencies in connection with various federal undertakings—e.g., in connection with federal health programs, the government seeks to generate beneficiary constituencies; in connection with transportation, functional activity constituencies; and in connection with programs related to housing and urban development, constituencies comprising affected local governmental jurisdictions.

The state has the potential for creating a profound metropolitan presence that may be far greater than the bottom-up influences or those that result from federal policies and practices. The state has the constitutional responsibility for nearly all major local functions. Increasingly, the states are beginning to exercise these functions beyond merely providing financial assistance or serving as a conduit to and negotiator with the federal government. They are providing continuing oversight, direct control, and sometimes even front-line involvement. State after state has explored, or is exploring, substate districting, with a view to establishing a consistent districting plan for all state departments and agencies. These substate districts often coincide with the metropolitan urbanized areas and come closer to approximating defensible metropolitan "governing" units than units that might be created on a bottom-up basis. Metropolitan government may come into being by indirection (top down), rather than by direction (bottom up). It is possible that in the future an "assistant governor" could be appointed to coordinate and oversee such a state subdistrict, with the help of a professional and political staff and possibly even an advisory council. The election of a "substate" governor and a regional council conceivably might then not be far behind. In various parts of the country, such councils—often with a low profile and limited visibility and power—are already in existence. The state metropolitan presence is likely to be a more acceptable alternative, generating its own loyal and growing constituency, since it may be perceived as less of a threat to the small, local political jurisdictions than bottom-up mechanisms assumed to be dominated by the central city.

Implementing Metropolitan Governance

Issues of metropolitan governance are a critical factor in considering issues of management capacity and service delivery. There are, in addition, a host of both top-down and bottom-up devices and measures to deal more directly with achieving (horizontal) executive authority, and (vertical) client, consumer, and beneficiary services. The former include a series of structural and organizational devices, staff changes and supports, and methodological tools and approaches. Staff aides have been appointed at the local level, sometimes given imposing titles, and charged with responsibility for coordinating and expediting the diverse activities of government. A related effort at the federal level was President Lyndon Johnson's "convening order," which charged one department head—the Secretary of Housing and Urban Development—with responsibility for convening other related department heads in the hope that this would represent a painless means of achieving policy and program coordination. The effort fell substantially short of the goal.

Simple organizational forms include a deputy or deputies and assistants appointed either across a whole range of government agencies, over grouped activities—such as public works, environment, economic development, and the like—or over particular target groups or missions. Initially, these deputies and assistants are assigned expediting and coordinating functions. Not uncommonly, however, particularly at the state and federal levels, the staff assembled around the governor or the president grows in such proportions that it creates a major conflict among central executive staffs and ministerial departments and agencies and their respective staffs. The growth in the size of the executive staff is generally accompanied by an associated increase in power, to the point where control and direction are centrally asserted, even if functions and performance are left to the ministerial (departmental) groups. That such a tug and pull can reach extreme proportions was shown during the Nixon administration with the political domination of the "ministries" by the president's executive staff.

Central executive authority, building on the British model and fully legitimated, first at the federal and then at the state and local levels, places heavy reliance on the budget-making authority subsequently expanded to include management and budget. In the search for centralized authority it is this budget-making authority that is the pivotal activity. No longer, however, does the executive have a monopoly on the budgetary "expert" capacity, since budgetary staffs are now attached to most legislative bodies at nearly every level of government, resulting in a further need for reconciliation to avoid or overcome conflict.

Other staff measures frequently introduced are the creation of "superdepartment" heads with command power over a series of designated and subsumed agencies, departments, and functions. These superdepartment heads may represent ministerial reorganizations or consolidations, or may be incorporated as part of the central executive authority. In the latter case, they constitute a kind of kitchen cabinet—a control point—and, together with the budget and management group, oversee the chief executive's governing universe.

At the state level—and even more so at the local level—the planning and development activity is no longer carried out by a series of coordinate functional agencies, but is now the responsibility of a central, executive office. It therefore becomes another major executive instrument for asserting central control. Its function is to plan and program growth and change directions for and across the governing system, with no subject matter constraint. The executive generally seeks to sharply delineate distinctions between operations and planning. The planning function therefore is withdrawn from the ministries and incorporated as a central function and control instrument leaving to the ministries basic responsibility for operations and implementation.

While all of the references here are to the governmental structure and system, a comparable situation exists in the not-for-profit and corporate sectors. The circumstances and characteristics of centralized executive authority are applicable to large-scale organizations where management capacity needs to be exercised over structural and functional space and territories, and in connection with a range of activities, professions, specializations, and organizational subdivisions. In a large hospital, private agency, service enterprise, corporate activity, or retail or industrial empire, the devices of centralized executive authority are very similar.

Among the other top-down organizational devices utilized by the executive are a series of structural changes. Some of these changes are inconsistent, create conflict, and become counterproductive. The goal is to crosscut activities more effectively, enhance horizontal capacity, and strengthen executive authority. The structural changes include the creation of superdepartments through the collection or consolidation of related departments, agencies, and activities. Mayor John Lindsay, in New York, and, at the federal level, President Nixon and President Carter proposed the creation of a number of gargantuan departments around a set of themes like community development, economic development, and other broad-brush programs that would collect and assemble functional departments and activities. A whole set of diverse reorganization proposals to consolidate functions—as in the case of the Department of Health, Education and Welfare (HEW)—are offered on the theory that this is the best way to enhance functional integration. Some approaches disaggregate functions by narrowing the jurisdiction and focusing more sharply on a designated function, as in the case of the Department of Education. Not uncommonly, a major modification or a total reversal in the approach to organizational structure is proposed or undertaken. Consider the shift in the Department of Health, Education and Welfare to the Department of Health and Human Services and the jeopardy to the continued existence of the Departments of Education and Energy. Still other arrangements aggregate dispersed functions by collecting them in one agency, as in the case of the Department of Energy. Invariably, the superdepartments, as in the New York experience, do not succeed in reducing the size of the large-scale bureaucracy. They may, however, reduce the number of critical contacts that are imposed on the executive. The superdepartments add another layer to the organizational pyramid, thereby increasing the distance between the beneficiaries and the decentralized components of the system on one hand and the centralized departmental decision makers and the executive on the other. In the process, the price the executive pays for reducing organizational contacts is more powerful functional bureaucracies, potentially representing more aggresive adversaries who may threaten centralized, executive control.

There is little evidence to support the respective arguments for departments organized around themes, territories, or functions. It might, on its face, appear that organization around broad-based themes and missions or around neighborhoods and communities is better suited to executive enhancement than organization-utilizing functions as its basic principle. But the Department of Housing and Urban Development (HUD) belies the assertion. HUD is perceived sometimes as the department for community and metropolitan development and improvement and sometimes as a functional agency for housing and support facilities. HUD is a weak and ineffectual agency of little value in enhancing executive capacity—let alone community development or improvement, or housing and commercial and economic development—in any major or meaningful way. Similarly, economic development is buried in an inconsequential Department of Commerce, which is perceived as a special interest agency. The department has done little to strengthen its executive authority or to serve the broader public interest. With respect to economic development activity, its successes have generally been in connection with projects that would have been undertaken without public intervention, or under circumstances that, even when well-intentioned, had little or no chance of success.

Generally, departments and agencies organized around functions threaten and, on occasion, undermine executive authority and central and horizontal capacity. Frequently, the more effective and efficient the functional agency, the greater the challenge to central control.

Increasingly, executives are looking to and relying on analytical instruments, sophisticated professionals, and methodological tools and approaches to help provide the horizontal, executive capacity. This trend is reflected in the use of councils of economic advisers and in proposals to introduce councils of social advisers. It can be seen as well in efforts to introduce systems of social accounting; in the increased reliance on economic, social, and related indicators as measures of change and achievement; in the use of cost-benefit and cost-effectiveness analyses; in the introduction and application of systematic procedures for establishing need and allocating resources across functional jurisdictions; and in the growing utilization of evaluation and related mechanisms. We see evaluation used more and more as an instrument of management control, allocation, and programming, rather than solely as a postauditing device.

Historically, we have relied on politics and negotiation or on the marketplace as the principal means of decision making. But systematic decision making is increasingly based on analytical and "rational" approaches that are explicable and transferable. The new technologies and methodologies can be described, are communicated and replicated, and are presumed to be objective and evenhanded.

Reliance on technical and analytic methodologies now constitutes a principal means for achieving horizontal capacity and asserting executive authority. In large measure this is due not only to the glamour of the current computerized approaches, but also to the fact that these approaches are usually quantifiable and, therefore, appear to increase accountability. It is also presumed that since these approaches are quantifiable they can be made more economical and efficient. Most importantly, however, they generally leave intact existing systems, practices, and actors. They can be superimposed and introduced without fundamentally threatening the survival of the status quo. Therefore, improvement is a prospect, even if it is illusory, and while organizational conflict may arise, the adversaries can generally be assured that they will be left intact and free to fight again another day.

Centralized establishments at all levels, and in both the public and private sectors, have frequently sought to deal with the failure to achieve horizontal capacity by abdicating responsibility through the delegation, distribution, and transfer of dollar resources or power, or both, to other coordinate authorities, to functional activity systems, or to administrative subdivisions. We see this in the case of block grants and general and special revenue sharing, where responsibility for activities such as welfare, higher education, transportation, or other troublesome and costly functions has been transferred to other levels of government. Such transfer of responsibility accounts for the introduction of modified forms of community self-determination, as in the case of schools, police boards, or other functions in various cities in the country; measures to decentralize power and increase autonomy of subordinate field units and organizations; and similar efforts. No matter what their merits or advantages, rarely do such attempts to distribute resources and power by transference to another authority resolve the problem of responsibility. Rather, the transference frees one authority and fixes another with the problem-solving responsibility. The receiving entity or authority may provide a climate better suited to problem solution, but rarely is it better equipped financially, professionally, or politically to discharge the responsibility, even when dollars and other resources accompany the transfer. The shift of the balance of power in the local decision-making process makes a resolution of conflict or support for an allocation possible. However, there will now be a risk of distorting a program's purposes, reducing its benefits, diluting its standards, and creating a new set of dysfunctions and inequities.

Delivering Goods and Services

A number of measures utilizing the bottom-up approach at or near the firing line of goods and services delivery have been advocated. These approaches attempt to cope with the vertical extension of the functional activity systems and with its dysfunctional effect on the ultimate recipients, to connect disparate and semiautonomous functions and to join them holistically, thereby overcoming the proliferated and disjointed services delivery network. They seek to establish links among an increasing number of valued specialists whose jurisdictions are becoming more and more discrete. Of considerable importance is the desire to moderate the overwhelming effects of large-scale organization widely distributed over space and characterized by detachment, anonymity, and anomie. Key goals are the reduction in the distance between recipient and central authority and the refashioning of the decision-making process so that the beneficiary and consumer are able to influence (if not share) decision-making authority with the producers and providers of services.

The structural and organizational mechanisms to decentralize power include (a) creating smaller, more manageable, and accessible units; (b) bringing functions closer to the people and thereby increasing organizational responsiveness; and (c) changing the way in which goods and services are made available, delivered, and triggered by users and beneficiaries.

One approach to achieving these purposes is to develop mechanisms that seek to alter the spatial organization of the governing and corporate system through establishing semiautonomous decentralized units. An illustration is the creation of "little city halls" that may be charged with varying degrees of power and assigned a range of functions. In some cities, local community boards—advisory or governing—are chosen either by appointment, giving the board limited power, or by at-large elections, which provide the officials elected with more elaborate power. Sometimes the local boards are empowered to engage specified staff and to discharge them—to disperse dollars and other resources, to enter into third-party contracts, to perform or have performed specified services; sometimes they are empowered to act as intermediary and negotiator with a host of relevant public and private individuals, agencies, and groups.

A related mechanism is the consolidated service center, a descendant of the earlier settlement houses and functionally akin to a little city hall. Here public and private services charged with the responsibility for a designated geographic area are brought together, at least physically, in a visible setting, usually within the same structure. The physical collection of activities, however, is rarely matched by any systematic integration.

Ideally, collecting the various actors serving a prescribed territory within a decentralized setting makes possible a series of functional and beneficiary relationships. The consolidated service center is usually a microgoverning component within a larger macrogovernmental functional network located outside the service area. In the perception of the local citizens it represents the public presence.

Community organizations and community corporations are the two principal bottom-up devices that are created by local initiative to rationalize large-scale organization, moderate the tendency toward centralization, modify functional autonomy, and challenge provider domination. With increasing frequency, the community organization is reaching beyond political activism. It has assumed the prime role as consumer representative in dealings with the functional systems, and in sanctioning and legitimating the delivery system itself. It cross-cuts the range of services horizontally and interfaces with the critical private and public agencies, organizations, and groups. The community group serves to coalesce the political, economic, social, and spatial forces. It is not surprising, therefore, that to community residents, local organization is not simply a patriotic experience in democratic participation, but rather the means to consolidate power, to achieve access, to influence the ways in which goods, services, and resources are distributed and allocated, and to offset and shape the nature of decision making.

These factors and this spirit account for the wide support for community organizations. The pressure for community self-determination is based, in many respects, on the suburban model of presumed independence, power, and self-expression. The case for self-determination is predicated on the theory that self-esteem, self-governance, personal investment and identification, and a sense of community are not simply casually desirable or preferable, but essential and critical to community revitalizaton. Community organization consequently is viewed as the catalyst that is likely to turn the system, the group, and the individual around, and provide the chemistry that makes the benefits of knowledge useable for a population heretofore resistant and untouched. Community organization can thus provide access to services and other advantages for a population not previously reached by traditional, conventional, and top-down governmental and functional policies and practices. Community organizations promote participation in formulating, articulating, and delivering goods and services, as a way to increase the probabilities of fulfilling the potential advantages and benefits of programs and services. They stress indigenous institutional and community development through the creation and reinforcement of a sense of community achieved by the efforts of the citizens themselves, rather than by relying on large-scale service providers, public agencies, or major institutions.

Community-based corporations are another evidence of community self-determination. Whereas the community organization is an assertion of political power, the community corporation is an assertion of economic or functional and professional power. The stress on economic power is reflected in the significant increase in the number of newly created community-based economic development corporations brought into being with the support of foundations, the federal government, and private financial and corporate interests. The assertion of functional and professional power is evident in the day care centers, manpower and training programs, social services, and related service delivery systems created under the auspices of community corporations.

Community corporations can serve as a political device as well, constituting a viable and effective micro form of local governance. One idea that has been advanced would extend their function even further by creating a community-based and -controlled research corporation that would sponsor and support independent and objectively undertaken research, distinguished from other legitimate research efforts only by its aegis. The corporation could establish a research agenda, influence the framing of the research questions, assure community involvement in the research inquiry, and facilitate the use and dissemination of the research results. The objectivity of the research would match that of comparable academic, institutional, governmental, or corporate studies.

When central power is transferred to another governmental unit lower in the hierarchy, political decentralization results. When central functions are transferred to another unit lower in the hierarchy, administrative decentralization results. Little city halls and consolidated service centers can represent either political or administrative decentralization, depending on how the power and functions are distributed.

The consequences that result from introducing one or another of these alternative methods to distribute power are uncertain. The comparative advantages of particular mechanisms for achieving sanction and meeting prescribed goals and purposes will vary with the particular circumstances. The relative effects of alternative forms of centralization and decentralization, and of the distribution of power among hierarchical layers and diverse constituencies, remain to be assessed.

Not uncommonly the little city halls and the multiservice centers precipitate the creation of one or more advisory technical and governing councils. Governing councils consist of the key executives sharing the common setting. The technical councils usually comprise the chief professional staff members who deal with such matters as evaluation, standards of performance, information gathering, record keeping, and the like. Advisory councils usually consist of either one or a combination of types of users, interested or affected community residents, and civic-minded citizens. At the outset they are generally assigned a limited role and possess little power. However, it is not unusual for these councils to acquire muscle, grow in influence, and ultimately be merged into a governing group.

Intervention Strategies as Power

Intervention strategies that influence the allocation of resources, as well as the mechanisms for their delivery, affect the distribution of power. Whether the public intervention is entrepreneurial in scale, as in the case of public housing and public schools, and involved in the direct provision of services, or is exercised through less visible devices, as in the case of interest, credit, and investment practices that affect housing and industrial location and development, it will have profound impacts on the pattern of power. Sewer and water grant provisions, highway location decisions, and interest and credit restrictions are likely to have more far-reaching effects on the distribution of power and on the location, scale, and character of human settlement activity than is commonly perceived. There are also diverse methods by which resources are allocated: directly, through producer or consumer housing subsidies; or indirectly, through favorable financing terms and arrangements designed to attract lenders, financing institutions, builders, and other relevant actors.

The most extensive and prevalent bottom-up devices to assist recipients and beneficiaries in dealing with the complex network of functional bureaucracies are related to the delivery of goods and services. These devices may exist or may be introduced in various combinations in connection with any of the top-down and bottom-up structural and organizational alternatives discussed earlier. Each represents an effort to extend the benefits and enhance the quality of goods and service delivery, and to provide the beneficiary and recipient with the capacity to "work" the proliferated and disjointed system. The intention of the various devices is to help the user diagnose problems in the semiautonomous multiple and disconnected functional systems and to make possible service and treatment packages that cut across these systems horizontally in the combinations necessary for prognosis and problem solution. The executive (top down) and the user and recipient face a parallel dilemma and challenge: they find themselves at the mercy of a highly proliferated network that they seek to master through some sort of holistic response.

Information and Referral (I and R) is an elementary device designed to facilitate the user's entry into the service delivery system and to channel the user along the principal paths to and among its components. In its simplest form, I and R operates within a single agency, providing information and directing users to appropriate units within the agency, usually following a preliminary and tentative interview or diagnosis. I and R is frequently used, however, for far more ambitious purposes. For example, I and R may be charged with the responsibility for distributing users among a number of diverse service delivery functions and agencies. Thus an individual may seek service from a particular service agency, and thereby be assured he will have access to the range of selected service agencies, for example, health, manpower, and other needed sources of assistance and support. I and R may be decentralized among each of the service delivery components, with entrants channeled as appropriate across the vertical network; or I and R may exist as a separate entity, and perform the entry and distribution function for the entire service network.

In this latter case, a diagnostic capacity is frequently incorporated to serve the entrant better by improving the quality of the referral process. Thus, by taking on sophisticated diagnostic activities, I and R can become more than a clerical and mechanical procedure. In addition, I and R can be and has been used to maintain the individual's link to the delivery systems over time. The individual may be referred to more than one delivery system at any point ranging diagnostically beyond the stated purpose that precipitated the initial visit, and causal factors and collateral symptoms may be explored so that the entrant is dealt with adequately. The I and R function can be accompanied by a variety of tracking arrangements. For example, central records and files may be maintained on the individual. These are used as "control" devices to provide a modicum of oversight on the functional activity systems and to maintain both a holistic view of the referent and of his experience with the delivery network. In a growing number of instances, this increases the systematic review of service delivery performance and the accountability and responsiveness of providers through assessments that are undertaken periodically across the range of functional activity systems.

In many cases a cadre of beneficiary or client representatives (variously designated) is added to the staff to function as ombudsmen who help the entrant-referent maneuver and "work" the system. In some cases the ombudsman becomes an advocate identifying with the beneficiary-client rather than with the institution or organization. In the case of the ombudsman-advocate, the user-beneficiary-client may remain the charge of an assigned representative over time, to provide familiarity and continuity.

The ombudsman-advocate may be a part of the structured and hierarchical order, attached to I and R or to a comparable component to help lubricate the system and facilitate beneficiary use and service provider performance. Frequently, the I and R role and the ombudsman function are an outgrowth of, and are performed by, a distinct outreach entity. The outreach entity may exist under the aegis of, and be attached to, a particular service delivery function, or be legitimated by a group of service delivery providers who invest the outreach function in a semi-independent body under their joint sponsorship. This latter approach seeks to achieve coordination among the sponsoring providers and a holistic perception and "treatment" of the user-beneficiary. These attempts have a positive by-product: they bring the recipients into the system.

Outreach, in its simplest form, is frequently achieved through the addition of a group of community representatives, community workers, or community agents. Their duties are usually limited to field contacts in which they serve as a liaison and bridge connecting home and service. At best, they reach out for a service market and improve access and facilitate the use of the delivery network. More ambitious efforts have resulted in establishing semi-independent and decentralized outreach facilities that are located in close proximity to the place of residence of groups of existing or potential users-beneficiaries and are sometimes connected with one function but more generally with a range of functions. Contacts with community organizations and programs of education and information and referral are usually among the basic activities of these groups. However, many of them take on advocacy and politically related functions, including a host of community and resident-related roles that go beyond service provision and frequently involve planning, development, housing, municipal housekeeping, and similar activities.

A number of these outreach groups assume diagnostic functions as well, many of which are performed by a trained core staff that is sometimes augmented by relevant specialists. In all cases, however, they have backup facilities and elaborate arrangements for the provision of support and specialized professional services.

While outreach, I and R, and ombudsman-advocacy functions are often part of an administratively decentralized network, it is not uncommon for them to be performed as part of a politically decentralized network as well. Outreach not only performs prescribed service functions but constitutes a means of exercising and exerting control over the professional service systems. Outreach becomes the device by which political influence and power are exercised by a community organization or user-beneficiary groups that in fact take on many of the characteristics of an informal microgovernment. These functions and activities can be initiated or undertaken by one or a group of functional delivery systems, a consolidated neighborhood or community service center, a "little city hall" or more formal microgovernment legitimated and sanctioned by the community, a community organization, or a community corporation.

These diverse efforts at connecting goods and services delivery at the point of provision, and creating a linking mechanism to connect the beneficiary to the system, can constitute the means for a host of possible relationships and functions varying in potency and potential. For example, the efforts will at least make possible increased contact among and between providers and can consolidate the influence and power of the beneficiaries. These new relationships can also be the basis for technical exchange and consultation going far beyond contact and information, and can include research packages involving multiple functions, systematic evaluation of provider performance, and accountability measures. In rare cases, an effort has been made to pool power and dollar resources and to distribute functions and make budget allocations across activity areas, thereby overcoming categorical and jurisdictional rigidities at the neighborhood or community level. This latter goal is generally sought by community groups and users as a means to gain access to and facilitate service performance by exercising control and power over the system's resources and activities. While communities and beneficiaries are frequently co-opted by the providers and by the functional systems, they also seek to co-opt the provider's instruments (sometimes they succeed) by the use of and control over many of the tools of professional service providers—research, evaluation, and budget and resource preparation and allocation.

Antidotes to Overspecialization

Instrumentalities like the ombudsman, the advocate, information and referral, evaluation, research, and the like are efforts at overcoming specialization—without necessarily replacing it or diluting its benefits. More frequently, the purpose is to preserve and accommodate specialization while simultaneously achieving a horizontal, cross-cutting capacity among the diverse and competing functional activities. Most of these efforts, and the devices and mechanisms proposed for achieving them, take on a generalist quality, sharply juxtaposed to specialization and functional diversity. The decentralized entities earlier referred to— neighborhood and community service center, little city hall, community organizaton, community corporation—are examples. Other mechanisms that have been advanced and explored seek to achieve this same purpose by the introduction of generalist practitioners, sometimes from the top down and sometimes from the bottom up.

These attempts to create generalist practitioners may represent a most promising long-term prospect for providing sustained employment opportunities for the upwardly mobile among the residents of the service area and the beneficiaries and recipients. As these new categories of professional generalists (as well as their spin-off specialties) emerge, they are bound to be a useful method for assuring both status and dignity, as well as jobs and income. For these reasons there is merit to the deliberate and systematic identification of functions within the traditional professional jurisdictions that can, with appropriate training, be performed by these new cadres.

The top-down response to the concept of a generalist with integrative and horizontal capacity is to assign this functions to a case manager, a nurse practitioner, a policy analyst, a development officer, a field supervisor, or other equivalent cross-cutting professional. The bottom-up, consumer-beneficiary response to dealing holistically with the individual and his needs is through the outreach worker, the community representative-agent, the ombudsman-advocate, or other equivalent role. These roles are closely related to the emergence of the paraprofessional in nearly all functional areas. The paraprofessional is either himself a beneficiary or is drawn from the same socioeconomic class or service areas as the beneficiaries. This is done in an effort to achieve a maximum degree of communication and inspire confidence, credibility, and responsiveness. Taking the paraprofessional from the client group presumably serves two functions: it increases the effectiveness of the advocacy approach and helps to create employment opportunities, particularly where the beneficiaries are financially disadvantaged. The argument frequently advanced is that neighborliness or current or prior client status is a critical qualification.

The "lay" generalists or paraprofessionals can, with experience and limited and systematic training, constitute a new professional category— one endowed with status and with prescribed duties and skills that can be acquired and communicated. Other professions have emerged historically as a result of comparable developmental processes. The New Deal era provides extensive evidence of this phenomenon. It is not an exaggeration to claim that the affluence and growth of the middle class in the post–World War II era are at least in part the result of just such occupational changes set in motion by the New Deal. Each profession is encumbered by an excess of functional baggage that intrudes on and obscures its more sophisticated and distinctive core functions. This excess functional baggage can be removed from the professional jurisdiction at little or no jeopardy to the profession. Often, the functions that are transferred are either routine and repetitive or no longer consonant with the host profession. Nevertheless, the functions are of sufficient importance to make possible the establishment of a new professional activity area.

The growth, maturity, and sophistication of knowledge and the professions continually increase both specialized knowledge and the number of specialists. Invariably, this heightens the need for integrating that knowledge by packaging specializations in combinations relevant to problem resolution. This process achieves a synthesis that in the past has led to the emergence of a new professional group backed up by a feed-in body of consolidated knowledge. The new generalist-professional usually grows out of an existing professional jurisdiction. At the outset, the generalist is at the mercy of the specialist, commanding less respect and status, since the generalist stage is more primitive in conception and in practice. The newly born generalists tend to be less sophisticated and tutored, often relying on *art* at the expense of science. People with more limited qualifications are attracted to the generalist role. In time, however, the "primitive" generalist achieves degrees of sophistication that may demand higher skills than are required by the specialist. This is so because the generalist is ultimately expected to integrate and enlarge on the specialized knowledge by producing a new creative threshold and conceptual order that will rationalize the existing system and connect the specializations. The threshold is a synthesis constituting the new thesis, which subsequently spins off new sets of specializations. The metamorphosis of the generalist from primitive to sophisticated practitioner is usually accompanied by the obsolescence of many of the existing specialists and specializations. Pressures for self-examination and for finding a more defensible and marketable base to justify its continued existence grow inside and outside of each of the specializations.

The methods by which the goods and services are delivered can enhance the prospects for their full and constructive reception. There is confirming evidence that in the case of the dependent population a supportive environment and familiar liaisons and bridges will not only improve access, but may be the essential element in the delivery and acceptance of the service. A hostile environment in which benefits and services are reluctantly and punitively delivered and provided is destructive to the recipients and is counterproductive.

In addition to the more formal mechanisms, such as outreach, advocacy, community organizations, and the like, voluntarism has begun to exert a major influence. Voluntarism is helping to provide emotional and material reinforcement by creating networks of family members, former and current clients and beneficiaries, and public-spirited citizens. Increasingly, these actors and constituencies are becoming important elements in an elaborate service support system. Sometimes they operate as an informal and shadow network influencing the organizational structure and behavior of the providers and the more formal delivery network.

The Capacity for Quality Control

Among the factors that need to be taken into account in determining how benefits, goods, and services are delivered is the issue of how the service population is defined and prescribed. An assessment of the relative advantages and disadvantages of a universal versus a narrow, target-group approach, especially in the public arena, raises difficult political and psychological choices. In a period of limited public resources, and with the reluctance to expand public involvement, a powerful case can be made for limiting benefits and services to that part of the population without adequate alternatives or resources. However, experience has demonstrated that targeting the dependent population and segregating and earmarking their benefits often result in an inferior service and product. This narrow approach is frequently able to achieve sanction only by a massive effort that overcomes opposition with the help of reluctant supporters and benefactors. Furthermore, this approach results in benefits and services callously provided, widely depreciated, and often even devalued by their beneficiaries.

The disadvantaged are understandably suspicious of unconventional mechanisms and organizational arrangements and devices, no matter how innovative, creative, and farsighted. It is for these reasons that many health system organizational inventions to extend and enhance medical delivery are resisted. Generally speaking, new ideas first need legitimation by advantaged groups with resources and with alternative options and choices. Universalistic approaches achieve these purposes, at least at the outset. They assure sanction and have broad acceptance and appeal. In conception they are both class and color blind. Clearly, they reduce the dollars available to serve the most disadvantaged and dependent. However, if one sees the total dollars expended for a public goods-benefit package in relation to the gross national product and in relation to an individual's disposable income, then the level at which the dollars are collected, allocated, and distributed is basically an accounting issue, even if political and philosophic differences are raised and need to be faced.

How is the benefit and service delivery system triggered? The method by which access is achieved has a central influence on the character and quality of the delivery: Is it purchased by a direct payment or by insurance coverage (as in the case of health services)? Is there limited access to a particular segment of the population (as in the case of many welfare programs)? Or is there universal access (as in the case of education)? The debate on the use of cash vouchers in education, housing, or any other appropriate service should focus on the relative advantage of separating the source of the payment from the benefit or service it purchases or provides. Thus, in connection with health, the fact that some people are self-payers, others are covered by insurance programs, and still others by public reimbursement programs, would not ostensibly affect the kind, quantity, or quality of the benefit or its provision. Consequently, there may be merit in converting beneficiaries and recipients into consumers able to compete in the marketplace through the use of cash vouchers or their equivalent. By this one device the recipient may be provided an enabling capacity, and the private market an incentive to produce goods and services.

The triggering mechanism that is adopted can influence if not determine the degree of positive benefit to the recipient. Alternative triggering devices have a differential impact in setting in motion the process most likely to be effective in putting in place all of the critical components of the delivery system, and with the fewest negative by-products and counterproductive consequences. However, arguments as to the preferred triggering device can frequently beg the essential questions. Although the selection of one or another trigger mechanism may rest on philosophical, political, or analytical grounds, in essence it constitutes a strategy based on a set of assumptions. The intervention that is selected presumably has the greatest likelihood of generating and meshing the range of collateral and coordinate delivery components that comprise the system. This is especially the case if the aim is to extend the benefits broadly, to make them available widely, and to assure the maximum possible success. From this vantage point, the challenge is to convert service delivery systems into a mass-production industry or enterprise.

Accordingly, the triggering devices become strategies rather than philosophies, tested by their probable success in materializing the system. The "mass production" delivery system needs to be concerned with supply, demand, personnel and staffing, costs and financing, and, most important, quality control. In all fields, but especially in the human service area, the importance of quality control is directly related to the success of achieving service provision on a mass scale.

Concentrating attention on the triggering mechanism or on any other single system component is to beg the delivery issue and divert interest and attention away from the system and its performance. The philosophical or political bias of the decision maker will determine which of the preferred components is stressed and which triggering mechanism is selected. Thus, one group—often the public body—may opt for increasing the supply of the good or service; another—often the private sector and the marketplace advocates—may opt for expanding demand; another—often special-interest groups and professionals—may opt for increasing the quantity of dollars, resources, and staff that is made available. Experience has demonstrated, however, that concentrating on the trigger mechanism at the expense of the coordinate system components will preclude the achievement of goals and purposes. The assumption that the triggering mechanism will set in motion a process that materializes these collateral components, and thereby the system, is little more than a faint hope. For example, an increased demand by the lower-income population, even when cash vouchers or other forms of consumer subsidy are made available, has not increased the housing supply sufficiently to meet and satisfy the demonstrated need. For a host of reasons, some of them manipulative, increasing demand without actively attending to the other system components will simply result in price rises and will continue, if not sharpen, short supply. In addition, it will expand rather than reduce the distance between the user and the benefit. If all of the components are not tended to, the selected triggering mechanism benefits only those whose narrow self-interests are served: the providers who derive personal gain, the bureaucrats who gain power and control, and the philosphic and political advocates who gain status, prestige, and influence. There is merit, however, in weighing the alternative advantages—tactically and strategically—among the range of components from which the appropriate triggering mechanism is selected. Whether a supply or a demand strategy is chosen for a given plan of action, for example, will affect the degree of rippling effect. There is no conclusive evidence that a so-called market or public approach has a valildity independent of other contributing factors, or that it is possible to avoid examining and accounting for other elements in the complex "mass production" delivery network. The challenge is to create a system, not to agree on a triggering mechanism or to determine the more widely held philosphical preference. The public or private character of the system is less important than the public and private contributions to the system. The key actor in any mass-oriented service or mass-produced product is likely to be quality control and the organizational and other arrangements that are structured to achieve it. The capacity for quality control, in the course of mass provision, may have a far greater influence than philosophical or political advocacy.

Organizing the Service System Efficiently

The process of entering, organizing, and connecting the service system is of great importance to the successful and satisfactory packaging of a delivery network. The interests, pressure, and power of constituent groups are often far more influential in determining the character of the delivery system than are demonstrated need or rational and systematic organizational structure and the requirements of management control. User, client, and beneficiary perception and influence frequently account for a particular organizational form as the basis of the delivery organization. These include the geographic area, the particular function, the target group, or the mission or problem. Thus the delivery system may be organized around a neighborhood, community, or other territory. Another approach is to organize it around a function—e.g., health, mental health, education, job training, economic development, or other major activity area. Sometimes a target group constitutes the organizing principle—in most cases either the elderly or the young, although not uncommonly an ethnic or special interest group, such as the American Indians, the Spanish-speaking population, the handicapped, etc. Finally, there are a growing number of cases in which a problem like poverty, or a mission like nutrition, captures the public interest and is then used as the organizing principle for delivering services.

In the extreme, each ordering theme can represent a fully developed network of delivery components organized around the particular rallying principle. Each can then be further subdivided, either by territory, subject, or relevant population. Thus, a functionally dominated and oriented delivery organization is likely to be decentralized by territory; a target group orientation, subdivided by functional needs, and then perhaps by territory. A basis exists for each of these forms under different circumstances and at different times. The challenge is to rationalize, reconcile, and connect these forms and to reduce overlap and avoid the waste and conflict of duplication. The danger exists—and it is only occasionally avoided—that a whole set of duplicated and competing systems will be created. The system components that need to be connected into a matrix suggest themselves logically. For example, each target group is dependent on the range of available functions to some degree; each function touches on all target groups; a geographic area seeks to incorporate the range of functions to serve all target groups; and most problems and missions include and depend for solution on functions, target groups, and geography in some system of relationships.

Occasionally, several fully developed delivery systems exist side by side, each providing a mosaic of services and each competing with the other. Thus, for example, a job training center, mental health center, or nutrition center is created, each of which takes on family counseling and social services, day care, physical and mental health, transportation, and a host of related activities. Functional differentiation is not necessarily the most effective basis for administration and organization.

Various techniques have been utilized and advanced to avoid system replication. In the extreme, attempts to eliminate functional bureaucracies, either by direct action, as in the case of sunset legislation establishing dates for program termination, or by systematic and scheduled program reviews, as in the case of zero-based budgeting, have been adopted. Less extreme measures include the use of coordinators, expediters, and liaison officers, who are usually situated in a central or executive office and are conventionally charged with target group responsibility to assemble functional and territorial delivery systems or draw on existing systems, thereby avoiding separation and duplication. Sometimes the target group coordination occurs at the top, infiltrating the ongoing service delivery activities of the governing or operating unit. At other times the target group coordination occurs at the bottom, at the point of delivery, and occasionally includes the delivery of a limited number of direct services.

Functionally oriented service systems tend to be controlled centrally, relying on decentralized administrative subdivisions. Functionally oriented systems clash sharply with territorially based, politically decentralized systems, reflecting vertical and horizontal approaches and differences. Functionally vertical systems challenge the semiautonomy of territorial systems seeking to achieve horizontal integration. Territorially independent units challenge the preeminence and domination of functional, professional, and bureaucratic establishments. Efforts at reconciliation and accommodation between the two approaches include devices to achieve linkages and connections either at the top or at the bottom. In some situations functions retain their vertical separation and integrity at superior levels in the hierarchy. They provide guidance and direction and build the knowledge base, but are without direct and vertical power and control over the hierarchically nested layers. They leave to these latter groups the right of independent action both to integrate functions horizontally across the range of activities at each successive hierarchical layer, and to assume responsibility for delivering the goods, services, and benefits. A reverse approach is often utilized to achieve an acceptable accommodation. This approach seeks to maintain horizontal, territorial control at superior levels in the hierarchy, leaving vertical performance nearer the point of delivery and assigned to lower hierarchical layers.

Where a problem or a mission constitutes the organizing principle, an organization may be created on a crash or transition basis, established either independent of or temporarily drawn from the existing functional or territorial establishments. The mission- and problem-oriented systems tend generally to constitute an interim arrangement pending the transfer of activities to the normative agencies, institutions, and organizations upon completion of the mission or solution of the problem.

A more fundamental approach may lie in systematically determining and differentiating between core and specialized characteristics and activities, on the one hand, and secondary supportive activities, on the other. It is important to determine for each target group, for example, those activities that are most appropriately undertaken and discharged directly by the associated delivery system, and those that are secondary and supportive, and therefore better undertaken by other systems; and for each territorially oriented system, to differentiate between critically related core activities and those that are better undertaken by vertical functional systems.

Organizational structures—territorial, functional, target group, and mission or problem—can be left intact, thus avoiding conflict with advocates, interest groups, and bureaucrats and their constituencies and relying instead on such devices as outreach, informational and referral mechanisms, ombudsmen, community agents, client representatives, community organizations and community corporations, and other techniques to cope with the proliferated jurisdictions and the complex maze. These connective devices can achieve a modicum of integration and a holistic approach, as well as serve both diagnostic and therapeutic purposes. Sometimes these devices and mechanisms merely constitute appendages that at best facilitate and lubricate the system without profoundly affecting it; in other circumstances they represent major influences, fundamentally altering institutional and systemic performance and profoundly changing the nature of the decision-making process.

In the former, more modest case, the measures represent the addition of a set of services that may help cushion change; in the more ambitious case, the measures may be more far reaching and may be instrumental in affecting institutional and systemic change.

The consolidation alternative is most difficult conceptually unless a knowledge base exists that provides some ground for fusion among diverse functional areas. The simple consolidation of functions that attempts to merge two full-blown entities which wish to protect and maintain their individual integrity often results in an unmanageable and inefficient enterprise. Fundamental and conceptually defensible fusions among two or more functions should grow out of restatements and redefinitions rather than out of administrative convenience. A redefinition of function creates a new synthesis at a higher level in the conceptual hierarchy. In addition to the conceptual problems raised by the desire to overcome the proliferation and conflict among an ever-growing number of functions, management, administrative, and structural problems also present an imposing challenge. Frequently, we seek to achieve administratively what we are unable to deal with, understand, or clarify conceptually. The administratively related problems highlight the strategic and fundamental differences that exist between service-oriented approaches and the approaches that seek to affect institutional and structural change. The service-oriented approaches have been emphasized in the discussion. They are designed to increase efficiency and to make functional provision more effective without altering the basic patterns of power or modifying the nature of decision making. The service-oriented approach relies on mechanisms for coordinating and for expediting, through new administrative forms, and other devices to reduce the distance between the provider and user in order to increase the sensitivity and responsiveness of the big bureaucracy and improve the capacity of the beneficiary to enter and "work" the system. Unfortunately, these devices frequently have been instituted for the administrative convenience of the provider rather than as a "diagnostic" response to improve service delivery to the recipient.

The Search for Fresh Organizational Forms

These three elements—conception, organizational structure and management, and political pluralism and sanction—constitute the action agenda and are the essential ingredients in imposing an order and discipline on the expanding and free functioning bureaucracies. The central task is to establish relevant interdependencies, define the operative system, establish its boundaries and limits, and provide closure. The size of the knowledge base and reliance on the academic or professional expert have not enabled us to define the problem, close the system, and satisfactorily either diagnose the underlying causes or prescribe treatment for the symptoms. Therefore we utilize surrogate and other indirect devices to buy time, pending greater understanding or the sanction to do what otherwise cannot be done, or to try to achieve by indirection what cannot be achieved by direction.

Revenue sharing and block grants are examples of such surrogates. The transfer of dollars downward in the governmental hierarchy seeks in theory to decentralize decision making, moderate the effects of the detached and anonymous bureaucracy, overcome categorical allocation, blunt the dominance of the functional bureaucracies, and bring decisions closer to the beneficiaries and to the constituencies. Ostensibly, the result is a better match between problems, needs, and resource allocation; and it simultaneously tips the scale of influence toward the populace at the expense of the professional and bureaucratic provider. Another related fiscal surrogate, seeking to do by indirection what is difficult or impossible to do by direction, is the use of accounting as the means to achieve control through systematic measures that impose and relate performance and cost benefit criteria.

Pressure to alter the structure of service delivery may in time come from the private sector entrepreneur. These private sector actors may exert more influence on service delivery than the beneficiary group, the professional bodies of providers, or the administrative agencies, bureaucrats, or functionaries heretofore associated with the delivery system. The systemic conversion of one human service field after another from elite-status locations in agency and professional offices to "storefront" shopping center locations is having, and will continue to have, a profound effect on service delivery. The commercialization of human services is accelerating the development of their mass character and rapidly extending and universalizing access to them. Marketplace controls are being incorporated as a normative phenomenon, radically altering the fundamental nature of the service delivery system and the roles of its respective actors. The character of the associated professionals is being transformed, as are the constellation and hierarchy of direct-service providers. This transformation has begun to occur in dentistry, in optometry, and, in its early stages, in law. It is also seen in connection with the medical laboratory and diagnostic components of the health field. One need only take note of the mass marketing of the so-called tax expert vis-à-vis the accountant and the tax lawyer to observe the change.

What is occurring is the segregation of functions, profession by profession, that relegates to the traditional professional group the complex, exotic, refined, and highly specialized functions. The professions retain their analytical and scientific activities and functions, and at the same time act as backup and referent. Those functions that can be are standardized, routinized, and reduced and limited to mechanized and mechanical performance before being consolidated, packaged, and marketed. The net effect is the standardization of services, delivered by modestly trained cadres of mechanics and technologists, back-stopped by highly trained professionals, and supported by the latest technology. Mass-produced services provide easy access and dependable delivery. In the process of providing services on a massive scale, professional practice is redefined, creating new professional groups and new occupations.

The changes in the nature and form of service delivery sharpen the challenge and the issues involved in assuring that quality control is achieved and sustained. Sometimes because of a legitimate concern with quality, and sometimes because traditional professionals seek to defend their turf against intrusion and assault, protests are voiced by professional groups and administrative agencies. There is, for example, a growing resistance to attempts at job reclassification and to efforts by administrators to acquire the right of staff reshuffling and reorganization. For these and other reasons there is resistance as well to attempts at redistributing functions, overcoming traditional jurisdictional lines, and redeploying and maneuvering across the service network. This resistance has its counterpart in the industrial sector, where efforts at increasing productivity and quality control through changes in conventional practices and in job classifications are challenged by institutional groups faced with the perceived threat that might come from efforts to change the decision-making process by increasing the form and degree of worker and provider participation.

Manufacturing industries are faced with the need to determine the relative advantages of, for example, connecting and controlling local or regional sales offices by centralizing decision making to assure consistency and uniformity versus allowing local or regional sales offices relative freedom and autonomy (and thereby encouraging them) by decentralizing control and decision making. A limited number of studies of the industrial experience seem to suggest that decentralizing power is more profitable. It lends itself to competitive and lucrative rivalry, to quantifiable assessment of comparative performance and outcome, and to greater consumer satisfaction. Comparable horizontal and vertical pressures exist in the educational and medical areas as well. These pressures are reflected in the tensions between generalized and specialized knowledge, general and specialized health care, and general and special education.

It is fascinating to observe, for example, the decline in the test scores on those scholastic examinations that presumably measure general college readiness and aptitude and the concurrent rise in the achievement scores for a range of individual specialized subjects. This at least suggests a further reinforcement of society's vertical tendencies substantively and administratively. It is also a sign that the vertical imprinting is being perpetuated by the educational providers and producers, by the knowledge transmission belts, and by the nature of academic training.

These phenomena are influenced by the construction of knowledge and by the form and content of professional practice. The organization of service delivery reflects the relative state of diagnosis and treatment. Diagnosis is the product of specialized vertical knowledge; it is based on symptoms that can be tracked and quantified. Prognosis and treatment, on the other hand, tend to be embedded in a complex gestalt, the product of interacting and interdependent factors existing in an uncertain relationship that lends itself to descriptive and qualitative assessment. It is not surprising, therefore, in the face of the organization of knowledge and of professional practice, that we are far more tutored and informed than we are prescriptive and remedial.

Resolving the tension between the expansion and consequent specialization of knowledge and the pressure to solve problems and develop administrative and management capacity is the great challenge. Resolving the tension will require the integration of knowledge and functions within a new configuration. Existing content areas and functional jurisdictions manifest organizational forms that reflect prior social and economic states and are responses to earlier problem constellations. New conceptual formulations represented by fresh organizational forms that recombine knowledge and functions in a way that is appropriate to the technological age are now required. The reformulations will reflect goals and processes that can constitute organizing principles for distributing functions, allocating and deploying resources, and planning and programming activities. The adequacy of the new conceptual threshold will be determined by whether the response that is thereby fashioned succeeds in resolving problems, enhancing management capacity, and moving the agenda to the subsequent theoretical and conceptual threshold. Currently, we consciously or intuitively recognize the inadequacy of traditional ways of organizing knowledge and functions. We are uncertain, however, of the more appropriate alternative. Whether the actions that result from the new conceptualization advance both understanding and capacity is the relevant issue.

CHAPTER 7

The Professional and Practical Consequences of Big Bureaucracy

The New Private and Political Populism

he growing demand for a restructuring of the bureaucratic systems has set the stage for a reexamination of the ways in which decisions affecting public policy are made. The assaults on bureaucracy are generally double pronged: they arise from a fear of the governmental intrusion that allegedly goes hand in hand with massive governmental programs and from a fear of the overwhelming financial burdens associated with the provision of the benefits themselves. Governmental involvement and welfare and dependency programs are closely linked in the public mind. The underlying assumption is that the costs of providing these lower-class benefits can be reduced or eliminated without sacrificing the benefits and advantages that accrue to the middle class and that ostensibly can be provided by other less onerous and costly means. These concerns have been advanced and fed by "conservatives" whose philosophical outlook and political self-interest have been and are being served by such arguments and allegations.

These assertions are a snare and a delusion. The assumption that transferring services to the private sector will allow them to be delivered with the ease and simplicity involved in selling and buying a tie or a bag of groceries is unfounded. The production and delivery of benefits and services depend on an elaborate network and support system that needs to be connected vertically and extended over vast spaces. Only large-scale organizations can provide benefits and services—whether they are delivered by the public sector, the marketplace, or by voluntary agencies. Each sector must deal with the same attendant problems of management, quality control, and consumer satisfaction—and at reasonable and defensible costs.

The rallying cry to fight big government has distorted our perspective, has diverted our attention from the critical challenges, and has resulted in a general weakening of the political and social fabric. It has fed the conservative argument that each and every governmental activity should be replaced by private entrepreneurial devices on the theory that the marketplace is a more efficient, economical, and evenhanded provider than the public agency. The approach proceeds on the premise that the pricing structure is a more responsive control mechanism than the budget process, and that consumer behavior is a better regulator than are legal and administrative procedures. This premise misses the point completely—big bureaucracy, not big government, is the threat. As a matter of fact, the reverse may be the case. "Big" government may be necessary if "big" bureaucracy is to be checkmated and held accountable. Representative government, even with its current imperfections and lack of assertive power, at least constitutes a minimal check and constraint on big bureaucracy, whether it is operating in the public or the private sector.

It is frequently asserted that allocations in the marketplace are more evenhanded and less arbitrary than in the public sector. But is this so? While there are dramatic examples of the influence of market behavior on particular enterprises, these enterprises are usually run by new entrepreneurs who have either lacked the resources, talent, or capacity to produce or merchandise, or who have been unable to withstand massive attempts by established competitors to undermine them during the enterprises' formative stages. With the large established enterprise, market behavior generally influences packaging, merchandising, or advertising, but rarely affects practices and policies in any profound way. In addition to "seductive" attempts to improve the company's image and make its product more alluring, any significant changes in policies and organizational structure are directed at increasing profit margins rather than at customer convenience and satisfaction. In the big private bureaucracy, prices are artificially influenced, resources are controlled, and production levels, supplies, and inventories are arbitrarily manipulated to adjust prices.

Entrepreneurial machines tend to develop lives of their own. The administrations and managements of large private enterprises are no more or less invested in the businesses they are overseeing than are the administrations of the public agencies or departments. There is no real difference between the public and private sectors with regard to their "sense of proprietorship." In both sectors it is becoming difficult to enter the system and impossible to be removed from it.

In the public sector, a whole series of measures have been proposed and are being implemented to contain and constrain the big bureaucracy, to increase its responsiveness to the users and beneficiaries of its services, to provide the executive with the ability to cross-cut the range of functions horizontally and thereby create and enhance governing capacity. These measures are all directed toward strengthening government vis-à-vis big bureaucracy (i.e., by constraining the professional, the administrator, the agency, and the function). In the private sector these distinctions tend to be blurred, since their enterprises are increasingly under detached and unresponsive management control that is subject only to minimum constraint and accountability. In the public sector it is still valid to distinguish between administration and bureaucracy, and between governance and executive power. These distinctions make it possible to discuss popular and user control, the integration and coordination of functions and purposes, and the various means to achieve and exercise them.

In many respects the distinctions between the public and the private sectors themselves are disappearing. In the big cities the pressures for governments to be labor intensive are being replaced by the need to economize and become efficient as a condition of survival. It has become necessary for cities to introduce new technologies and new administrative practices and systems in their own housekeeping and maintenance functions: fire, police, public works, garbage collection, etc. It should be noted that while these may be welcome changes, since waste and inefficiency are hardly defensible, without compensatory measures we might well anticipate unfortunate social consequences. These profound changes imitating private sector practices are not fully understood or appreciated.

What is more, the public sector is increasingly beholden to the private sector. The financial community, in the role of fiscal agent, is a necessary counterpart in the government's efforts to maintain its fiscal integrity and capacity to govern. In nearly all activities and functions, the public and the private sectors exist in interdependent relationships. The private sector depends on direct and indirect subsidies, on special understandings and arrangements, and on access to government programs to sustain its ability to exist and to operate successfully. The public sector not only has developed dependency relationships with the financial community but also has made special arrangements with the private sector for the delivery of a range of goods and services and the performance of a host of functions. The public sector has discovered that this not only makes management and administrative sense but good political sense as well. In many respects, what the functional enterprises within government have done is to adopt private sector franchising practices. The public sector provides seed money and continuing financial support and specifications for the services and functions it wants performed and

establishes the criteria and standards to assess the practices and performance it has commissioned. Though on the one hand the private
sector holds the government in financial bondage, on the other hand it is
an action instrument for the big bureaucracies of government. Indeed this
relationship increasingly has become the critical element in determining
whether a particular establishment, enterprise, service area, or industry
can or will survive.

This fragile mutual dependence has evolved as both a necessary
precondition of action and a defensible and critically important strategy.
The private sector exists by public franchise, taking on many of the
characteristics of minigovernments; in many other instances, as in the
case of the multinational oil cartels, the private sector franchises governments whose existence depends on their good offices and their prevailing
policies and practices. Private sector examples are everywhere: the financial community and the oil industry come immediately to mind. They
facilitate, checkmate, or possess oversight powers on the policies and
practices of government. They share, in fact at least, the responsibility for
governance in ways that are nowhere prescribed constitutionally or
legislatively. By these actions and practices they dilute and reduce popular control and popular will. While the question of which sector is more
beholden to the other is a matter of debate, the fact is they exist in a
life-support embrace.

It is clear that decisions in both the public and the private sectors are
being made by technicians and professionals with similar training, values, skills, and goals. We have organized our public life jurisdictionally
by function, by profession, by gigantic organizational agglomerations
that exist in a semiautonomous galaxy of relationships taking on the
character of a dual government and with minimal deference to the
governing hierarchies. This pattern of bureaucratic giantism is further
overlayed and compounded by the entanglement and complex connection between the public and the private sectors.

In nearly every part of the private sector, mass markets have resulted
in the creation of private bureaucracies, which have not only grown in
size but have multiplied and grouped themselves into complex interconnected networks. Economies and efficiencies have been achieved by
extensive internal regulations dictating and controlling behavior, and by
other devices that have served to make goods and services available on a
massive basis, but have left little room for individual adaptation, justice,
or equity.

The growth of large corporations, as well as of agencies and departments, has led to the expanded influence and power of the professional
and has brought us close to a new kind of syndicalist state in which
society is controlled not by federated bodies of workers but by groups of

professionals. The syndicalist state that is currently approximated is an outgrowth of the massive expansion in the service and benefit sector. While the early apostles and advocates of the syndicalist position postulated an idealized condition with no need for government, in the new public-private bureaucratic alliances participatory and democratic components are bypassed.

The new private and political populism is largely a reaction to these syndicalist tendencies; populism sees bureaucracy and professional domination as the natural consequences of approaches that have increased public intrusion into every aspect of human activity. Political candidates who advocate major legislative enactments reminiscent of the New Deal and post–New Deal periods are rejected as prehistoric men. Yet the mystical charismatic leader who justifies his or her wish to impose a punitive order on moral grounds, or the one who with an elusive magical quality claims that the reordering of institutional relationships will somehow restore individual values, is hailed. In the first instance, populism focuses on human evil, on the deviousness and malevolence of the decision maker; in the second instance, it is predicated on the evils that inhere in the system—on complexity, scale, and misguided or misdirected purposes. Both populist streams constitute reactions to detached and massive bureaucracy, to specialization and technical expertise, and most particularly to anonymous and faceless decision making. The populist stance suggests that individuals are no longer willing to place themselves at the mercy of the system and to organize their lives in accordance with institutional functions that require compartmentalizing needs, services, and goals to accommodate professional and institutional administrative arrangements.

Generalization and Specialization

Here we see a replay of earlier historical phases, phases that will most certainly recur again. The generalist phase, in every sphere of activity and at every stage in time, represents primative states of knowledge and managerial capacity. In every profession generalization has meant a lack of differentiation and conformity; prognosis rather than diagnosis; and descriptive, reportorial, and comprehensive examination rather than insightful, selective, and systematic analysis. In the hard sciences the general practitioner illustrates the early phase of professional development. City and urban planning and social welfare, among the soft science professions, have, until recently, used comprehensive and descriptive tools in the absence of more refined knowledge of cause and effect relationships. The expansion of knowledge has generated diverse and multiple areas of specialization. Specialization has brought administrative proliferation and, as a result of substantial population growth, gigantic bureaucracies as well, which in turn have spawned even more specialties in an effort to achieve linkage and legitimacy. The individual served by these specializations no longer exists as a holistic entity. The public or the elected executive, faced with the array of specializations among and between functions, struggles to discover new administrative and organizational techniques to manage the network. What results are more generalized approaches—in government, in the service area, or in the private sphere—that cut across the diverse specializations and functions. Since knowledge, wisdom, and experience are limited, the early response in the search for horizontal cross-cutting capacity tends to be intuitive rather than systematic, debatable rather than demonstrable, hopeful rather than factual. The techniques are usually historical, reportorial, crude, and descriptive. The administrative measures stress structural form rather than substance. As wisdom, knowledge, and capacity increase, new orders of specialization will emerge out of our primitive general state which will again create fresh conflict and yet again raise new integrating challenges.

Currently, specialization has more status than generalization; however, the growing concern with proliferated functional performance has highlighted the inefficiencies and dyseconomies associated with jurisdictional separation, in which the specialty is assessed as one element in a larger institutional and systemic framework. A far more favorable assessment results when the examination is limited to the specialization's prescribed functions. Proposals have been advanced, some of which are now operational, to achieve interconnections between, and cohesion among, specialties and yet preserve specialized functional patterns. Clinics, health maintenance organizations, and comprehensive service centers are such devices. In addition to performing as service providers, they link the specialties administratively, and thereby seek to achieve the benefits associated with generalized patterns through the skillful management and integration of special talent brought together in shared physical settings, without diluting or homogenizing the specialty.

Out of specialization comes conflict. Faced with a host of problems, sophisticated specialized knowledge generates "apostolic" positions as to the most appropriate intervention strategies. Activities and functions identified with particular specializations are alternatively advanced as constituting the critical key to solving the range of urban problems, e.g., schooling, job training, environment, or motivation. Since these specialty-oriented strategies are themselves interlocking components of a larger network, each inevitably extends the boundaries of its overlapping subject matter into related specialized areas, culminating in a massive power struggle among competing specializations, as they extend their sphere of influence in a complex web of conflicting strategies. With this approach, problems have no closure and activities constitute events rather than climaxes; problems are not solved, only restructured. From this specialized vantage point problem solution is dependent on steady increases in the specialists' power and resources; and administrative organization is relied upon to facilitate delivery of the services associated with the particular specialization. The stress tends to be on expanding user demand as a means of enhancing the specialists' marketability, and evaluation is largely a self-serving exercise in which success is judged by growth measures reinforcing the specialization's reach and influence.

The extent of specialization has reached such proportions that ours is now a syndicalist society with a dual nationalism—governmental citizenship and occupational and professional membership—that can lead only to competing loyalties. The executive faces a mammoth task in rationalizing and managing the multiple functional bureaucracies whose loyalties cut across governmental layers; and the individual citizen is at the mercy of these specialized networks. They are manifested in diverse and discrete service delivery systems operating out of decentralized outposts controlled at central points that are substantially distant organizationally from the people being served.

The syndicalist character of our society is reflected not only in public practice but in the private sphere as well, and it is reinforced by the interlocking character of the two sectors. Activities in one sphere affect, are affected by, and are dependent on the other; and occupational and professional commitments establish loyalties across public and private boundaries independent of personal "contractual" relationships.

At the local level, where there is an overlay of intricate and complex activity webs on mushrooming urbanized areas, the management and governance problems are compounded and multiplied. The dependent populations seek to acquire the power and capacity to secure access to services and resources and to assert a degree of control over the dollars and knowledge in the custody of the highly specialized and fractionated service delivery network. The challenge is to devise instruments that transform the specialized and diverse delivery components into a human service delivery system and to reduce conflict in order to promote the reconciliation process. Persistent conflict among professional subsystems threatens each system and can, in time, destroy it.

The historical separation between the social welfare and environmental professional highlights the disabilities that inhere in professional and specialty arrangements which proliferate and artificially fracture indivisible subject matters. Space and function are mirror images of each other; yet, we maintain these distinctions and others as if they possessed a separable and absolute validity. The marriage or fusion of these approaches would establish a new "generalized" threshold. Subsequent orders of specialization can be anticipated as the generalized knowledge base expands. Fresh future challenges to integrate the specialties will inevitably emerge from the historical cycle.

Professional Jurisdiction and Power

Much of a profession's energies, as it seeks to consolidate its base, are directed toward first expanding beyond its limits and then more carefully defining, refining, and rationalizing its jurisdictional claim. These latter tasks move the profession toward more careful delineations of the problems it seeks to address, the constituencies it seeks to serve, and the scale and scope of the subsystem jurisdiction that sanctions its definition. Jurisdictional warfare often results as each profession seeks to define and close its subsystem, whether it involves mental health, the elderly, poverty, corrections, law enforcement, social services, job training, the environment, or some other problem.

The possession and command of knowledge do not mean changes in policy setting, despite the presumption that, since knowledge constitutes a force for change, a profession possesses the inherent capacity to impose its will by the control and transmission of information. The interaction among decision makers and citizens and clients is the more critical component in determining a change in course. In the face of complexity the political process is dependent on the knowledge base of the professional if it is to function and perform effectively. It is not the adequacy and availability of knowledge or the primacy among alternative knowledge goals that are the critical factors; it is arriving at value choices, achieving sanction precedent to action, and managing the knowledge base and delivering on its benefits. This latter management component and the planning capacity that defines it are discussed in chapter 9. The greatest challenge may lie in acquiring the means for the "public management of disorder." Professionals tend to represent a force for rationalizing the status quo, as each group standardizes and normalizes its activities in order to achieve sanction and survive. As professionals become increasingly technologically aware, they compete with the political forces for control and domination. The influence of technology on the professions is reflected in the growing reliance on methods, tools, techniques, and instrumentation at the expense of direct, and "hands-on," service provision. An example is the health profession, which substitutes technology for social and human services. Further, a mastery of methodology is not necessarily evidence of intellectual capacity. Consider the costly professional research that "digs up the flower to examine its roots."

When professionals perceive, conceptualize, and solve problems by using technology and instrumentation without serious attention to moral or social issues, we see indications of a punitive state. The technocratic conversion of the professional commonly breeds self-serving professional witchcraft. As the professional technocrats (and bureaucrats) seek to build defenses against external assault, they develop an elaborate rhetorical network, solving problems by redefining what is dysfunctional and what is normative. Functions that are initially collected to build a pyramid of power are subsequently exported to other subsystems, thereby shifting responsibility in the face of failure and as a way of coping with incapacity or incompetence.

Each profession has been subjected to skepticism and cynicism, the inevitable result of sponsoring public programs that in time lose their evangelistic appeal when disillusionment follows in the wake of false promises and lost expectations. No profession is exempt. Every profession has experienced the pleasure and exhilaration attendant on the launching of a new program and has been forced to endure the pain and indignity resulting from the need to defend and abide its practices and consequences.

The diminishing good will toward the professions has been accompanied by an increased competition among the professions and bureaucracies for available and shrinking resources. Limited resources and increased skepticism have reduced or eliminated the permissible margin of tolerated error and imperfection in professional and bureaucratic practice. It is less possible to excuse, obscure, or absorb incompetence and/or waste. Using professional rhetoric as a protective strategy no longer works. Professions are less able to rely on chaos as a security blanket with which to cloak and diffuse responsibility; orderliness and clarity leave the profession starkly naked and clearly responsible. Confusion has all too often constituted a cover for a profession's incapacity. The professionals' defense that all issues are complicated, therefore difficult to solve, permits them to sidestep and avoid a clear and direct public statement.

Professional abuses account in large part for the fact that the professions are suspect and under attack. The public is no longer mesmerized by jargon and witchcraft. It feels emboldened to question, if not challenge, professional premises and performance. The growing readiness to equate professionals and bureaucrats brings professionals into further disrepute. The professionals' persistent—and often excessive—self-interest has dulled their luster. The public is becoming persuaded that the professional is essentially a craftsman selling a skill in the same fashion as every other craftsman—plumber, cabinetmaker, tailor, tool and die maker. That the skills required by the professional may be more complex and time consuming to acquire accounts for, if not justifies, the higher salary and greater approbation. It does not, however, give the craftsman-professional any special claims to civic virtue and veneration.

In the health field escalated costs are at least in part the result of an elaborate financing system based on a complex set of incomprehensible and often extraneous statistics, using insurance not for consumer protection but as a pyramiding pricing device. The complicated bookkeeping practices obscure the actual dollars exchanged by invisible networks that hike actual beneficiary and consumer costs. This complex network enables the medical practitioner, for example, to multiply his charges. Medical practitioners influence (if not determine) the rates charged by hospitals and the allowable costs reimbursed by insurance companies. Yet they pile on added consumer charges. These patterns may constitute a deliberate conspiracy perpetrated on the users and the general public. In some form the pattern is duplicated in nearly every field.

There are other practices that have proven even more invidious in eroding public confidence in the professions. Two illustrations warrant attention. The widespread tendency is for the professional bureaucrats, speaking on their own behalf or through their agencies and organizations, to attack the practices and policies that they themselves have established, endorsed, and sustained. They view the consequences of these practices and policies with alarm, as they seek to mobilize public opinion in crusades against them. Rarely, however, do the professionals/bureaucrats accept or acknowledge any authorship or responsibility for the practices, policies, or consequences they come to abhor. The fire fighter, it turns out, is the arsonist. This is a phenomenon common to public officials. It is prevalent in, but not limited to, the fiscal and economic area. We see it in Federal Reserve Bank practices. We observed it, for example, in the attitude of former President Carter's chairman of the Council of Economic Advisers and in the White House aides to Carter who were ready, after they left office, to lead us out of the wilderness into which they had brought us. The public figures who oppose policies for which they were once responsible, and who now turn their opposition into a career on the basis of their "demonstrated expertise," the former White House officials who become television commentators, the army of university professors turned consultants—all are further examples of this "expert class." The most dramatic and notorious culprits are those professionals, bureaucrats, and intellectuals associated with the Nixon administration who have since distanced themselves from him with the same devotion to their own self-interest that drew them to him in the first place.

This expert class is enlarged by an even more destructive group of intellectuals and professionals: the nonpracticing expert/critic, as distinguished from the academic scholar with a record of knowledge building.

The nonpracticing expert/critic is one of that growing body of intellectuals and professionals who have made careers of hovering over the activities of others, nitpicking and tweaking, provoking and courting, and waiting eagerly to gloat over imperfections and failures that they often incite and that enrich them in the process. Memorable examples can be drawn from all fields.

It is not surprising, therefore, that private and public agencies are created to certify the adequacy and quality of professional performance in the face of the growing disaffection and loss of trust in professional knowledge and commitment. A "shadow" structure is brought into being on the premise that performance is only possible with an elaborate system of checks and balances. The right is always reserved—and it is increasingly being factored in—to assure that one gets what is promised or appropriated. Participatory activities, consumer and beneficiary groups, and structural reorganizations are frequently introduced, not to solve problems directly, but rather to checkmate professionals and bureaucrats and hold them responsible.

The Challenge of Professionalism

The new practitioners produced by the phenomenal growth of the knowledge base and the expansion of science and technology are a special class of professionals. They are a breed of technocrats, craftsmen, and organization men and women who deliberately seek to distance themselves from the people affected by their activities. They tend to be amoral, using acquired information and skill as tools in the performance of their tasks and as weapons for self-aggrandizement. They are particularly susceptible to ego inflation by the politically and economically powerful. These anonymous technocrats and professionals are conditioned to believe that their only moral obligation is to knowledge and empiricism. These technicians and professionals have helped bring both sectors (but especially the public sector) to their knees. Their detached, anonymous, and all too frequently arrogant behavior has bred frustration, anger, and cynicism on the part of citizens and program beneficiaries. There is no individual, family or group, consumer or client who has escaped a debilitating experience at their hands.

The unintentional offenses committed by academic and non-academic researchers may match or exceed those committed by these technocrats and professionals. Legal and administrative defenses have been developed to cope with professional misconduct and malpractice. However, we have not yet developed the capacity to deal with misguided sincerity, particularly by dedicated, zealous, and crusading scholars and researchers. The scholar all too frequently relies on a conception of reality that is advanced as if it were verified truth. In many instances, university-based research is predicated on framing questions that are calculated to please the clients and sponsors rather than to derive the truth or to advance understanding. It is as if university research has become part of a vast public relations enterprise.

The research effort is compromised in many ways. It is often assumed that a methodologically pristine research design provides a systematic understanding of what exists and is already known, or has already taken place and has now been replaced. The research effort usually succeeds only in refining nineteenth-century ideas, rather than in plowing new ground and pointing in fresh directions. The most extreme evidence of this scholarly "shell game" can be seen in the academic policy arena. If an academician/researcher has exotic quantitative and mathematical skills, has mastered sophisticated technologies and methodologies, and is promoting and plying these skills in the policy arena—i.e., addressing policy-related questions—there is a prima facie assumption that the person is a policy expert. The arrogant stance he or she communicates is magnified by these people and object counters, and confirmed by the analytical character and quality of the study effort. Universities accept the assertions since they are useful market devices in the quest for research funding. The repetitive claims of analytical excellence are applied to what are largely mechanical, procedural, and technical tasks. The goal is to imbue the tasks with an intellectual mystique and worth that are belied by close examination. Not only are the tasks menial and the research questions slanted to reflect researcher bias, but the methodologies impose a discipline that limits the examination to factors that are quantifiable, even if they are irrelevant or inconsequential. Thus, while the research is reduced to manageable proportions, the significance and validity are diminished.

The methodologists establish their claims to policy analysis by producing statistical tabulations without ever having grappled with issues, wrestled with ideas, or evaluated alternatives and consequences. The measurement of attitudes and behavior comes to constitute the whole of understanding, analysis, and policy direction. The statistician is valued more than the thoughtful person or the idea itself. Many sociologists and social welfare scholars claim to be policy makers because they have engaged in survey "fun and games." These academicians are wrong more often than they are right. They regurgitate macrostatistics supporting executive and legislative "atrocities" about the clientele they have just finished measuring. Various studies reduce the human experience to mathematically measurable terms and thereby obscure the individual's nonmeasurable needs and requirements. The policy consequence is that

measurable interventions are likely to be selected, even if they are ineffectual. The research tendency is to measure input if you can't measure
output, a practice that inevitably leads to policy positions that perpetuate
the status quo.

The posture of maintaining the status quo accepts and confirms the
perfect state of the "controlled environment" and sees change as dysfunction and a movement toward deviation and pathology. Research is
used to legitimate the conviction that the victim is the cause; that the
target, the beneficiary, the client is the recalcitrant, unresponsive variable
to be manipulated and conditioned. The maladaptive quality of the
system, the institutions, and the practices is rarely recognized as the
critical variable in the early stages of change. Only at critical junctures and
at profound and threatening moments do recognition and awareness
result in a fundamental change in perception and in behavior.

We are beginning to recognize that the massive research programs
that ostensibly document dysfunction, thereby making the case for major
legislative programs, lead to distorted public policy. Required are policies
and interventions to facilitate the accommodation and to cushion its
effects; to help introduce and strengthen new institutional and structural
networks, support systems, and social and spatial arrangements. The
prevalent tendency, however, has been to shore up prior institutions and
systems, and to assert and impose funding, programmatic, and operational criteria oriented toward organizational, structural, social, and
spatial arrangements presumed to be normative, but no longer applicable
or defensible.

Public disaffection and dissatisfaction with public and private intervention are largely the result of these misjudgments and miscalculations.
They are the consequence of the inadequate perception of the academic,
professional, and bureaucratic advocates of the misdirected programs
and policies rather than of the inherent failures of a system in transition.
The public distrust has turned into general opposition to public involvement. One can only hope that this attitude is a temporary one and that the
quality of intervention will be addressed once again. Modest evidences of
changes in attitude and policy on the part of the public are apparent. Both
public and private programs are increasingly being directed toward
institutional and systemic changes, rather than toward remedial approaches. This is observable in connection with the elaborate ways in
which the decision-making base has been broadened to include the
spectrum of affected individuals and groups. It is now recognized that an
increase in productivity and in modernization will only be achieved by
changing the roles and relationships of the central actors involved in and
affected by these processes.

Conclusion

Quantitative methodologists, "counters" plying their craft in the policy arena, have access to the inner governmental circles and hold privy positions. The presumption is that methodological skills endow them with a more significant point of view than that of theoretical scholars, experienced practitioners, or elected officials. Unfortunately, information has been confused with knowledge, knowledge with wisdom, technique with scholarship, and scholarship with objectivity. These scholars are lab technicians and sperm collectors, rather than immunologists and scientists. Instead of introducing simple concepts to describe and explain complex phenomena and relationships, these academics and professionals prefer complex concepts to describe and explain simple phenomena and relationships.

Professionalism at its best represents both an art and a science. The skilled professional has a command of the political system and seeks to serve and strengthen popular and political decision making. The professional is a part of the political process—yet stands apart from it. In highly politicized agencies, or in agencies where competing political forces have arrived at an accommodation, professionals and technicians are frequently shielded and are thereby enabled to proceed almost anonymously to plan, program, and manage highly complex subject matter and functions. The result is a managerial approach to governance. Where no political accommodation exists, professional roles undergo steady deterioration and a loss of status and dignity. Professionals tend to be the target of a governing board's political byplay. Politically divisive boards evoke the worst in their members, and the professionals are often their victims. These boards are either unable to act, or act in defiance of the public will. Thus, power is either arbitrarily bestowed and irresponsibly and arrogantly exercised or withheld, immobilizing the agency. Generally, these boards consist of political careerists of inferior caliber who are beholden to others and subsist on spoils. The most destructive board members in a politically devisive and abrasive agency, however, are traditionally not the political hacks but the arrogant and successful businessmen currying political favor and the labor leaders whose tunnel vision is confined to the interests of their constituency.

An increasing number of individuals use their professional base to establish political beachheads. Even the citizens and civic leaders who have traditionally maintained their distance from the political figures and their organizations are not above the fray. The result is a fusion between the public and political interest as professional and civic leader turn politician. The professionals who accept political appointment become subject to the sponsor's domination and manipulation and are ready to do his bidding. Appointing professionals to political positions is a way to avoid strengthening potential political adversaries. The damage to the political system is considerable, however, since it designates political leaders by fiat and anointment and permits power to be consolidated arbitrarily by destroying political opposition.

The damage to the professional role and its public perception is even more devastating. Political-professional distinctions are destroyed, and, in the process, government and the public are denied the advantages that derive from a separation between the political and professional roles. Without this clear separation, knowledge is neutralized, suspect, and even corrupted. Experience has generally demonstrated the validity of Lord Acton's assertions regarding the corrupting influence of power by professionals turned politicians. The sudden and artificial acquisition of power by professionals unaccustomed to its use, and awarded it as an unearned privilege, deludes the recipient, who tends to become arrogant, oppressive, and exploitive. The power of the professional turned politician is derived without a demonstrated political constituency; the professional is answerable to no one except the sponsor. After the sponsor has passed away or is defeated, the swaggering attitude of the politician-professional becomes even more onerous and oppressive; all moderating influences have been removed. Public and democratic rule is clearly threatened by the challenging and attacking of elected officials by the politician/professionals, as if their positions were established by some supreme authority.

The inevitable professional and bureaucratic excesses and the public reaction and criticism of them have led to a reexamination of the decision-making process. The growing demand for a restructuring of the bureaucratic systems has set the stage for more profound and far-reaching changes. The capacity of the professions to adapt and shape their subsystems to match the requirements of the target populations they seek to serve and the problems they seek to solve is sharply constrained (1) by the jurisdictional limitations imposed by the feed-in disciplines and their knowledge base and (2) by the necessity to achieve a management and governing capacity. These content and operational constraints argue for sharply defined professional and jurisdictional limits. However, the gap between the specializations and the administrative compartments and a more holistic theory to match knowledge with human need is widening.

The challenge is to determine whether accountability is to be achieved by more efficient management and administrative mechanisms, including greater reliance on bureaucracy, professionalization, and technology; by increased reliance on strengthened and centralized governing instruments; or by an expansion in participatory and decentralized forms and increased beneficiary, consumer, and citizen controls. To link these diverse approaches, to draw these factors and components together, an approach that inevitably comes to the fore is planning, best understood in relation to social welfare.

CHAPTER 8

Social Planning, Social Welfare, and Social Policy

T

Planning and Social Welfare: Similarities and Differences

he fields of planning and social welfare emerged in the latter part of the nineteenth century as direct responses to the industrialization of our cities and to waves of immigration that brought people to these urban centers from other parts of the country and from abroad. From its inception, social welfare was committed to serving the populations in the industrializing city through civic and religious voluntary organizations whose programs were directed toward the amelioration of the noxious environment that created social and physical deprivation and hazards for individuals and families. The aim of early social welfare activity was to support and facilitate the individual's efforts to cope with the problems of poverty and social dislocation. Its historical mission was to reduce or ameliorate financial, material, physical, and family problems by offering personal support and services. Environmental interventions, both spatial and social, were undertaken as part of a conscious effort to reinforce, expand, and extend individuals' capacities and opportunities so they could effectively exercise choice and independence. Social welfare was in the forefront of the movement to enact legislation that would regulate tenement structures and occupancy. It was identified with housing code enactment and enforcement, the introduction of public health and sanitation measures, and many social programs and laws that sought to improve the physical and social living environment. Social welfare directed a part of its efforts to institution building and to community organizations and consolidation.

The result was a network of settlement houses, family and child welfare agencies, and hospitals—all of which delivered important sur-

147

vival support services—and programs that sought to enrich the safety, stability, and qualilty of daily existence. The voluntary social welfare programs sought not only to lessen hardships but also to relieve the dreary and harsh environment and to motivate, reinforce, and accelerate the aspirations and upward mobility of the population, particularly the young. The ethos of voluntary social welfare was rooted in a belief in "man's" perfectibility, in society's receptivity, and in a degree of opportunity that would make possible the realization of individual potential and personal fulfillment and achievement. Individuals could be expected to influence and shape external events through the institutional and community instruments and organizations created by and for them.

The stress on the individual, the family, the group, and the community was a person-centered orientation; it inevitably resulted in social welfare's strong commitment to and identification with the residents, their areas, and their life styles and circumstances. The success of voluntary social welfare was measured by the social and physical mobility of the groups it served. Frequently, these groups moved up the socioeconomic ladder and left their first neighborhoods. The social welfare institutions then had to reorganize to serve new populations in new ways or face extinction.

In contrast to social welfare, planning stressed the pivotal role of the environment and its impact on social behavior and stress. The planning response to the industrializing city was to replace it or escape from it. Planning assumed that if it were possible to alter the environment or to create the idealized environment, in which land uses existed in a happy and harmonious equilibrium, the course of human experience and its prospect would be enhanced, if not assured. The faith and commitment of planning was in the perfectibility of the environment and in its potential for influencing human behavior and social institutions. Planners believed that improving and changing the quality of the "place" would inevitably improve the quality of life for the individual. For the planner, the dysfunctional and brutal environment constituted an obstruction to the achievement and fulfillment of the aspirations of the individual and the family. The life style and physical living space of economically depressed populations were perceived as evil and destructive impediments requiring action to remove and replace them with new structures that would house fewer residents in settings with more light and air. In the view of planners, institution building and community organization were devices mobilized to transform or materialize the desirable and perfected environmental end state. Planning fundamentally directed its attention to the utilization of land and to spatial relationships—an orientation that has continued despite substantial modification. In its early stages, the planning field focused on the creation of "garden cities"; it emphasized monumental structures, pathways, and spaces. It stressed capital and public works facilities, the infrastructure and its facilitation, and the efficient functioning of the "system." Spatial order was presumed to precede, impose, and reinforce social order. The social consequences of planned intervention was either outside the purview of planning or were casually classified as unfortunate by-products assumed to be correctable and remedial by modest and unobtrusive measures.

Although social welfare was historically imbedded in the problems of the city, planning traditionally had a distaste for density, diversity, and concentration that produced a strong bias *against* the city. Although this bias has been sharply moderated recently, a dogged devotion to a prime concern with space and how it is utilized, rather than with people and their occupancy of the space, still persists.

Many of the historic differences between the fields of planning and social welfare stem from the fact that planning has more generally been publicly funded, whereas social welfare has been largely influenced and controlled by private voluntary funds from civic leaders and philanthropists. Planning has historically been detached from direct engagement with the groups it has affected and has tended to perform in an advisory role to decision makers and service providers, whereas social welfare has been directly engaged in providing service and relating on a personal level with the groups to be served. It is not surprising, therefore, that planning is identified with "statism," and social welfare with "localism." Planning has historically been concerned with macroscales and has been attracted to ever widening territories as the most appropriate universe for intervention; in social welfare, the reverse has been the case. Social welfare has focused on microscales, and it has been more comfortable with reducing the territorial base. Planning has tended to increase the distance between the professional practitioner and the people affected by planned interventions; social welfare has tended to narrow this distance. Planning seeks to address problems and issues that presumably warrant an extension and expansion of the macroperspective and the large geographic horizon; social welfare controls scale in order not to lose or obscure individual and group identities, uniqueness, and differences.

Each field relates to the same social and urban systems and to the identical and relevant populations affected by these systems. However, each field defines the issues and poses its central questions in a different way. The tendency in planning is to emphasize efficiency criteria and to focus on an improved climate and functioning environment in the interests of a relatively more affluent population. Social welfare has emphasized equity criteria in the interests of the dependent, aspiring, and relatively less advantaged population. These differences also influence the manner in which each field approaches its subject matter, the programs each relies on, and the strategies each calls into play. The scale of the planning universe, and accordingly its prevailing "mind set," inclines the field toward a "global" solution that is then disaggregated. The local and individualized social welfare orientation tends toward limited and incremental solutions that are then aggregated.

From another perspective the differences between the fields are "generational rather than conflictual" in that they are best accounted for cyclically. Each field represents an approach that is appropriate to particular socioeconomic groups at different stages in their life cycle, to geographic areas at different stages in time, and to individuals and families at different points in their social and economic development. Conflict between the fields may result from obscuring this difference or failing to perceive it, and from competition for public attention, priority, territory, and limited resources. Or the battle may be over which is the more deserving or appropriate population group to be served, rather than over the most relevant and defensible strategy or program. The professionals in each field have entrenched attitudes and belief systems that resist change because of the potential threat to careers and turf. Public perceptions and stereotyping tend to foster the isolation of the fields from each other.

Social welfare is classified as a humanistic activity, whereas planning is assumed to be a far more technological one. Social welfare has been identified with the poor, the disadvantaged, and the ethnic minority groups, and has reached out to serve them. Planning has been identified with the middle class and the relatively more affluent. Social welfare has relied substantially on the right of the populations and areas being served to set their own goals of self-determination; planning has been committed to "futurism" and has sought to materialize an idealized reality through rational, objective, and systematic approaches to attaining its goals.

The social welfare field has sought to develop and nurture relationships with the individual, the family, the group, and the community. Its primary subject matter and the accompanying tools that have emerged have stressed the direct and indirect provision of services and have focused on program development and program implementation. Planning has focused on the structure and operation of an impersonal service, urban, or administrative system. Planning has sought to anticipate the future course of the system, to forecast changes in it, to determine the constraints and opportunities available to influence it, and to develop a blueprint for its inevitable, deliberate, or preferred end state. The stress on process by the social welfare field, and the stress on product by the planning field, profoundly affect existing and potential intervention strategies.

The focus of social welfare on deprivation, disability, pathology, and marginality is an inevitable consequence of the field's client-referent group, which in turn accounts for the concern with diagnosis/assessment and understanding of the problem or dysfunction and its genesis, and with the motivations and behavior of the affected population. Planning has focused on the "normative state" and on its facilitation, and on prognosis—i.e., the plan, the proposal, and the solution. Other differences include the weight that social welfare has historically assigned to redistributive mechanisms that are tilted toward benefits and "output," as distinct from the planning tilt toward "input" and allocating resources. The social welfare microapproach results in a bias toward decentralized organizational forms and devices, whereas the planning macroapproach creates a bias toward centralized organizational forms and devices.

Citizen Involvement

Social welfare has historically looked to people and their organizations and institutions as its constituency, with heavy stress on participation to fuel and lubricate the social welfare process. Planning, too, is coming to recognize increasingly the importance of citizen involvement in programs and projects.

Highly centralized and even authoritarian societies and private enterprises are beginning to acknowledge the importance of encouraging and providing maximum opportunity for participation to enhance performance and achieve quality control, while continuing to concentrate and centralize ultimate decision making. The pattern is especially noticeable in Japan and is increasingly seen in the private sector in the United States. In addition to its effort to comprehend and manage the complex urban system, particularly in the inner city, planning has been reexamining its relationship to citizens and to communities. It is no longer sufficient to view citizen participation deferentially or as a way to develop sanction and overcome political resistance. The issue of citizen involvement relates to the nature of the decision-making process. Access to resources, social accommodation, and compatible spatial patterns reflect the distribution of public and private power. The increased number of community organizations and their rising expectations are the result of profound apprehensions about the promise and potential of representative government, of professional and agency performance, and of the role of the individual in society. Community organization has become a major means by which people have attempted to effect sweeping institutional and governmental change. It has sought to replenish the spirit of bypassed populations in the cities and to mobilize these populations to help find solutions to urban problems. Thus, community organization is not a device to be manipulated by specialists, but a democratic and egalitarian movement, a fundamental instrument of constructive social and political change.

Though planning and social welfare approaches have both come to regard citizen involvement as a priority, planning has traditionally looked to the more formal and official organizational structures and establishments as its constituency and has relied on either an overt or a covert consensus among the elite and power structure. A fascinating difference between the two fields flows from this characteristic. Social welfare has ascribed advantages and has strong commitments to *cultural* pluralism and little patience with *political* pluralism, which, in its view, has obstructed the adoption of a relevant and defensible social agenda and has prevented or delayed the introduction of redistributive benefit mechanisms. Planning, on the other hand, has accepted *political* pluralism as a fact of life (sometimes even imbuing it with fervent democratic values) and has resisted *cultural* pluralism as an obstruction to progress and an intrusion, dilution, and diversion.

In programmatic terms, these differences and distinctions have resulted in social welfare approaches that have been oriented toward relative change, on the theory that people improve their circumstances by stages, and imperceptibly, rather than in a single step at one moment in time. Social welfare has emphasized social mobility and spatial stability as strategies to reinforce aspirations along with area enrichment. Planning has stressed absolute rather than relative change on the theory that the perfected environment is not only desirable but that it can also constitute a positive instrument to achieve order and equilibrium among functions and activities that would, in turn, enhance the quality of life and constructively influence human behavior and experience. In contrast to social welfare, planning has emphasized spatial mobility and social stability, i.e., the movement of people and goods (consonant with long-held urban theories about succession and segregation) without sacrificing order and certainty, along with a substantial confidence in the inevitability if not the desirability of homogeneity.

There are various ways to conceptualize and define the environmental and social welfare fields and the planning approaches that are associated with each. Table 1 compares the major characteristics of each field, the relationships between them, and the changes that will influence future intervention and programmatic strategies.

Commonalities and Directions

The buzz words commonly used in the fields of environmental and social welfare planning are order, alternatives, choice, allocation, distribution, forecasting, predictability, interdependence, circularity, and consequences. Both environmental and social welfare planning have assumed

Table 1

Environmental Approaches	*Social Welfare Approaches*
Technology	Humanism
Macro-orientation	Micro-orientation
Stress on external factors	Stress on internal factors
Rational decision making	Decision making by negotiation
Efficiency	Equity
Political pluralism	Cultural pluralism
Comprehensiveness	Selectiveness
Effecting change	Cushioning change
Experts	Citizenry
Government	Community
Absolute measures	Relative measures
Stability	Mobility
Ends	Means
Planning product	Planning process
Methods	Values
Materializing the future	Modifying reality
Affluence	Poverty
Normativeness	Dysfunctionalism
Disaggregation	Aggregation
Space and uses	Program and services
Elitism	Participation
Centralization	Decentralization

a variety of roles, including the technical role, the broker role, the mobilizer role, the advocacy role, and the synthesizer role. The diverse constituencies of both environmental and social welfare planning include consumers and beneficiaries, producers and providers, coordinate and collegial professional and administrative agencies, funding sources, and units of government. Planning in each of the respective areas tends to be oriented toward either the doable, the desirable, or the achievable; toward the diagnostic or the prognostic; and toward the descriptive or the prescriptive. The planning process generally proceeds from an objective to a performance standard, to measurable criteria, to the identification of obstacles and blockage points, and finally to programs and to implementation. The fields can be perceived as parallel vertical activity areas, with quite distinct orientations, highly differentiated central functions, and separate and identifiable subject matter content that helps to delimit their respective boundaries and establish their jurisdictional scope. Environmental planning, for example—commonly referred to as city, urban, metropolitan, or regional planning—is concerned with land use and space and with facilities and infrastructure.

It is clear, however, that the character, role, and function of environmental planning are changing in many ways that are removing it from its traditional spatial and land use focus toward broader interests and concerns with the quality of life within the urban setting. Three adaptations are especially significant:

1.   The field is being transformed from an activity dominated by and absorbed with space utilization and with the transportation linkages and communication channels among space users to an activity seeking to combine spatial and social goals and realities. In the Model Cities program of the 1960s and in its successor programs, for example, the intent was to integrate physical, social, and economic planning within a unified community development system.

2.   The growing reliance on systematic methodologies and analytical techniques is refashioning the field into a professional instrument for comprehending and programming the urban complex holistically, and this is shaping the future role of the profession. Increasingly, the field is charged with the responsibility for resolving conflict among diverse constituencies, and with systematically examining and recommending intervention strategies drawing on diverse public and private activities (in housing, employment, education, and the like) in appropriate combinations.

3.   Planning agencies in an expanding number of jurisdictions are being assigned programmatic responsibility for connecting, relating, and reconciling the multiple and diverse coordinate planning and development functions of government.

Concurrently, social welfare planning is coming to suggest the detailed and highly specific blueprints for the delivery of services and for community organization and other participatory devices and forms. Social welfare planning is committed not only to participation but to process—in the course and conduct of an undertaking rather than solely in its achievements or completion.

A highly distinctive quality of social welfare may be its stress on lubricating the system, facilitating the interaction among the actors and events, and coalescing the critical stages in the decision-making process. It utilizes planning to help identify and establish goals and to spell out and assess alternatives rather than to prepare a "packaged" product or "war plan" to deal with pressing issues or a pending crisis. Planning, in this latter context, operates on the assumption that goals and other key guidelines are stated, are apparent, or can be explicated; what is required is a rational, systematic, and analytical examination and blueprint to achieve a predetermined end. Social welfare–related planning stresses means rather than ends and gives heavy weight to the use of the planning instrument to convene, coalesce, and rationalize human, institutional, and organizational interrelationships and accommodations.

The extension and consolidation of the social welfare/planning universe—i.e., the act of drawing together the multiplicity of related though widely ranging human resource–related services and activities, augmented by major community support efforts and devices for citizen and professional participation—would achieve a fresh synthesis and reformulation.

The reformulation would seek to define a new system of environmental and social welfare relationships by connecting relevant social sciences and behavioral and spatial factors in a new gestalt, drawing on administrative and management theory and the emerging "control" technologies for both intelligence and muscle. The refashioned pattern of relationship would seek to weave connections among the related though diverse feed-in disciplines. Ideally, the *social planning system* thereby conceptualized would cease to be another coordinate vertical activity. It would be transformed into an important executive instrument, constituting a horizontal activity cross-cutting the system and its functions. Effective guidance and control would thus be provided, and the highly sensitive and critical factors affecting and influencing change and growth directions would be fused and forged into a compound rather than a mixture. *Social planning,* along with fiscal management, would represent the key components for guiding the system and would be sharply detached and distinct from the coordinate and vertical specialized and operating activity areas.

In contemporary practice, each field uses cross-cutting and encompassing approaches to conceptualize the urban system, and each offers a set of interventions and management strategies to influence growth and change. To some extent both fields reflect the fundamentally diverse technological and humanistic courses of action available to society: macro- or microanalysis and intervention directed toward person or place; spatial or social strategies, such as ghetto enrichment or ghetto dispersal; and public works or human service programs.

The objectives and achievements of each field, and their relationship to each other, reflect the vast knowledge and experience that must be integrated if the contemporary social and urban system is to be managed. The integration of this knowledge and experience will establish the threshold and parameters for a refashioned synthesis. Coalescing the knowledge base of these two fields could increase the prospects for more effective problem resolution and, further, enhance the capacity of the urban system for continuing constructive adaptation.

The crosscurrents and tensions between and among particular functions, disciplines, and activities are played out in the interaction between the environmental and social welfare fields. The "turf and subject" conflicts between these fields have been reduced or could be resolved in one of the four organizational and planning modes depicted in figure 2.

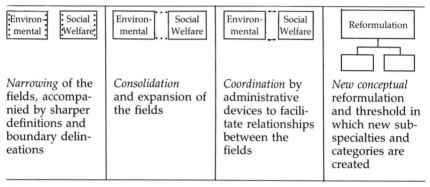

Environ-mental : Social Welfare	Environ-mental Social Welfare	Environ-mental Social Welfare	Reformulation
Narrowing of the fields, accompanied by sharper definitions and boundary delineations	*Consolidation* and expansion of the fields	*Coordination* by administrative devices to facilitate relationships between the fields	*New conceptual* reformulation and threshold in which new subspecialties and categories are created

Figure 2. *Alternative Environmental and Social Welfare Conceptions*

The new conceptual reformulation could, in time, constitute a social planning and policy capacity representing an amalgam of the environmental and social welfare fields, spinning off new subspecialties consonant with this refashioned theoretical base.

These tendencies are already observable in hyphenated specializations that cross-cut both fields in an attempt to address the social and economic problems of the marketplace. The trends have been accelerated by the desire to transfer and apply the technological and methodological skills to the public and private sectors. Centers and institutes have been created around either a particular subject or function or an encompassing theme, replicating the horizontal and vertical organizational orientations discussed in chapter 3, in connection with the matrix there described. These centers and institutes are organized along one of the four alternative models diagrammed in figure 2. This pattern can also be observed in colleges and universities, where similar entities have been created and where a vast and complicated bureaucratic academic network has resulted. The special function centers comprise the academic equivalent of the vertical bureaucracy in the public sector and in the gigantic corporate sector. The consequence will very likely be that, over time, divisive organizational loyalties will develop, rigidifying rather than melding professional differentiations.

One or another of the diagrammed models is explored or introduced either when it is assumed that prevailing practices and policies do not reflect the current state of knowledge, application, and delivery, or when there is dissatisfaction with some aspect of achievement, performance, or response. Conceptual reformulations are frequently achieved by creating umbrella and cross-cutting centers and institutes as a means of drawing on diverse professional jurisdictions and specialized knowledge areas. The organizing theme around which these more ambitious models are based, draw from and connect the environmental and social welfare fields and are likely to speed the prospect of achieving a social planning and social policy capability, as well as an organizational capacity, for its delivery and undertaking.

Devising Strategies for Change

Spatial planning and social planning represent mirror images of each other, and each is more effective and productive when it is recombined into an indivisible functional activity. To maintain independent identities is artificial and serves the professional rather than the beneficiary. A major impetus for effecting these modifications and reformulations has come from the increased commitment to devising strategies for change and to identifying and fashioning workable redistributive mechanisms. The aim is to secure the necessary sanction to achieve social purposes. Frequently, securing sanction requires that a "marginal concession game" be played—i.e., that there be a steady flow of concessions and advantages that can, on occasion and without continuous vigilance, preempt the more ambitious purpose: the creation of profound change mechanisms.

Ideally, the parallel purposes of cushioning change and effecting it are reinforced by coalescing spatial and social orientations. Each such purpose, independent of the other, inevitably results in a diversion of energy and resources. An excessive commitment to cushioning change may sanction the status quo and institutionalize existing organizational relationships and power balances. An orientation that is heavily weighted toward effecting change may tend to reject existing systems, to minimize the usefulness of attempts to accommodate aspiration and upward mobility over time, and to give little weight to or ignore the social problem by-products that undiluted change generates at any given moment.

The key functions that have long been associated with planning (and have been potent forces for change) are now undergoing recombination and consolidation. These functions have been modified and redefined in three basic ways. First, "city" planning no longer has very much status as a formal or universal designation. More prevalent terms are urban, metropolitan, or regional planning. The change in terminology is only partially a matter of rhetoric. More important, the change reflects a shift in the scale and scope of the universe being examined and the relevant and defensible infrastructure and operational framework of that universe. "City" is a static spatial and geographic designation, whereas an "urban," "metropolitan," or "regional" designation reflects the urbanization process and the changing patterns and profile of human settlement.

The second shift is the break with conventional subject matter. Frequently, the traditional planning function, while often facility related, extends beyond the land-use subject matter to include the whole range of services relevant to planning, including human service areas such as day care, law enforcement, and the like. Names of planning agencies have been altered to reflect these enlarged and altered activities, functions, and expectations. There is an effort to reduce the stress on product and assign greater weight to planning as a method. Increasingly, the planning function is viewed as universally applicable to a range of activities. To a considerable extent, planning represents a disciplined procedure that can be communicated and duplicated in many fields of human endeavor and constitutes the means by which diverse fields can be related and interwoven. Planning is not limited to a prescribed content; the content can be acquired or made available to the planning organization by others. Planning is a systematic method with widespread applicability.

The third factor, which is a direct outgrowth of the other two, is the shift away from the semiautonomous role of planning, which traditionally was separate from and outside of the hierarchical structure of government and had only limited advisory functions. The historical assumption was that its autonomous and advisory role would free planning from political influence, safeguard it from the intrusions and compromises that direct engagements would impose, and assure the continuity of an organizational unit of government predominantly, if not exclusively, concerned with the future. The planning function that traditionally was performed by a quasi-independent and autonomous agency has been transferred to and incorporated into a department or agency integral to the hierarchical structure. And while an independent planning commission is sometimes retained for quasi-administrative or quasi-judicial purposes, the principal planning functions have been placed within a formal departmental unit. The separate and advisory planning role has been replaced by assigned responsibilities and duties consonant with the needs of the jurisdiction and related directly to the chief executive.

Planning has become a part of the decision infrastructure. The stress in planning has shifted to immediate and short-range issues and to the pressures, conflicts, and problems faced at any moment in time. While planning generally continues to be charged with responsibility for attending to the future, these traditional purposes are inevitably compromised or sacrificed by the stress on the pending problem, crisis, or decision.

Planning is increasingly being assigned missions and charged with problem resolution. Most significantly, as planning has become a pivotal component in the executive's organizational network, the "product" is being deemphasized and the "process" is gaining in importance. Planning has become the lubricant that facilities the functioning of the system, rather than the producer of blueprints that constitute snapshots of desired or desirable end states. Many of the plans being produced take on the characteristics of armistices or treaties of understanding among diverse, competing, and sometimes adversarial groups, rather than designs for an ideal future or results of a systematic and objective analysis that can constitute a guideline for change and growth.

The net effect of these tendencies is to reinforce the technical orientation of planning and emphasize the refinement of the methodological skills on which it depends. The stress on process is well-suited to planning, which has historically emphasized the integration of knowledge, rather than its creation or production.

Thus, traditional planning with its urban-environmental and land-use orientations has been influenced and modified by activities and pressures from the social welfare sphere and by its increased reliance on process and its concern with method and technique. When goals, values, and preferences are given heavy weight, concern with equity- and allocation-related questions is inevitable. These issues are intrinsically political in nature and, more frequently than not, move planning into the active public if not the political arena. Stressing methodology and technology, on the other hand, implies a value-free, or at least a presumed neutral and detached performance in which planning stands apart from the fray, making its skills available in connection with goals and purposes defined and determined by others, assisted and facilitated by the planning professional and technician.

Significant changes in planning have come as well from within the field itself. Increased knowledge and a heightened civic consciousness and sophistication have led to increasing emphasis upon and attention to political, social, and economic considerations. The premise that spatial relationships influence behavior and social organization clearly suggests that an understanding of behavior and social patterns is crucial to an understanding of the character and quality of spatial arrangements and their distribution. For example, sustaining and reinforcing communities are likely to be considered higher priorities than space allocation or occupancy-related functions and goals. Spatial and community diversity is a natural result of understanding and accepting variations in individual and group behavior and makes the traditional planning emphasis on the "good and absolute" environment obsolete. Conventional planning assumptions about the value of the separation of land uses are similarly being reexamined. A heightened consciousness of individual and social diversity results in a more selective and differential treatment of environmental, community, and spatial components than was characteristic of the historical, comprehensive, and saturation approaches. These social concerns lead in one short step to a need for incorporating participatory forms in the planning process as well as an increase in "social sensitivity." The net effect of all of these factors is an increased populist quality in planning, an extension of the planning constituencies, and the increased influence of citizens and beneficiaries in establishing planning agendas and directions and reducing the dominance of professionals. The shifting power balance in planning has led to a growing emphasis on efforts to relieve immediate burdens and resolve short-range problems, conflicts, and crises. Long-range and futuristic orientations have given way to incremental and short range approaches, to problem anticipation and problem solving, and to analytical planning directed at facilitating decision making.

The historical planning objective of creating the "perfect environment" has been replaced by the contemporary conviction that space and its deployment have no validity independent of social and economic differences and considerations. Plans and planning activity are tested not only for their analytical rigor (and by efficiency criteria), but for the degree to which they enhance opportunity and reduce social and economic disparities. Relative measures of change—i.e., change over time and by stages—have replaced absolute measures of change—i.e., change in relation to one's desired and preferred status and condition. Selective planning—developing operational and manageable packages to achieve predetermined goals rather than detailed blueprints to materialize an idealized future—is the prime focus. Land use, transportation, and related planning activities are perceived as instruments of social and economic policy and as prospective programs and strategies to cushion or effect change.

These adaptations have placed greater stress on urban, individual, and target group dysfunction than had been the case in traditional planning where the focus was almost exclusively on the normative system and its practices. The increased attention on remedial measures to deal with those dysfunctions also tended to redirect the historical planning agenda toward associated needs, causes, and effects. Thus, the planning focus is increasingly slanted toward collateral functional activities and the planning of human services and their delivery; toward economic development and the eradication of poverty through education and job training; toward intervention strategies such as ghetto enrichment or ghetto dispersal; toward public works or education measures; and toward a stress on particular life-cycle stages. Alternative models that have been advanced to effect change represent different strategies and set in motion distinct planning methods and approaches. Among these alternative models are the "treatment" model, which is predicated on overcoming and remedying the dysfunctions and pathologies of the system; the "power" model, expressed either as a bottom-up phenomenon through the assertion of community organization, or as a top-down phenomenon through city- or metropolitan-wide political organization and activity; the "professional" model, which relies on demonstrated capacity and performance manifested in an assumed analytical and research capability and in a professionally dominated service delivery system; and the "economic" model, which emphasizes economic development, job generation, and other allied and associated activities to increase and enhance the productive and purchasing capacity of individuals and communities.

External phenomena have refashioned and altered the climate and framework for planning and have profoundly changed the traditional planning field and its practices. The deterioration and decline of older central cities, the metropolitanization of urban areas, and the regional redistribution of people and activities have sharply shifted the geographic focus and the territorial universe for planning and redirected its attention from new growth and expansion to preservation, redevelopment, and restoration. Severe socioeconomic differences between the population and the changing demographic distribution have brought a series of poverty- and dependency-related problems to the surface and have targeted particular population groups—the dependent, the aged, the young, most notably the young blacks, and others—as requiring priority attention if stability is to be achieved and order maintained. These pressing social and economic issues have visibly altered the planning agenda and forced the field to turn its attention to the resolution of these problems by whatever jurisdictional alliances and strategies are deemed appropriate and feasible. The simultaneous effort to fashion mechanisms that can serve as management instruments to cut across diverse and competing functions and provide executive oversight for a complex governmental structure is the heart of today's planning agenda.

CHAPTER 9

A Changing Agenda for Urban Planning

Profound technological changes are likely to alter societal patterns and life styles. Commercial, office, and banking practices may be radically affected by intricate communication systems that will ultimately influence transport patterns. New forms of energy and methods of sewage disposal could eliminate the need for conventional power plants, chimneys and power stacks, sanitary sewers, and arterial grid systems.

Together, these changes are bound to remove many of the existing constraints in land use development, such as structural location, lot sizes, building layout, and right-of-way alignments, and may well revolutionize economic locational theory and other pivotal social science conceptions. Similarly, it may be possible to create vertical cities (assuming social and political sanction) that would markedly alter spatial patterns and introduce new methods of material and product distribution. These changes would result in major shifts in marketing and in plant locations. Furthermore, climatological and pollution control and related opportunities would flow from the experimental and ultimately selective use of geodesic domes. The feasibility of megastructures, which could incorporate all major daily functions within a single building or complex, would lead to a profound refashioning of social patterns and land usage and, in the process, would require a massive reordering of traditional professional roles, including the probable emergence of a socioarchitect or other new and as yet unknown professional. Or, in contrast to a pattern of increasing densification, an alternative redistribution of population might emerge, with equally profound implications for conventional professional practice forms and associated academic training requirements.

162

In any case, executive capacity will be reinforced by the transformation of urban planning into an instrument which is (1) oriented toward methodology and systems; (2) geared to problem solving and to missions; (3) located horizontally in the governmental structure; and (4) charged with the responsibility for preparing plans and programs across the system that affect and shape change and growth. This transformation will comprise the most effective means available to society to absorb, digest, and adapt to technological change and to the new problem constellations.

The increasing growth of government is of particular significance. It is estimated that government now constitutes a larger job-creating industry than does manufacturing—one in four of the new jobs created since World War II has been in government.

Additionally, the changing pattern of urbanization provides another important contextual component. The metropolitanization of the large urban areas is widely recognized. Population, jobs, and activities are now distributed over space and in a new spatial configuration. The metropolitan area consists of a galaxy of subcities growing out of a collection of major shopping centers and market sheds. The new settlement profile is accompanied by a redistribution between the central city and the subcities of functions, population types, and social problems. These emerging settlement patterns describe the metroplex conception that will characterize the twenty-first–century urban network.

Along with these new metropolitan forms, the population of smaller metropolitan areas and of nonmetropolitan areas has been increasing. More significant is the spectacular growth of the sun belt and the low-density regions of the South, Southwest, and West, and the alarming decline of the Midwest and Northeast. Of particular note is a new regional awareness that is recasting the historical territorial consciousness. The metropolitan universe and the regional universe are being interposed as critical components in enhancing hierarchical and planning capacity.

The challenge, therefore, is not to planning but to democracy itself: to find the means to cope with massive change and to make the necessary adaptations in a manner that is responsive and sensitive to the needs of a diverse population and a pluralistic society.

The Planner's Role

The new and emerging directions are not viewed here as the mechanistic incorporation of technological and scientific innovations but rather are advanced to reinforce and enhance executive and governing capacity. It is becoming increasingly clear that there is a need to create executive as well as citizen and consumer capacity at each geographic level because that is the only effective means of achieving social, economic, and community goals. The dilemma is not a lack of professional and technological know-how. Rather, it is an inability to define goals reflecting the interaction between citizens, the private sector, and government and to develop integrated plans and programs that allocate resources and activate program instruments unconstrained by conventional functional jurisdictions. Current frustrations are in major part a product of governmental fragmentation. The executive (and the citizenry) in the face of the fragmentation is incapable of assessing alternative program and activity combinations, proposing defensible resource allocations, or evaluating program effectiveness.

Charles Merriam has said that free enterprise (we can substitute democracy) has more to fear from lack of planning than from its effective and appropriate use. Planning can provide the means by which the public, and ultimately the executive, assures its control over the decision-making process in the face of massive technological change, increasing professionalization and mechanization, an expanding distance between the individual and the decision maker, and rising personal and family expectations and aspirations.

These profound transformations can provide the occasion for planning's greatest achievements, but only if planning will remove its traditional institutional and narrow subject-matter constraints and fulfill its promise as the professional facilitator of change and of growth. Failing to meet this challenge will provide other professions with the opportunity to do so. For the need to find and fashion a "professional" able to harness programmatic opportunities and resources and to serve and strengthen the executive is demonstrable and inevitable.

Planning is a creative means to contain and control the vast network of activities and agencies. Currently, legislatures are often relegated to the status of dignified advisory boards, and executives to the status of conveners, coordinators, or chairmen of the board as a result of their dependence on, and domination by, bureaucratic and professional establishments. Planning can constitute a critical element in restoring electoral and political determinism.

New dilemmas and issues, many of which cannot now be foreseen, will emerge from and be created by the future patterns discussed here. These by-products will demand fresh governmental and professional adaptations. But planning, if it is to fulfill its destiny—as the profession born of society's need to influence and manage change—must come to view adaptation and accommodation as the fuels that generate its continued existence. In large part, it is this sequence of events that is responsible for the new direction planning is taking. To date, however, these efforts have been halting and premature. They continue to be circumscribed for three crucial reasons.

1.   Conceptually, planning continues to be too firmly wedded to its physical facility origins. Space utilization still persists as the field's central focus, despite the addition of professionals from the social sciences who have extended and enhanced the planning capacity.

2.   Administratively, planning efforts continue to be constrained by the place of the profession in the organizational structure—despite significant changes in executive and legislative intent and purpose, including an increase in the numbers of advisory plan commissions that have been given departmental or other comparable status and have been placed in the executive chain of command, and the growing number of consolidations among developmentally related agencies.

3.   The limited success in achieving integral relationships among functional activity systems.

The requirements of the urban system demand that the modest changes in the role and character of planning be sharpened, extended, and accelerated. While these comments are directed specifically at planning within local governmental jurisdictions, they are applicable to the federal and state levels as well. To facilitate planning performance, what is required is:

• a forthright expression that planning is not a neutral force in the urban (or social) revolution. The all too prevalent identification of planning with the status quo refutes the very basis of its existence. If planning is to survive, it must be identified with change, mobility, and aspiration. The task is not the simplification of the planning process but its complication by a deep and profound involvement in and commitment to social change.

• a broadening and deepening of the base of planning beyond its traditional focus on space utilization. The deployment of physical facilities represents only one of the many available instruments in planning and programming the urban system. Planning has the capacity to examine and recommend alternative methods for resolving social and economic issues, to develop strategies for deployment of public resources, and to call activity systems into play in whole or in diverse combinations.

Three by-products would result from such an expansion of the planner's role. First, the chief executive would be helped to respond to identifiable problems, assess alternatives and their implications, and allocate resources uninhibited by the constraints built into the present jungle of administrative, multiactivity systems. Such an approach would obviate the current concern with proliferated functions, which obscures understanding by diverting energies and attention to institutionalized subject areas (welfare, health, education, etc.) and away from specific issues and problems, such as disadvantaged youth, or unemployment, etc. Not only would the character of planning shift, but its role and relationship to the activity systems would be changed by interposing planning horizontally as a programming and planning aid to the executive. Variable goals, instruments, and program opportunities would be interrelated, unrestrained by the rigidities associated with existing functional activity areas.

Second, planning would be more determinative than predictive in its character and performance. There would be an increased reliance on diagnosis and treatment rather than on trends and forecasts that inhibit the capacity to influence public action and decision making. Trends and forecasts are obviously essential tools in diagnosis and treatment, but they inevitably are precedent to action; they do not necessarily culminate in action.

Third, exploring the impact of public activity would be seen to be as important as defining the initial task. Responsibility for the indirect and long-range effects of public action is frequently obscured by the pressure to provide immediate remedial relief to urgent public issues. The effects of public programs have sometimes been more severe than the problems that initially brought the programs into play. As is the case in science, the side effects of public programs require careful investigation. We often charge ahead with public programs that profoundly affect people's lives as though we were installing a new set of tires on an automobile. Planning labors in the vineyards of the public interest must be tested by the degree to which the lives of citizens are enriched by opportunities for improvement and advancement.

Public programs concerned with urban reconstruction have undergone a series of developmental stages in response to our cumulative experience and as a result of the interplay between divergent goals and purposes. Two major streams have traditionally characterized public and professional concern with questions of urban reconstruction: social welfare and the environment. They have been dealt with in detail in the previous chapter. These streams frequently overlap and intertwine, representing disparate orientations that have yet to be fully reconciled. A conceptual reformulation is taking place that fuses spatial and social welfare planning, drawing on their historic antecedents and recombining traditional physical and social instruments in new relationships. The field of planning is increasingly concerned with social and economic disparities and with the use of space as an instrument of social policy rather than as an end in itself. Among the consequences of the social and spatial fusion are an expanding concern with criteria of equity and efficiency, with poverty and dependency as well as with affluence, with relative change rather than with absolute achievement, and with behavioral influences and consequences in place of static effects. The combined impact of these changes has been to sharpen governing mechanisms by providing the executive with a horizontal and systemwide capacity that emphasizes the integrating rather than the coordinating role of planning. Planning accordingly becomes a governing, administrative, and management tool in addition to a guidance system.

A Federated Approach

While planning tends to conceptualize its universe as a system, it may be more realistic to challenge and modify this perception. The universe may not be an integrated and unified organizational and institutional structure but rather a collection of loosely connected subsystems that depend on good will and on executive and administrative mechanisms to achieve varying degrees of mutual tolerance and accommodation. Efforts to create systemic solutions in the public, private, or academic sphere are usually aborted or blunted by the lack of strong constituencies and the inability to overcome resistance from these entrenched subsystems and from their associated professionals and functionaries. In health, transportation, economic development, energy, and the environment, the functions have grown to such proportions that new federated approaches have been devised to relate and connect these agglomerations to and with the more formal governing entities at all hierarchical levels. Professional and bureaucratic resistance has discouraged more ambitious attempts to recombine and coalesce these diverse functional activity areas into a unitary system. Failure to achieve a unitary approach has resulted in federated arrangements that retain the division of responsibilities and powers and dilute central authority as the subsystem components are preserved. The subsystem resistance to unification is reinforced by the organizational problems that inhere in imposing a unitary system on a complex and diverse network of multiple functions distributed over space—a network that defies manageability.

Achieving a unitary system may constitute a generational problem, because the subsystems themselves have experienced a phenomenal growth in their knowledge base and in the institutional and organizational structures created to produce and deliver their services. Each subsystem is engaged in linking and connecting its diverse constituent components. For example, the health subsystem, whose component parts include hospitals, clinics, medical practitioners, and financing institutions and devices, reaches out for its own federated form to overcome more finite and narrow jurisdictional activities. Ultimately it seeks to create a "unitary subsystem" as a first-order achievement. Any success in moving toward the development of a more comprehensive, overall system is dependent on the prior consolidation of the subsystem components themselves. Another example is the academic sphere, where unifying and unitary cross-cutting and horizontal mechanisms, such as centers or institutes for urban or regional studies, have been preempted, either by special subject and functional activity "subsystem" centers or by a horizontal (unitary) system center that is able to survive only by relying on a collection of vertical subsystem projects.

Planning has had to accommodate to these organizational arrangements since the increasing attempts to interconnect the subsystems themselves as key units of a total system depend on federated rather than centralized approaches. Federalism suggests equivalency among its federated parts; a division of functions and powers, and a balance—albeit frequently uncertain and unsettled—among the partners. Each of the federated components possesses an identity and a claim to continued existence and influence. Consequently, decisions cannot be imposed—except at peril and with risk—but are, rather, dependent on sanction and on a continuous process of interaction with generally indeterminable results. The influence exerted by any federated partner is likely to vary and shift at any moment, and each stage is cumulative, altering and momentarily "fixing the state" preceding the next interactional phase.

A federated approach stands in sharp contrast to a highly centralized approach with a hierarchical arrangement, in which components constitute decentralized units within a pyramidal organization. The essence of federated arrangements is political structure, with the decentralized units and layers possessing orders of independence that dilute central authority. In contrast, in centralized organizations, management mechanisms and devices tend to achieve degrees of dominance over administratively decentralized activities.

Legislative enactments or agency programs in the United States organized pursuant to the highly centralized and hierarchical model, as in the case of the massive functional bureaucracies, are subject to severe criticism and attack. Since such efforts are frequently the product of a strong moral commitment to a social or economic goal, the failure tends to be grand and heroic. On the other hand, enactments and programs that respect the federated system are usually less grandiose and inspirational, imperfect in their construction, even less perfect in their undertaking, and quite often accompanied by more subdued rhetoric. In a centralized state, goals tend to be predetermined, and planning is the *means* to achieve them. In a decentralized and pluralistic system, planning is the *process* by which goals are achieved.

The federated principle has been extended far beyond the issue of the federal-state relationship. The principle applies to the relationships between virtually all governing entities: federal-city, state-city, and the like. We extend the principle to the relationships among the central city and all of its metropolitan parts, as well as among the state and its subregions. The approach is also applied to the central city in relation to its communities and neighborhoods; it is considered the most effective means to reach an accommodation among competing populations and geographies.

The increasing effort to involve citizens in the planning process and to gain their participation in the decision-making process has frequently led to the creation of new forms of microgovernance. Planning has been used to reconcile macro forms at the scale necessary for problem solving and micro forms at the scale required to engage people. There has also been a dramatic shift in emphasis from comprehensive to selective planning approaches, from a stress on product to a stress on process, from an elite to a popular or, at least, pluralistic consensus, and an increased dependence on methodological, analytical, and evaluative techniques.

Far more critical is the growing concern with intervention strategies that have become the single most important consideration influencing the planning approach, process, and product. The intervention strategy constitutes the organizing principle; it imposes a discipline on the planning cycle from conception to blueprint to undertaking and impact. The intervention strategy has facilitated the connections among intelligence, order, and execution, combining knowledge and content with enactment and undertaking.

The tendency to view planning in a decision-making and hierarchical context, to include both the vision and its materialization in the planning horizon, and to test the planning performance by humanistic as well as technological criteria has sharpened a series of conflicts and dilemmas. This is dramatized by the differences that continue to exist between incremental, improvised, and piecemeal approaches, on the one hand, and large-scale and grand designs, on the other. In more rational systems, planning and policy are shaped and guided by normative principles and experiences from which defensible public positions are extrapolated. In the short run, any sharpening of issues and distinctions, and any increased clarity, will probably be accomplished at the expense of stability. Inequity and maldistribution of goods and services are made tolerable so long as the governing entity is able to maintain stability by brokering and negotiating among unequal and competing constituencies. Pluralism, if it is to be sustained in the face of inequity, is dependent on uncertainty and on a lack of clarity. Unfortunately, uncertainty and the need to broker among unequal partners also result in deliberate distortions, as aberrations and dysfunctions become the basis for establishing public policy, since such distortions themselves become negotiable instruments and currency in the bargaining and pacification process.

The most ambitious challenge to planning (and to society) lies in the efficient, economical, and equitable delivery of public-related goods, services, and benefits. The issue is how to provide public works (schools, transit, roads, sewers, housing, parks, etc.), social and public services, and other amenities consistent with the principles of a free society with the least drain on individual and family expenditures. Put differently, we have yet to find the means to produce and deliver the package of benefits and services that cannot be provided by conventional exchange and transfer systems. Acrimonious and spirited debates are taking place in connection with the intervention alternatives appropriate for the public and private sectors, centralization and decentralization, incremental and long-range approaches, and the like.

Planning and urban development and restoration approaches are closely related, even though they can be distinguished and separately assessed. Among the sometimes devastating effects of urban development interventions are the distortions that result from the inevitable pressure for a proven "payoff" from public intervention, and from the consequent narrowing of poverty-related benefits and services. In both of these cases the trend toward measuring effectiveness has circumscribed the planning prospect and potential in both depth and range. For example, the tendency to target all public action and to assess its leveraging effect has narrowed, if not eliminated, a concern with social objectives, since the so-called defensible interventions—those that meet the targeting and leveraging tests in fullest measure—are those with the smallest risk, the greatest probability of success, and, therefore, the least need of assistance.

At the other extreme, the tendency to limit services to the hard-core poverty group will lead to devaluation of the service by a return to the public housing syndrome. We learned from this and comparable experiences that a service for the poor becomes a poor service. The return to a particularistic approach will limit developmental opportunities to the affluent, in the first instance, and to the poor, in the second instance, by a policy of segregation and containment. The same particularistic policy is used differently but with similar effects. It is a return to the protectionism and elitism of the nineteenth and early twentieth centuries. Bonuses for the propertied and affluent, alms for the poor.

The most promising prospect made possible by the linking of planning and intervention is the opportunity it provides to move toward a *simultaneity* in planning. The characterization of planning as a series of interdependent components and elements fails to grasp the essential unity among these components and elements. Similarly, referring to planning as the "science of juxtaposition" falls short of capturing the quality of "oneness" of the juxtaposed factors and forces. The infrastructure and the system defy easy description. We comprehend these factors as integral to the system and as a totality, yet we find it necessary to disaggregate and arbitrarily sequence the events and elements in order to describe and communicate our meaning. The fact is, however, that the relevant collection of forces and factors is intellectually and emotionally indivisible. The unity and simultaneity of their impact and effect on planning are the substantive and spiritual counterpart and manifestation of what Joyce and others sought to achieve in literature, what Picasso and others were all about in modern art. Simultaneity in planning represents the inescapable and connected presence of those elements that describe and impact on the system. The system infrastructure comprises a unity in which comprehension, guidance and manipulation, and management and undertaking are facilitated by enhanced planning capacity. While traditional reliance on interdependency, coordination, and other descriptive characterizations reflects the pluralistic and complex nature of the urban system, these categories do not adequately portray the unitary quality represented by the system's constellation at any given moment.

The changing and temporal nature of what constitutes the unitary state of the pluralistic and complex urban system is an elusive concept. However, it constitutes an important recognition and accounts in major part for the otherwise inexplicable, erratic, and often dysfunctional experience with programs undertaken pursuant to legislative enactments that were initially widely hailed and supported. The nature and the quality of the urban system are constantly changing. The gestalt and configuration that reflect the system's pluralistic and complex network of relationships are manifested in different and altered states as they evolve.

Planning as Synthesis

Construction of the "plan package" is rarely achieved by the addition and accumulation of functions, but rather depends on their careful selection, weighting, and matching. What must be sought is an appropriate combination of factors and functions that can be brought together in a form resembling a chemical compound rather than a mixture. In this spirit, the ideal product constitutes a holistic entity whose parts are indistinguishable elements of an indivisible and defensible whole. Clearly, this state will only be arrived at over time and through systematic research efforts and through analysis of recorded and shared experiences. Further, the desire to connect and relate functions in combinations that seek to achieve predetermined goals is observable in the attempts to arrive at appropriate and meaningful relationships between social and spatial planning and to use knowledge from the behavioral sciences to achieve a new conceptual planning threshold.

Planning is able to play a very useful role in a highly specialized society since it is particularly suited to integrating information and knowledge. In most professions, the span of attention is limited to defined roles and functions and prescribed knowledge and subject matter, and there is a tendency to tighten the lines of demarcation. In planning, however, the tendency is to flirt continually with new boundaries and with new subject matter alliances. In sharp contrast, other professions narrow and constrict their span of attention in the interest of deepening their understanding. The planner, in the desire to be inclusive, may achieve comprehensiveness at the expense of comprehension. The knowledge and understanding needed to support relevant relationships among all the elements in a comprehensive package are sometimes lacking. The gaps in understanding causal relationships reflect the imperfect state of applied research in the social and behavioral sciences, particularly in the public sector. It is hoped that in time the gap between "reach" and "depth" will narrow and close and that the defensible comprehensive envelope can be continually refined.

These countervailing pressures to assure inclusiveness and relevance, on the one hand, and to limit and bind the subject matter by containment and closure, on the other hand, create a serious tension in the profession. Some groups within the profession seek to retain its generalist character; others seek to convert the field into a specialization by asserting a set of functional limits with prescribed roles and activities; and others are either content, process, or methodologically oriented. Most significant, divisions exist between the traditionalists, who continue to stress the futuristic character of planning, and those who place great stress on the analytical and technological opportunities and potential provided by the field.

Very little human activity escapes the attention of the planner: education and training, housing, energy, environment, community and economic development, commerce and industry, transportation, health, human services, management and administration, recreation and community facilities, etc. The social, political, economic, and behavioral context for all such human activity is of major interest also. Yet the planner is constantly challenged to demonstrate the connections between the diverse subject matter components. Certainty grows as knowledge expands. Recognition that a relationship exists among particular factors—e.g., training, jobs, industrial development, and the environment—does not a priori establish the character of the relationship or weight the components comprising the relationship. The nature of specialized and fragmented research may create distortions that limit the understanding needed to connect the key components. The sheer quantity of information and its uneven distribution among particular subjects may result in a biased understanding, since the importance of respective subjects will not necessarily correlate with the availability of information.

In addition to connecting subject matter and achieving new generalized ordering principles that can facilitate the reintegration of knowledge, concomitant efforts are conventionally directed toward the consolidation of proliferated specialized jurisdictions through a variety of other top-down and bottom-up administrative and management devices.

Planning suggests intervention, manipulation, power, and decision making. It is real, even though in the United States there are few legal supports to give planning muscle. Where these legal supports exist, frequently they either lie dormant because of fear of insufficient public support or they are neutralized by political reality or professional timidity. Yet, even in the absence of legal supports, planning affects private and public action and does so in widely diverse settings and circumstances. The very act of planning depends on and stimulates the involvement of people and institutions. Even though the *planning* process is undertaken cautiously and timidly, it alerts and mobilizes the public. The process inevitably brings issues and conflicts to the surface, and, although both inquiry and conclusions may be deliberately understated, the questions posed and the short- and long-term answers sought help to elevate the public debate. Adversarial positions frequently begin to coalesce, often as a direct response and reaction to the planning undertaking, even when efforts are made to avoid them. It is not uncommon for constituencies of varying stripes to emerge, mobilize, or consolidate as a result of a planning activity, thereby generating a level of participation either consciously sought by the planners or their sponsors, or in spite of them and in the face of their affirmative opposition.

The plan represents a force at each stage in its preparation, as does the planning process itself, with or without an ultimate planning product. The plan, independent of its quality, is a statement, a position; and while it may lack the promise of fulfillment, it constitutes an endurable and reproducible document. The plan and the process take on a life of their own, acting as a rallying cry for private and public interests that either support or oppose any or all of its elements. As in the political realm, the plan and the process are persistent, and persistence has a way of winning out, whether or not it is supported by logic and rational judgment. Time is always planning's ally.

Most important, however, the plan, the planners, and the planning process represent a professional mystique that incorporates data and information, diverse knowledge, rational analysis, detachment and objectivity, and "intelligence" and guidance. Planning represents professional power—along with political power and economic power. No longer does anyone question the massive and pervasive influence exerted by professionalism, by the expert, and by his knowledge. Private and public councils and councillors convene only in the company of their experts; no decision is made without the inclusion of experts at every stage in the process, and no deliberation proceeds without their substantial involvement. The experts' influence, and the coordinate and profound role they have assumed in the structure and functioning of society, is evident and is dramatized in connection with foreign affairs, fiscal and monetary policy, and critical domestic issues. During the Ford administration it was the experts at the Center for Disease Control—not the political forces—who made highly questionable policy on the swine serum and were held accountable. This is also the case in connection with nuclear energy and nuclear plant location and a growing number of other subject areas. The extent of the expert's influence can be observed in the frequent blurring of lines among the three "powers," as the professional (the expert) crosses over into the political and the economic spheres. Planning represents professional power, expertise, and knowledge. The activity and process are legitimated and assigned attributes often far beyond their demonstrated capacity to perform or deliver.

In simple terms, decision making can be classified as based on either a Picasso-like, Bismarckian, or Jeffersonian approach to planning. The Picasso approach stresses the planning artistry, emphasizing the skills and talents of the intervener, which may not always be comprehensible or lend themselves to easy replication and transmission. This position argues that truly effective and distinctive planning is the exclusive province of "maestros," that planning cannot be systematized and rationalized, or taught to and understood and practiced by "ordinary" planning practitioners. Lay citizens therefore have little hope of comprehending the field or its product. The Bismarckian approach depends on strong central authority, on the exertion of power, and on an imposed organizational structure that demands conformance and compliance. Bismarckian planning emphasizes authoritarian approaches, imposed either politically or professionally. The Jeffersonian approach to planning has increasingly begun to take hold. This approach stresses participation and small-scale planning on a human and humane scale.

We have already noted that modern urban planning was a response to the problems created by the rapid industrialization of Western European cities and the parallel problems that emerged in the United States in the late nineteenth and early twentieth centuries. Planning sought to remedy the imperfections of rapid economic, population, and urban growth by shaping and reconstructing a healthful living and working environment. Consonant with this remedial spirit, and as a reaction to the chaotic and disturbing state of the industrial city, planning has historically been perceived as a "soft" activity whose goal was to materialize a hoped-for future with an uncertain relationship to the existing and probable reality. The stress in planning, whether remedial or futuristic and visionary, was on the efficient meshing and functioning of the system's parts.

A series of factors have altered and extended the overriding efficiency criterion by which the profession guided and gauged its own performance and by which it was judged by others. These changes have enhanced its attraction and distinction and reaffirmed its role as a people-oriented profession. In its early history, analyses and proposals were initiated and pursued without regard to socioeconomic status, race, or family status. A given plan sought to maximize its marketplace potential and tax yields and benefits, avoiding any concern and responsibility for the consequential socioeconomic effects. This deliberate avoidance ostensibly provided evidence that the plan was blind to class and race and to other socioeconomic differences. The theory on which the plan was based was presumed to be a detached and objective standard of absolute spatial and environmental excellence and achievement.

The effect of changes in planning practice has been to broaden the basic planning criterion to include equity as well as efficiency-related considerations. Increasingly, plans and planning are being guided and tested in terms of their social consequences. This accommodation is but a short distance to approaches that seek affirmatively to achieve social objectives and deal constructively with the consequences of marketplace behavior. The lines begin to blur between planning intended to cushion change and planning intended to effect change. A growing concern with social change inevitably generates a concomitant concern with constituencies and with various forms of participation. What develops in the early deliberate stages are certain expected questions, including: Who is the planner's client? Is the plan based on an elite consensus? Who participated in the plan's formulation? The reactive attitude can grow and mature (and frequently has done so) to the point where affirmative assurances are sought that representative constituencies exist, that they can be created where they do not, and that participatory devices for involvement in the planning process can be introduced to help shape its product. In this spirit, planning becomes the means by which the popular will can be expressed on a continuing and normative basis, and the legitimated means to effect change without threatening the American system of governance.

The recent and growing concern of planners with equity-related factors has interestingly enough, although not surprisingly, brought them back full circle. There is an increased recognition that in the final analysis equity is closely linked to efficiency-related factors, particularly in a period of diminishing resources. These and other factors have made problems of allocation more difficult, almost in direct relation to the pressing need to find workable and politically acceptable redistributive mechanisms. In a sense, waste and inefficiency represented a hidden tax, tolerated to support the unskilled in labor-intensive activities in the private as well as the public sector for purposes of achieving necessary social accommodations, a kind of indirect tax-supported work-welfare program. Private and public institutions, including governments and major private corporations, are themselves discovering that they can only survive by stringent and vigorous economies and efficiencies—and in most cases these measures are essential components in achieving and delivering on an equity-related agenda.

Among the profession's most distinctive and attractive qualities is its virtuoso character. Planning in all respects represents orchestration—whether in the deployment of a diversely trained and talented staff, in the mix of subject matter, in the connections to the variety of coordinate professions, in the relation to the private and public sectors, in the interplay between politics and information, in the selection and use of intervention strategies, in the manipulation among a diet of categorical governmental programs, in the contact with and influence on the range of affected actors, or in the sweep in scope and time of its vision and panorama of the future. Orchestration is individual and private; even when undertaken publicly and visibly, it is a personal achievement calling upon very personal talents. Events did not just happen, nor were they random; they could be accounted for—and, what is more, they could be influenced and redirected. If explanations were not readily available, they were at least being sought and were achievable. The field sought to achieve order, and to do so not by imposing authority arbitrarily but by a demonstrated, defensible, and inherent logic, which was tested by the degree to which it facilitated function. It was neat—the pieces fit. The process was nourished by a provocative and stimulating range of subject matter content and by the challenge to connect the subject matter by testing and reaching out for causal and interdependent relationships among facts, factors, and functions.

These qualities have been enhanced with the increased reliance of the field on science and technology. The highly descriptive nature of planning, and the stress on fancifully developed future scenarios which was its historic orientation, has been replaced and modified by systematic and rational analytical approaches, sophisticated models, games, and systems, and other modern technology.

The planner is still the orchestrator, but he or she now performs with a computer instead of a baton. Planning stands at a fascinating interface, between art and science, humanism and technology.

Selected
Bibliography

CHAPTER 1. CONTEMPORARY ISSUES IN POLICY AND PLANNING

Berry, Brian J. L., and Meltzer, Jack, eds. *Goals for Urban America*. Englewood Cliffs, N.J.: Prentice-Hall, 1967.
Blumenfeld, Hans. "The Modern Metropolis." In *Cities. A Scientific American Book*. New York: Alfred Knopf, 1965.
———. *The Modern Metropolis*. Cambridge: MIT Press, 1967.
Brooks, Michael P. *Social Planning and City Planning*. Chicago: American Society of Planning Officials, 1970.
Davidoff, Paul; Davidoff, Linda; and Gold, Neil N. "Suburban Action: Advocate Planning for an Open Society." *Journal of the American Institute of Planners* 36 (January 1970):12–21.
Downs, Anthony. "Key Relationships between Urban Development and Neighborhood Change." *Journal of the American Planning Association* 45 (October 1979):462–72.
Erber, Ernest, ed. *Urban Planning in Transition*. New York: Grossman, 1970.
Frieden, Bernard J. "The Changing Prospects for Social Planning." *Journal of the American Institute of Planners* 33 (September 1967):311–23.
Friedman, John, and Miller, John. "The Urban Field." *Journal of the American Institute of Planners* 31 (November 1965):312–20.
Galbraith, John K. *The Affluent Society*. Boston: Houghton Mifflin, 1958.
Gans, Herbert J. *People and Plans: Essays on Urban Problems and Solutions*. New York: Basic Books, 1968.
Gorham, William, and Glazer, Nathan, eds. *The Urban Predicament*. Washington, D.C.: The Urban Institute, 1976.
Harrington, Michael. *The Other America*. New York: MacMillan, 1962.
Lowenstein, Louis K., and McGrath, Dorn C., Jr. "The Planning Imperative in America's Future." *Annals of the American Academy of Political and Social Science* 405 (January 1973):15–24.
Lowi, Theodore. *The End of Liberalism*. New York: W. W. Norton, 1969.
Meltzer, Jack, and Whitley, Joyce. "Social and Physical Planning for the Urban Slum." In Berry and Meltzer, eds. *Goals for Urban America*.
Perloff, Harvey S., ed. *Agenda for the New Urban Era*. Chicago: American Society of Planning Officials, 1975.
———. "Common Goals and the Linking of Physical and Social Planning." In *Planning 1965*. Chicago: American Society of Planning Officials, 1965.

Rossi, Peter H., and Dentler, Robert. *The Politics of Urban Renewal.* New York: Free Press of Glencoe, 1961.

Thurow, Lester, and Thurow, Charles. "Equalizing Public Services." In Perloff, ed. *Agenda for the New Urban Era.*

Tunnard, Christopher. "The Planning Syndrome in Western Culture." *Annals of the American Academy of Political and Social Science* 405 (January 1973): 95–103.

Warren, Roland L. *The Community in America.* 2nd ed. Chicago: Rand McNally, 1973.

CHAPTER 2. THE URBANIZATION MOSAIC

Abbott, Carl. *The New Urban America: Growth and Politics in Sunbelt Cities.* Chapel Hill: University of North Carolina Press, 1981.

Abrams, Charles. *The City Is the Frontier.* New York: Harper and Row, 1965.

Barr, Donald A. "The Professional Urban Planner." *Journal of the American Institute of Planners* 38 (May 1972):155–59.

Berry, Brian J. L. "The Counter Urbanization Process: How General?" In Hansen, ed. *Human Settlement Systems.*

———. ed. *The Human Consequences of Urbanization.* London: MacMillan, 1973.

Berry, Brian J. L., and Kasarda, John D. *Contemporary Urban Ecology.* New York: MacMillan, 1977.

Blumenfeld, Hans. *The Modern Metropolis.* See Chapter 1.

Bolan, Richard S. "Emerging Views of Planning." *Journal of the American Institute of Planners* 33 (July 1967):233–45.

Bradbury, K. L.; Downs, A.; and Small, K. A. *Urban Decline and the Future of American Cities.* Washington, D.C.: Brookings Institution, 1982.

Brooks, Michael P. *Social Planning and City Planning.* See Chapter 1.

Brownell, Blaine A., and Goldfield, David R. *Urban America: From Downtown to No Town.* Boston: Houghton Mifflin, 1979.

Burgess, Ernest. "Urban Areas." In Smith and White, eds. *Chicago.*

Chinitz, Benjamin. *City and Suburb.* Englewood Cliffs, N.J.: Prentice-Hall, 1964.

Committee for Economic Development: *Redefining Government's Role in the Market System.* New York: Committee for Economic Development, 1979.

Dahl, Robert A. *Who Governs? Democracy and Power in an American City.* New Haven: Yale University Press, 1961.

Downs, Anthony. *Opening Up the Suburbs.* New Haven: Yale University Press, 1973.

Fine, Sidney. "The General Welfare in the Twentieth Century." In Schottland, ed. *The Welfare State.*

Frazier, E. Franklin. *The Negro Family in the United States.* Rev. ed. Chicago: University of Chicago Press, 1966.

Frieden, Bernard J. "Comment: Environmental Planning and the Elimination of Poverty" *Journal of the American Institute of Planners* 33 (May 1967): 164–66.

Friedman, John, and Miller, John. "The Urban Field as Human Habitat." In Gourne and Simmons, eds. *Systems of Cities.*

Gans, Herbert J. *People and Plans.* See Chapter 1.

———. *The Urban Villagers: Group and Class in the Life of Italian-Americans.* New York: The Free Press, 1962.

Glaab, Charles N., and Brown, Theodore A. *A History of Urban America.* New York: MacMillan, 1967.

Glazer, Nathan, and Moynihan, Daniel Patrick. *The Negroes, Puerto Ricans, Jews, Italians, and Irish of New York City.* Cambridge: MIT Press and Harvard University Press, 1963.

Gluck, Peter R., and Meister, Richard J. *Cities in Transition: Social Changes and Institutional Responses in Urban Development.* New York: Franklin Watts, 1979.

Gorham, William and Glazer, Nathan. *The Urban Predicament.* See Chapter 1.

Gourne, L. S., and Simmons, J. W., eds. *Systems of Cities: Readings in Structure, Growth and Policy.* New York: Oxford University Press, 1978.

Greer, Scott, and Minar, David W. "The Political Side of Urban Development and Redevelopment." *Annals of the American Academy of Political and Social Science* (March 1964):62–73.

Hammer, Philip. "Planning Imperatives." In Perloff, ed., *Agenda for the New Urban Era.*

Hansen, Niles M., ed. *Human Settlement Systems: International Perspectives on Structure, Change and Public Policy.* Cambridge, Mass.: Ballinger, 1977.

Hawley, Amos H., and Zimmer, Basil G. "Resistance to Unification in a Metropolitan Community." In Janowitz, ed. *Community Political Systems.*

Hayes, Federick O. R. "Citizen Access to Government." In Perloff, ed. *Agenda for the New Urban Era.* See Chapter 1.

Holleb, Doris B. "The Direction of Urban Change." In Perloff, ed. *Agenda for the New Urban Era.* See Chapter 1.

Janowitz, M., ed. *Community Political Systems.* New York: The Free Press of Glencoe, 1961.

Kahn, Alfred J. *Theory and Practice of Social Planning.* New York: Russell Sage Foundation, 1969.

Kain, John. "The Distribution and Movement of Jobs and Industry." In Wilson, ed. *The Metropolitan Enigma.*

Kemp, Michael A., and Cheslow, Melvyn D. "Transportation." In Gorham and Glazer, eds. *The Urban Predicament.* See Chapter 1.

Lewis, Oscar. *La Vida: A Puerto Rican Family in the Culture of Poverty—San Juan and New York.* New York: Random House, 1965.

Lowi, Theodore. *The End of Liberalism.* See Chapter 1.

McKelvey, Blake. *The Emergence of Metropolitan America, 1915 to 1966.* New Brunswick, N.J.: Rutgers University Press, 1968.

Metropolitan Governance. Washington, D.C.: National Academy of Public Administration, 1980.

Mills, Edwin. *Urban Economics.* Glenview, Ill.: Scott, Foresman and Co., 1972.

Moynihan, Daniel P. *Maximum Feasible Misunderstanding.* New York: Free Press, 1969.

————, ed. *Toward a National Urban Policy.* New York: Basic Books, 1970.

Muller, Peter O. *Contemporary Suburban America.* Englewood Cliffs, N.J.: Prentice-Hall, 1981.

Mumford, Lewis. *The Culture of Cities.* New York: Harcourt, Brace, Jovanovich, 1938.

Ostrom, Vincent; Tiebout, Charles M.; and Warren, Robert. "The Organization of Government in Metropolitan Areas: A Theoretical Inquiry. *American Political Science Review* 55 (December 1961):831–42.

Piven, Frances Fox, and Cloward, Richard A. *Regulating the Poor: The Functions of Public Welfare.* New York: Random House, 1971.

Rein, Martin. "Social Science and the Elimination of Poverty." *Journal of the American Institute of Planners* 33 (May 1967):146–63.

Schottland, Charles, ed. *The Welfare State.* New York: Harper and Row, 1967.

Schwartz, Barry. *The Changing Face of the Suburbs.* Chicago: University of Chicago Press, 1976.

Silberman, Charles E. *Crisis in Black and White.* New York: Random House, 1964.

Smith, T. J., and White, Leonard D., eds. *Chicago: An Experiment in Social Science Research.* Chicago: University of Chicago Press, 1929.

Sternlieb, George, and Hughes, James W. "New Regional and Metropolitan Realities of America." *Journal of the American Institute of Planners* 43 (July 1977):227–41.

Taeuber, Karl E., and Taeuber, Alma F. *Negroes in Cities: Residential Segregation and Neighborhood Change.* Chicago: Aldine Publishing Company, 1965.

U. S. Advisory Commission on Intergovernmental Relations. *Regional Decision Making: New Strategies for Substate Districts.* vol. 1. Washington, D.C.: U.S. Advisory Commission on Intergovernmental Relations, 1973.

Valentine, Charles. *Culture and Poverty.* Chicago: University of Chicago Press, 1968.

Vernon, Raymond. *The Changing Economic Function of the Central City.* New York: Committee on Economic Development, 1959.

Warner, Sam Bass. *The Urban Wilderness: A History of the American City.* New York: Harper and Row, 1972.

Warren, Roland L. *The Community in America.* See Chapter 1.

Weinstein, B. L., and Firestone, R. E. *Regional Growth and Decline in the United States: The Rise of the Sunbelt and the Decline of the Northeast.* New York: Praeger, 1978.

Wilson, James Q., ed. *The Metropolitan Enigma.* Cambridge: Harvard University Press, 1968.

————. "Planning and Politics: Citizen Participation in Urban Renewal." *Journal of the American Institute of Planners* 29 (1963):242–49.

Wood, Robert. "Intergovernmental Relationships in an Urbanizing America." In Moynihan, ed. *Toward a National Urban Policy.*

CHAPTER 3. COMPREHENDING AND MANAGING THE URBAN SYSTEM

Abels, Paul, and Murphy, Michael J. *Administration in the Human Services.* Englewood Cliffs, N.J.: Prentice-Hall, 1981.

Anderson, Martin. *The Federal Bulldozer: A Critical Analysis of Urban Renewal 1949–1962.* Cambridge: MIT Press, 1964.

Bahl, Roy, ed. *Urban Government Finance: Emerging Trends.* Urban Affairs Annual Review 20. Beverly Hills, Calif.: Sage Publications, 1981.

Black, J. Thomas. "The Changing Economic Role of Central Cities and Suburbs." In Solomon, ed. *The Prospective City.*

Bluestone, Barry, and Harrison, Bennett. *The Deindustrialization of America.* New York: Basic Books, 1982.

Bolan, Richard S. "Emerging Views of Planning." See Chapter 2.

Botkin, James; Dimancescu, Dan; and Stata, Ray. *Global Stakes: The Future of High Technology in America.* Cambridge, Mass.: Ballinger, 1982.

Boulding, Kenneth. "Boundaries of Social Policy." *Social Work* 12 (January 1967):3–11.

Brooks, Michael P. *Social Planning and City Planning.* See Chapter 1.

Committee for Economic Development. *Redefining Government's Role in the Market System.* See Chapter 2.

"Curriculum Essays on Citizens, Politics and Administration in Urban Neighborhoods." *Public Administration Review* 32 (Special Issue, October 1972).

Davidoff, Paul. "Working toward Redistributive Justice." *Journal of the American Institute of Planners* 41 (September 1975):317–18.

Davidoff, Paul, and Reiner, Thomas A. "A Choice Theory of Planning." *Journal of the American Institute of Planners* 28 (May 1962):103–15.

Donahue, W. T. "What About Our Responsibility toward the Abandoned Elderly?" *Gerontologist* 18 (April 1978):102–11.

Downs, Anthony. "Alternative Forms of Future Urban Growth in the United States." *Journal of the American Institute of Planners* 36 (January 1970):3–11.

Erber, Ernest, ed. *Urban Planning in Transition.* See Chapter 1.

Etzioni, Amitai. *Modern Organizations.* Englewood Cliffs, N.J.: Prentice-Hall, 1964.

Fayol, Henri. *General and Industrial Management.* London: Sir Isaac Pitman and Sons, 1949.

Fesler, James W. *Area and Administration.* Birmingham: University of Alabama Press, 1949.

———. "Centralization and Decentralization." In *International Encyclopedia of the Social Sciences,* vol. 2. New York: MacMillan, 1968.

Frankel, Charles. *The Democratic Prospect.* New York: Harper and Row, 1962.

Frieden, Bernard J. *The Politics of Neglect: Urban Aid from Model Cities to Revenue Sharing.* Cambridge: MIT Press, 1975.

Gottmann, Jean. *Megalopolis: The Urbanized Northeastern Seaboard of the United States.* New York: The Twentieth Century Fund, 1961.

Grabow, Stephen, and Heskin, Allan. "Foundations for a Radical Concept of Planning." *Journal of the American Institute of Planners* 39 (March 1973):106–14.

Grant, Daniel R. "The Metropolitan Government Approach: Should, Can, and Will It Prevail?" *Urban Affairs Quarterly* 3 (March 1968):103–10.

Greenstone, J. David, and Peterson, Paul D. *Race and Authority in Urban Politics: Community Participation and the War on Poverty.* New York: Russell Sage Foundation, 1973.

Gulick, Luther. "Metropolitan Organization." *Annals of the American Academy of Political and Social Science* 314 (November 1957):57–65.

Hammer, Philip. "Planning Imperatives." See Chapter 2.

Hawley, Amos H., and Zimmerman, Basil G. "Resistance to Unification in a Metropolitan Community." See Chapter 2.

Hayes, Frederick O. R. "Citizen Access to Government." See Chapter 2.

Holleb, Doris B. "The Directions of Urban Change." See Chapter 2.

Hudson, Barclay. "Comparison of Current Planning Theories: Counterparts and Contradictions." *Journal of the American Planning Association* 45 (October 1979):387–98.

"Issues in Deinstitutionalization." *Hospital and Community Psychiatry* 29 (1978):557–632.

Jacobs, Jane. *The Economy of Cities.* New York: Random House, 1969.

Kalba, Kas. "Postindustrial Planning: A Review Forward." *Journal of the American Institute of Planners* 40 (May 1974):147–55.

Krieger, Martin H. "Some New Directions for Planning Theories." *Journal of the American Institute of Planners* 40 (May 1974):156–63.

Lowi, Theodore. *The End of Liberalism.* See Chapter 1.

McNeill, C. A. "The Deinstitutionalization of Juvenile Status Offenders: New Myths and Old Realities." *Journal of Sociology and Social Welfare* 7 (1980):236–45.

Marshall, T. H. *Class, Citizenship and Social Development.* Chicago: University of Chicago Press, 1977.

Massey, Douglas. "Residential Segregation and Spatial Distribution of a Non-Labor Force Population: The Needy, Elderly and Disabled." *Economic Geography* 56 (1980):190–200.

MiKulecky, Thomas J., ed. *Human Services Integration.* Washington, D.C.: American Society of Public Administration, 1974.

Miner, John B. *Management Theory.* New York: MacMillan, 1971.

Mogulf, Melvin B. "A Modest Proposal for the Governance of America's Metropolitan Areas." *Journal of the American Institute of Planners* 41 (July 1975):250–57.

Nathan, Richard, and Fossett, James W. "The Prospects for Urban Revival." In Bahl, ed. *Urban Government Finance.*

Ostrom, Vincent, et al. "The Organization of Government in Metropolitan Areas." See Chapter 2.

Perloff, Harvey S., ed. *Agenda for the New Urban Era.* See Chapter 1.

Peterson, Richard A. *The Industrial Order and Social Policy.* Englewood Cliffs, N.J.: Prentice-Hall, 1973.

Piven, Frances Fox. "Planning and Class Interests." *Journal of the American Institute of Planners* 41 (September 1975):308–10.

Porter, David O., and Olsen, Eugene A. "Some Critical Issues in Government Centralization and Decentralization." *Public Administration Review* 36 (January/February 1976):72–84.

Rein, Martin. *Social Policy: Issues of Choice and Change.* New York: Random House, 1970.

Schorr, Alvin. *Slums and Social Insecurity: An Appraisal of the Effectiveness of Housing Policies in Helping Eliminate Poverty in the United States.* Washington, D.C.: U. S. Department of Health, Education and Welfare. Social Security Administration, Division of Research and Statistics. Research Report no. 1, 1966.

Solomon, A. R., ed. *The Prospective City.* Cambridge: MIT Press, 1980.

Thurow, Lester, and Thurow, Charles. "Equalizing Public Services." See Chapter 1.

U. S. Advisory Commission on Intergovernmental Relations. *Regional Decision-Making.* See Chapter 2.

Walter, S. Z. "Is There Any Benefit in Cost-Benefit Analysis?" *Quarterly Bulletin of the Intelligence Unit, Greater London Council* 21 (December 1972):5–10.

Warner, Sam Bass, ed. *Planning for a Nation of Cities.* Cambridge: MIT Press, 1966.

———. "Urban Constraints and Federal Policy." In Warner, ed. *Planning for a Nation of Cities.*

Warren, Roland L. *The Community in America.* See Chapter 1.

Weiner, Myron E. "The Implications of the Services Integration Movement for the Theory of Public Administration." In Mikulecky, ed. *Human Services Integration.*

Wholey, Joseph S. "What Can We Actually Get from Program Evaluation?" *Policy Sciences* 3 (September 1973):361–69.

Wood, Robert. "Intergovernmental Relationships in an Urbanizing America." See Chapter 2.

CHAPTER 4. DEVISING AN URBAN STRATEGY

Abrams, Charles. *The City Is the Frontier.* See Chapter 2.

Anderson, Martin. *The Federal Bulldozer.* See Chapter 3.

Auger, Deborah A. "The Politics of Revitalization in Gentrifying Neighborhoods: The Case of Boston's South End." *Journal of the American Planning Association* 45 (October 1979):515–22.

Bellush, Jewel, and Hausknecht, Murray, eds. *Urban Renewal: People, Politics and Planning.* Garden City, N.Y.: Anchor Books, 1967.

Blumenfeld, Hans. *The Modern Metropolis.* See Chapter 1.

Bowley, Deveraux, Jr. *The Poorhouse: Subsidized Housing in Chicago, 1895–1976.* Carbondale: Southern Illinois Press, 1978.

Brooks, Michael P. *Social Planning and City Planning.* See Chapter 1.

Clay, Philip F. "Managing the Urban Reinvestment Process." *Journal of Housing* 36 (October 1979):453–55.

Downs, Anthony. "Key Relationships between Urban Development and Neighborhood Change." See Chapter 1.

———. *Neighborhoods and Urban Development.* Washington, D.C.: Brookings Institution, 1981.

Erber, Ernest, ed. *Urban Planning in Transition.* See Chapter 1.

"Federal, State, and Local Response to Urban Problems." In *The President's*

1980 National Urban Policy Report. Washington, D.C.: U. S. Department of Housing and Urban Development, 1980.

Ferebee, Ann. "Successful Cincinnati." *Design and Environment* 3 (Winter 1972):40–45.

Fisher, Robert M. *Twenty Years of Public Housing: Economic Aspects of the Federal Program.* New York: Harper and Row, 1959.

Friedman, John, and Hudson, Barclay. "Knowledge and Action: A Guide to Planning Theory." *Journal of the American Institute of Planners* 40 (January 1974):2–16.

Gans, Herbert J. *People and Plans.* See Chapter 1.

Gelfand, Mark I. *A Nation of Cities: The Federal Government and Urban America, 1933–1965.* New York: Oxford University Press, 1975.

Glickman, Norman, ed. *The Urban Impacts of Federal Policies.* Baltimore: Johns Hopkins University Press, 1980.

Goetze, Rolf; Colton, Kent W.; and O'Donnell, Vincent F. *Neighborhood Dynamics: A Fresh Approach to Urban Housing and Development Policy.* Cambridge, Mass.: Public Systems Evaluation, 1977.

Harrington, Michael. *The Other America.* See Chapter 1.

Holleb, Doris B. "Housing and the Environment: Shooting at Moving Targets." In *America Enters the Eighties: Some Social Indicators.* Philadelphia: Annals of the American Academy of Political and Social Science 453 (January 1981):180–221.

———. "The Direction of Urban Change." See Chapter 2.

Jacobs, Jane. *The Death and Life of Great American Cities.* New York: Random House, 1961.

Laska, Shirley, and Spain, Daphne. *Back to the City: Issues in Neighborhood Renovation.* Elmsford, N.Y.: Pergammon Press, 1980.

———. "Urban Policy and Planning in the Wake of Gentrification." *Journal of the American Planning Association* 45 (October 1979):523–31.

Marcuse, Peter. "Housing in Early City Planning." *Journal of Urban History* 6 (February):153–71.

Massey, Douglas S. "Residential Segregation." See Chapter 3.

Meltzer, Jack, and Whitley, Joyce. "Social and Physical Planning." See Chapter 1.

Meyerson, Martin. "National Urban Policy Appropriate to the American Pattern." In Berry and Meltzer, eds. *Goals for Urban America.* See Chapter 1.

National Urban Coalition, The. *Displacement: City Neighborhoods in Transition.* Washington, D.C.: The National Urban Coalition, 1978.

Perloff, Harvey S., ed. *Agenda for the New Urban Era.* See Chapter 1.

Polikoff, Alexander. *Housing the Poor: The Case for Heroism.* Cambridge, Mass.: Ballinger, 1978.

Schorr, Alvin. *Slums and Social Insecurity.* See Chapter 3.

Semer, Milton P., et al. "Evolution of Federal Legislative Policy in Housing: Housing Credits." In *Housing in the Seventies, Working Papers,* vol. 1. Prepared by the Department of Housing and Urban Development, 1973.

Simon, Arthur. *Stuyvesant Town, U.S.A.: Patterns for Two Americas.* New York: New York University Press, 1970.

Smith, Neil. "Toward a Theory of Gentrification." *Journal of the American Planning Association* 45 (October 1979):538–48.

Smith, Wallace F. *Housing: The Social and Economic Elements.* Berkeley: University of California Press, 1970.

U. S. Department of Housing and Urban Development. Office of Policy Development and Research. *Displacement Report. Final: I. Introduction; II. Minimizing Involuntary Displacement in the Administration of HUD Programs; III. Recommendations for the Formulation of a National Policy on Displacement.* Washington, D.C.: U.S. Department of Housing and Urban Development, 1979.

Weiler, Conrad. *NAN Handbook on Reinvestment and Displacement: The Public Role in a New Housing Issue.* Washington, D.C.: National Association of Neighborhoods, 1979.

Witte, William A. "Reinvestment: The Federal States." *Journal of Housing* 36 (October 1979):459–60.

CHAPTER 5. MARKETABILITY: THE MAJOR DETERMINANT IN CLEARANCE AND RESTORATION

Abrams, Charles. *The City Is the Frontier.* See Chapter 2.

Altshuler, Alan A. *Community Control.* New York: Pegasus, 1970.

An Atlas of the Spring Hill Neighborhood of Pittsburgh. Pittsburgh: Pittsburgh Neighborhood Alliance, 1977.

Bailey, Robert Jr. *Radicals in Urban Politics: The Alinsky Approach.* Chicago: University of Chicago Press, 1974.

Barkey, Paul W., and Seckler, David W. *Economic Growth and Environmental Decay: The Solution Becomes the Problem.* New York: Harcourt, Brace, and World, 1972.

Brooks, Michael P. *Social Planning and City Planning.* See Chapter 1.

Clavel, Pierre, et al., eds. *Urban and Regional Renewal in an Age of Austerity.* Oxford: Pergamon Press, 1980.

Davidoff, Paul; Davidoff, Linda; and Gold, Neil N. "Suburban Action." See Chapter 1.

Downs, Anthony. "Key Relationships between Urban Development and Neighborhood Change." See Chapter 1.

———. *Opening Up the Suburbs.* See Chapter 2.

Ferebee, Ann. "Successful Cincinnati." See Chapter 4.

Fish, John. *Black Power/White Control.* Princeton: Princeton University Press, 1973.

Frieden, Bernard J. "The Changing Prospects for Social Planning." See Chapter 1.

———. *The Future of Old Neighborhoods: Rebuilding for a Changing Population.* Cambridge: MIT Press, 1964.

Gans, Herbert. *People and Plans.* See Chapter 1.

Gorham, William, and Glazer, Nathan. *The Urban Predicament.* See Chapter 1.

Hammer, Philip. "Planning Imperatives." See Chapter 2.

Laska, Shirley, and Spain, Daphne. "Urban Policy and Planning in the Wake of Gentrification." See Chapter 4.

Leven, Charles L., et al. *Neighborhood Change: Lessons in the Dynamics of Urban Decay.* New York: Praeger, 1976.

Long, Norton E. "Another View of Responsible Planning." *Journal of the American Institute of Planners* 41 (September 1975):311–16.

———. "Citizenship or Consumership in Metropolitan Areas." *Journal of the American Institute of Planners* 31 (1965):2–6.

Meltzer, Jack, and Whitley, Joyce. "Social and Physical Planning for the Urban Slum." See Chapter 1.

Mott, George Fox. "Communicative Turbulence in Urban Dynamics—Media, Education and Planning." *Annals of the American Academy of Political and Social Science* 405 (January 1973):114–30.

Neill, Desmond G. "The Unfinished Business of the Welfare State." In Schottland, ed. *The Welfare State.* See Chapter 2.

Peattie, Lisa R. "Reflections on Advocacy Planning." *Journal of the American Institute of Planners* 34 (1968):80–88.

Perloff, Harvey S., ed. *Planning and the Urban Community.* Pittsburgh: University of Pittsburgh Press, 1961.

Polanyi, Karl. *The Great Transformation: The Political and Economic Origins of Our Time.* 1944. Reprint. Boston: Beacon Press, 1957.

Polikoff, Alexander. *Housing the Poor.* See Chapter 4.

Rossi, Peter H., and Dentler, Robert. *The Politics of Urban Renewal.* See Chapter 1.

Simon, Arthur. *Stuyvesant Town, U.S.A.* See Chapter 4.

Smith, Neil. "Toward a Theory of Gentrification." See Chapter 4.

Smith, Wallace, F. "Forecasting Neighborhood Change." *Land Economics* 39 (August 1963):292–97.

———. *Housing.* See Chapter 4.

Smuts, Edward E. "Comments on the Economic Functions and Structure of the Metropolitan Region." In Perloff, ed. *Planning and the Urban Community.*

Suttles, Gerald. *The Social Order of the Slum.* Chicago: University of Chicago Press, 1968.

Trolander, Judith Ann. "Social Change: Settlement Houses and Saul Alinsky, 1939–1965." *Social Service Review* 56 (September 1982):346–65.

Vaughn, Susan J. *Private Reinvestment, Gentrification and Displacement: Selected References with Annotations.* Chicago: Council of Planning Librarians, 1980.

Walter, S. Z. "Is There Any Benefit in Cost-Benefit Analysis?" See Chapter 3.

Warren, Roland L. *The Community in America.* See Chapter 1.

Weiss, Marc. "The Legacy of Urban Renewal." In Clavel et al., eds. *Urban and Regional Renewal in an Age of Austerity.*

Chapter 6. Functional Networks and Dual Governance

Abels, Paul, and Murphy, Michael J. *Administration in the Human Services.* See Chapter 3.

Aiken, Michael, and Mott, Paul E., eds. *The Structure of Community Power.* New York: Random House, 1970.

Alinsky, Saul. *Reveille for Radicals.* 1946. Reprint. New York: Vintage Books, 1969.

Altschuler, Alan A. *Community Control.* See Chapter 5.

American Society for Public Administration. *Human Services Integration.* Washington, D.C.: American Society for Public Administration, 1974.

"Baltimore Institutionalizes Neighborhood Centers." *Neighborhood Government* (November 1973):4–6.

Bebout, John E., and Bredemeier, Harry C. "American Cities as Social Systems." *Journal of the American Institute of Planners* 29 (1963):64–76.

Blumenfeld, Hans. *The Modern Metropolis.* See Chapter 1.

Brooks, Michael P. *Social Planning and City Planning.* See Chapter 1.

Burke, Edmund M. "Citizen Participation Strategies." *Journal of the American Institute of Planners* 34 (September 1968):287–95.

———. *A Participatory Approach to Urban Planning.* New York: Human Sciences Press, 1979.

Campbell, Alan K. "Centralization or Decentralization." In Mathewson, ed. *The Regionalist Papers.*

Committee for Economic Development. *Reshaping Government in Metropolitan Areas.* New York: Committee for Economic Development, 1970.

Cox, Fred M.; Erlich, John L.; Rothman, Jack; and Tropman, John E., eds. *Strategies of Community Organization.* Itasca, Ill.: F. E. Peacock Publishers, 1972.

Dahl, R. A. *Who Governs?* See Chapter 2.

Demone, Harold W., Jr., and Harshbarger, Dwight. "The Planning and Administration of Human Services." In Schulbert, Baker, and Roen, eds. *Developments in Human Services.* vol. 1, pt. 2.

Doggett, Rosalyn P. "The Development Sector Approach to Regional Planning." *Journal of the American Institute of Planners* 35 (May 1969):169–77.

Eisenger, Peter K. "Control-Sharing in the City." *American Behavioral Scientist* 15 (September–October 1971):36–51.

Farkas, Suzanne. "The Federal Role in Urban Decentralization." *American Behavioral Scientist* (September–October 1971): 15–35.

Ferebee, Ann. "Successful Cincinnati." See Chapter 4.

Fesler, James W. "Approaches to the Understanding of Decentralization." *Journal of Politics* 27 (August 1965):536–66.

Forrest, John W. "The Georgia Department of Human Resources and Its Public: A Critique by a Federal Agency." In American Society for Public Administration. *Human Services Integration.*

Frankel, Charles. *The Democratic Prospect.* See Chapter 3.

Frederickson, H. George. *Recovery of Structure in Public Administration.* (Pamphlet #5). Washington, D.C.: Center for Governmental Studies, 1970.

Gans, Sheldon P., and Horton, Gerald T. *Integration of Human Services: The State and Municipal Levels.* New York: Praeger, 1975.

Grant, Daniel R. "The Metropolitan Government Approach." See Chapter 3.

Greenstone, J. David, and Peterson, Paul D. *Race and Authority in Urban Politics.* See Chapter 3.

Greer, Scott, and Minar, David H. "The Political Side of Urban Development and Redevelopment." See Chapter 2.

Grollman, Judith E. "The Decentralization of Municipal Services." *Urban Data Services*, International City Managers Association, 3, no. 2 (February 1971).

Gulick, Luther. "Metropolitan Organization." See Chapter 3.

Hallman, Howard. *Neighborhood Government in a Metropolitan Setting*. Beverly Hills, Calif.: Sage Publications, 1974.

Hammer, Philip. "Planning Imperatives." See Chapter 2.

Hayes, Frederick O. R. "Citizen Access to Government." See Chapter 2.

Herbert, Adam W. "Management under Conditions of Decentralization and Citizen Participation." *Public Administration Review* 32 (Special Issue, October 1972):622–37.

Jacobs, Jane. *The Death and Life of Great American Cities*. See Chapter 4.

Kahn, Alfred J. "Service Delivery at the Neighborhood Level: Experience, Theory, and Fads." *Social Service Review* 50 (March 1976):23–56.

Lauffer, Armand. *Social Planning at the Community Level*. Englewood Cliffs, N.J.: Prentice-Hall, 1978.

Levin, Melvin. "Planners and Metropolitan Planning." *Journal of the American Institute of Planners* 33 (March 1967):78–90.

Liebman, Lance. "Metropolitanism and Decentralization." In Wingo, ed. *Reforming Metropolitan Governments*.

Lindbloom, Charles E. "The Science of 'Muddling Through.' " *Public Administration Review* 19 (Spring 1959):79–88.

Lowi, Theodore. *The End of Liberalism*. See Chapter 1.

MacNair, R. H. "Citizen Participation as a Balanced Exchange: An Analysis and Strategy." *Journal of the Community Development Society* 12 (1981):1–19.

Mathewson, Kent, ed. *Reshaping Government in Metropolitan Areas*. Detroit: Metropolitan Fund, 1974.

Metropolitan Governance. See Chapter 2.

Middleman, Ruth R., and Goldberg, Gale. *Social Service Delivery: A Structural Approach to Social Work Practice*. New York: Columbia University Press, 1974.

Mills, C. Wright. *The Power Elite*. New York: Oxford University Press, 1956.

Mogulof, Melvin B. *Five Metropolitan Governments*. Washington, D.C.: The Urban Institute, 1972.

———. *Governing Metropolitan Areas*. Washington, D.C.: The Urban Institute, 1971.

———. "A Modest Proposal for the Governance of America's Metropolitan Areas." See Chapter 3.

Mumford, Lewis. *The City in History*. New York: Harcourt, Brace and World, 1961.

Ostrom, Vincent. "Operational Federalism: Organization for the Provisions of Public Services in the American Federal System." *Public Choice* 6 (Spring 1969):1–17.

Ostrom, Vincent, et al. "The Organization of Government in Metropolitan Areas." See Chapter 2.

Perlman, Robert, and Gurin, Arnold. *Community Organization and Social Plan-*

ning. New York: John Wiley and the Council on Social Work Education, 1972.

Perloff, Harvey S., ed. *Agenda for the New Urban Era*. See Chapter 1.

Porter, David O., and Olsen, Eugene A. "Some Critical Issues in Government Centralization and Decentralization." See Chapter 3.

Rein, Martin. *Social Policy*. See Chapter 3.

Rich, Richard C. "The Roles of Neighborhood Organizations in Urban Service Delivery." *Urban Affairs Papers* 1 (Fall 1979):81–93.

———. "Voluntary Action and Public Services." *Journal of Voluntary Action Research* 7 (1978):4–14.

Rosentraub, Mark S., and Sharp, Elaine B. "Consumers as Producers of Social Services: Coproduction and the Level of Social Services." *Southern Review of Public Administration* 4 (March 1981):502–39.

Rothman, Jack. *Planning and Organizing for Social Change: Action Principles from Social Science Research*. New York: Columbia University Press, 1974.

Schulbert, Herbert; Baker, Frank; and Roen, Sheldon R., eds. *Developments in Human Services*. New York: Behavioral Publications, 1973.

Tobin, Sheldon S.; Davidson, Stephen M.; and Sack, Ann. *Effective Social Service for Older Americans*. Ann Arbor: University of Michigan–Wayne State University, Institute of Gerontology, 1976.

U. S. Advisory Commission on Intergovernmental Relations. *Citizen Participation in the American Federal System*. Washington, D.C.: U. S. Advisory Commission on Intergovernmental Relations, 1980.

———. *Regional Decision Making*. See Chapter 2.

Verba, Sidney, and Nie, Norman. *Participation in America: Political Democracy and Social Equity*. New York: Harper and Row, 1972.

Warren, Roland L. *The Community in America*. See Chapter 1.

Washeris, George J. *Neighborhood Facilities and Municipal Decentralization*. Washington, D.C.: Center for Governmental Studies, 1971.

Weiner, Myron E. "The Implications of the Services Integration Movement for the Theory of Public Administration." See Chapter 3.

Weintraub, Susan G. *Councils of Government in the 1970s: A Selective Annotated Bibliography*. Council of Planning Librarians, no. 1187, December 1976.

Wheaton, William L. C. "Metro-Allocation Planning." *Journal of the American Institute of Planners* 33 (March 1967):103–7.

Wilson, James Q. "Planning and Politics." See Chapter 2.

Wingo, Lowden, ed. *Reforming Metropolitan Governments*. Baltimore: Johns Hopkins University Press for Resources for the Future, 1972.

Wolff, Reinhold P. *Miami Metro: The Road to Urban Unity*. Coral Gables: Bureau of Economic Research of the University of Miami, 1960.

Wood, Robert. "Intergovernmental Relationships in an Urbanizing America." See Chapter 2.

Yessian, Mark R., and Broskowski, Anthony. "Generalists in Human Systems: Their Problems and Prospects." *Social Service Review* 51 (June 1977):265–88.

Yin, Robert K., et al. *Citizen Organizations: Increasing Client Control over Services*. Santa Monica, Calif.: RAND Corporation, 1973.

Chapter 7. The Professional and Practical Consequences of Big Bureaucracy

Abels, Paul, and Murphy, Michael J. *Administration in the Human Services.* See Chapter 3.

Altshuler, Alan A. *Community Control.* See Chapter 5.

Baum, Bernard H. *Decentralization of Authority in a Bureaucracy.* Englewood Cliffs, N.J.: Prentice-Hall, 1961.

Beckman, Norman. "The Planner as Bureaucrat." *Journal of the American Institute of Planners* 30 (November 1964):323–27.

Beneveniste, Guy. *The Politics of Expertise.* Berkeley, Calif.: Glendessary Press, 1972.

Billingsley, Andrew. "Bureaucratic and Professional Orientation Patterns in Social Casework." *Social Service Review* 38 (December 1964):400–407.

Bolan, Richard S. "Emerging Views of Planning." See Chapter 2.

Braybrooke, David, and Lindbloom, Charles. *A Strategy of Decision.* New York: Free Press of Glencoe, 1963.

Dahl, Robert A. *Who Governs?* See Chapter 2.

Drezver, Stephen M. "The Emerging Art of Decision Making." *Social Casework* 54 (January 1973):3–12.

Frankel, Charles. *The Democratic Prospect.* See Chapter 3.

Frieden, Bernard J. "The Changing Prospects for Social Planning." See Chapter 1.

Gans, Herbert J. "The Need for Planners Trained in Policy Formulation." In Erber, ed. *Urban Planning in Transition.* See Chapter 1.

Gilbert, Neil. "The Transformation of Social Services." *Social Service Review* 51 (December 1977):624–41.

Harris, Britton. "The Limits of Science and Humanism in Planning." *Journal of the American Institute of Planners* 33 (1967):324–35.

Hunter, Floyd. *Community Power Structure: A Study of Decision Makers.* Chapel Hill: University of North Carolina Press, 1953.

Klosterman, Richard E. "Foundations for Normative Planning." *Journal of the American Institute of Planners* 44 (January 1978):37–46.

Kuhn, Thomas S. *The Structure of Scientific Revolutions.* Chicago: University of Chicago Press, 1962.

Lipsky, Michael. "The Welfare State as Workplace." *Public Welfare* 39 (Summer 1981):22–27.

Long, Arthur N. "The Growth of a Bureaucracy." *Western Political Quarterly* 12 (December 1959):932–38.

Meade, Marvin. "Participative Administration—Emerging Reality or Wishful Thinking?" In Waldo, ed. *Public Administration in a Time of Turbulence.*

Mumford, Lewis. *The City in History.* See Chapter 6.

———. *The Pentagon of Power.* New York: Harcourt, Brace, Jovanovich, 1970.

Needleman, Martin L., and Needleman, Carolyn E. *Guerrillas in the Bureaucracy: The Community Planning Experiment in the United States.* New York: John Wiley and Sons, 1974.

Reid, W. J. "Mapping the Knowledge Base of Social Work." *Social Work* 26 (March 1981):124–32.

Rondinelli, Dennis A. "Urban Planning as Policy Analysis: Management of Urban Change." *Journal of the American Institute of Planners* 39 (January 1973):13–22

Schwartz, Edward E. "Macro Social Work: A Practice in Search of Some Theory." *Social Service Review* 51 (June 1977):207–27.

Siporin, Max. "Practice Theory and Vested Interests." *Social Service Review* 52 (September 1978):418–36.

Social Casework: Generic and Specific: A Report of the Milford Conference. New York: American Association of Social Workers, 1929.

"Symposium on Alienation, Decentralization, and Participation." *Public Administration Review* 24 (January–February 1969):2–63.

Waldo, Dwight, ed. *Public Administration in a Time of Turbulence.* New York: Chandler, 1971.

Walter, S. Z. "Is There Any Benefit in Cost-Benefit Analysis?" See Chapter 3.

Warren, Roland L. *The Community in America.* See Chapter 1.

Webber, Melvin M. "Comprehensive Planning and Social Responsibility: Toward an AIP Consensus on the Profession's Role and Purpose." *Journal of the American Institute of Planners* 29 (November 1963):232–41.

Weiss, Carol H. "Efforts at Bureaucratic Reform: What Have We Learned?" In Weiss and Barton, eds. *Making Bureaucracies Work.*

Weiss, Carol H., and Barton, Alan, eds. *Making Bureaucracies Work.* Beverly Hills, Calif.: Sage Publications, 1977.

Wholey, Joseph S. "What Can We Actually Get from Program Evaluation?" See Chapter 3.

Yessian, Mark R., and Broskowski, Anthony. "Generalists in Human Service Systems." See Chapter 6.

CHAPTER 8. SOCIAL PLANNING, SOCIAL WELFARE, AND SOCIAL POLICY

Addams, Jane. *The Second Twenty Years at Hull House.* New York: MacMillan, 1930.

————. *Twenty Years at Hull House.* 1910. Reprint. New York: New American Library, 1961.

Alinsky, Saul. *Reveille for Radicals.* See Chapter 6.

Altshuler, Allan A. *The City Planning Process: A Political Analysis.* Ithaca, N.Y.: Cornell University Press, 1965.

————. "The Goals of Comprehensive Planning." *Journal of the American Institute of Planners* 31 (August 1965):186–95.

Arnstein, Sherry R. "A Ladder of Citizen Participation." *Journal of the American Institute of Planners* 35 (June 1969):216–24.

Banfield, Edward C. *The Unheavenly City Revisited.* Boston: Little, Brown & Company, 1970.

Barr, Donald A. "The Professional Urban Planner." See Chapter 2.

Bauchum, Rosalind G., Associates. *Urban Planning: A Selected and Partially Annotated Bibliography.* Chicago: Council of Planning Librarians, 1983.

Bolan, Richard S. "Community Decision Behavior: The Culture of Planning." *Journal of the American Institute of Planners* 35 (September 1969):301–11.

————. "Emerging Views of Planning." See Chapter 2.

————. "The Social Relations of the Planners." *Journal of the American Institute of Planners* 37 (November 1975):387–96.

Boulding, Kenneth. "Boundaries of Social Policy." See Chapter 3.

Brooks, Michael P. *Social Planning and City Planning.* See Chapter 1.

Brooks, Michael P., and Stegman, Michael A. "Urban Social Policy, Race and the Education of Planners." *Journal of the American Institute of Planners* 34 (September 1968):275–86.

Chapin, Stuart F., and Kaiser, Edward J. *Urban Land Use Planning.* Urbana: University of Illinois Press, 1979.

"Citizen Action in Model Cities and CAP Programs: Case Studies and Evaluation." *Public Administration Review* 32 (Special Issue, September 1972).

Davidoff, Paul. "Advocacy and Pluralism in Planning." *Journal of the American Institute of Planners* 31 (November 1965):331–37.

Davidoff, Paul, and Reiner, Thomas A. "A Choice Theory of Planning." See Chapter 3.

Demone, Harold W. "The Limits of Rationality in Planning." *Community Mental Health Journal* 1 (Winter 1965):375–382.

Dyckman, John W. "Social Planning in the American Democracy." In Erber, ed. *Urban Planning in Transition.* See Chapter 1.

————. "Social Planning, Social Planners, and Planned Societies." *Journal of the American Institute of Planners* 32 (March 1966):66–76.

Eldridge, W. D. "The Legitimation of Social Work Planning." *Social Service Review* 55 (June 1981):327–35.

Erber, Ernest. ed. *Urban Planning in Transition.* See Chapter 1.

Fagin, Henry. "Planning Organization and Activities within the Framework of Urban Government." In Perloff, ed. *Planning and the Urban Community.* See Chapter 5.

Fisher, Robert. "Community Organizing and Citizen Participation: The Efforts of the People's Institute in New York City, 1910–1920." *Social Service Review* 51 (September 1977):474–90.

Frieden, Bernard J. "The Changing Prospects for Social Planning." See Chapter 1.

————. "Comment." See Chapter 2.

Frieden, Bernard J., and Morris, Robert, eds. *Urban Planning and Social Policy.* New York: Basic Books, 1968.

Friedman, John. "A Response to Altshuler: Comprehensive Planning as a Process." *Journal of the American Institute of Planners* 31 (June 1965):195–97.

Fromm, Erich. "Humanistic Planning." *Journal of the American Institute of Planners* 38 (March 1972):67–71.

Gans, Herbert J. "Planning for Declining and Poor Cities." *Journal of the American Institute of Planners* 41 (September 1975):305–7.

————. *People and Plans.* See Chapter 1.

Gilbert, Neil, and Specht, Harry. "Process vs. Task in Social Planning." *Social Work* 22 (May 1977):178–83.

Glass, James J. "Citizen Participation in Planning: The Relationship between

Objectives and Technique." *Journal of the American Institute of Planners* 45 (April 1979):180–89.

Goodman, Percival, and Goodman, Paul. *Communitas: Means of Livelihood and Ways of Life*. 2d ed. New York: Vintage Books, 1960.

Grabow, Stephen, and Heskin, Allan. "Foundations for a Radical Concept of Planning." See Chapter 3.

Greenbie, Barrie B. "Social Territory, Community Health, and Urban Planning." *Journal of the American Institute of Planners* 40 (March 1974):74–81.

Gummer, Burton. "A Power-Politics Approach to Social Welfare Organizations." *Social Service Review* 52 (September 1978):349–61.

Hansen, Willard B. "Metropolitan Planning and the New Comprehensiveness." *Journal of the American Institute of Planners* 34 (September 1968): 295–303.

Harrington, Michael. *The Other America*. See Chapter 1.

Howard, John T. "City Planning as a Social Movement, a Governmental Function, and a Technical Profession." In Perloff, ed. *Planning and the Urban Community*. See Chapter 5.

Hudson, Barclay. "Comparison of Current Planning Theories: Counterparts and Contradictions." *Journal of the American Planning Association* 45 (October 1979):387–98.

Kahn, Alfred J. *Theory and Practice of Social Planning*. See Chapter 2.

Khinduka, S. K., and Coughlin, Bernard J. "A Conceptualization of Social Action." *Social Service Review* 49 (March 1975):1–14.

Klosterman, Richard E. "Foundations for Normative Planning." See Chapter 7.

Kotler, Milton. *Neighborhood Government*. Indianapolis: Bobbs-Merrill, 1969.

Krieger, Martin H. "Some New Directions for Planning Theories." See Chapter 3.

Krumholz, Norman. "A Retrospective View of Equity Planning: Cleveland 1969–1979." *Journal of the American Planning Association* 48 (Spring 1982):163–74.

Krumholz, Norman; Cogger, Janice M.; and Linner, John H. "The Cleveland Policy Planning Report." *Journal of the American Institute of Planners* 41 (September 1975):298–304.

Kuhn, Thomas S. *The Structure of Scientific Revolutions*. See Chapter 7.

Lauffer, Armand. *Social Planning at the Community Level*. See Chapter 6.

Leiby, James. *A History of Social Welfare and Social Work in the United States*. New York: Columbia University Press, 1978.

Loeks, C. David. "The New Comprehensiveness: Interpretive Summary." *Journal of the American Institute of Planners* 33 (September 1967):347–52.

Lowenstein, Louis K., and McGrath, Dorn C., Jr. "The Planning Imperative in America's Future." See Chapter 1.

Mayer, Robert R. "Social System Models for Planners." *Journal of the American Institute of Planners* 38 (May 1972):130–39.

Magill, Robert S., and Clark, Terry N. "Community Power and Decision Making." *Social Service Review* 49 (March 1975):33–45.

Mazziotti, Donald F. "The Underlying Assumptions of Advocacy Planning: Pluralism and Reform." *Journal of the American Institute of Planners* 40 (January 1974):38–47.

Meenaghan, Thomas M.; Washington, Robert O.; and Ryan, Robert M. *Macro Practice in the Human Services.* New York: Free Press, 1982.

Meltzer, Jack, and Whitley, Joyce. "Social and Physical Planning for the Urban Slum." See Chapter 1.

Meyerson, Martin. "Building the Middle-Range Bridge for Comprehensive Planning." *Journal of the American Institute of Planners* (Spring 1956):58–64.

———. "National Urban Policy Appropriate to the American Pattern." In Berry and Meltzer, eds. *Goals for Urban America.* See Chapter 1.

Mocine, Corwin R. "Urban Physical Planning and the 'New Planning.' " *Journal of the American Institute of Planners* 32 (July 1966):234–37.

Morris, Robert. "Persistent Issues and Elusive Answers in Social Welfare Policy, Planning and Administration." *Administration in Social Work* 6 (February/March):33–47.

Moss, J. A. "Unemployment among Black Youths: A Policy Dilemma." *Social Work* 27 (January 1982):47–52.

Neill, Desmond. "The Unfinished Business of the Welfare State." In Schottland, ed. *The Welfare State.* See Chapter 2.

Nelsen, Judith C. "Social Work's Fields of Practice, Methods, and Models: The Choice to Act." *Social Service Review* 49 (June 1975):264–70.

Peattie, Lisa R. "Reflections on Advocacy Planning." See Chapter 5.

Perlman, Robert. "Social Welfare Planning and Physical Planning." *Journal of the American Institute of Planners* 32 (July 1966):237–41.

Perlman, Robert, and Gurin, Arnold. *Community Organization and Social Planning.* See Chapter 6.

Perloff, Harvey S. "Common Goals and the Linking of Physical and Social Planning." See Chapter 1.

———. "New Directions in Social Planning." *Journal of the American Institute of Planners* 31 (September 1965):297–303.

Piven, Frances Fox. "Planning and Class Interests." See Chapter 3.

Piven, Frances Fox, and Cloward, Richard A. *Poor People's Movements: Why They Succeed, How They Fail.* New York: Pantheon Books, 1977.

Ponsioen, J. A. "General Theory of Social Welfare Policy." In Ponsioen, ed. *Social Welfare Policy.*

———, ed. *Social Welfare Policy.* The Hague: Monton and Co., 1962.

Rein, Martin. *Social Policy.* See Chapter 3.

Rondinelli, Dennis A. "Urban Planning as Policy Analysis." See Chapter 7.

Smith, Russell, and Zietz, Dorothy. *American Social Welfare Institutions.* New York: John Wiley and Sons, 1970.

Smuts, Edward E. "Comments on the Economic Functions and Structure of the Metropolitan Region." In Perloff, ed. *Planning and the Urban Community.* See Chapter 5.

Spiegel, Hans, ed. *Citizen Participation in Urban Development.* Washington, D.C.: Center for Community Affairs, National Institute for Applied Behavioral Science, 1968, 2 vols. Vol. 3, Fairfax, Va. Learning Resources Corporation/NTL, 1974.

Strange, John H., ed. *Public Administration Review* 32 (Special Issue, September 1972).

Titmuss, Richard M. "The Social Division of Welfare." In *Essays on the Welfare State*. Boston: The Beacon Press, 1963.

Tunnard, Christopher, "The Planning Syndrome in Western Culture." See Chapter 1.

U. S. Advisory Commission on Intergovernmental Relations. *Citizen Participation in the American Federal System*. See Chapter 6.

Walker, Robert A. *The Planning Function in Urban Government*. 2d ed. Chicago: University of Chicago Press, 1950.

Warren, Roland L. *The Community in America*. See Chapter 1.

Webber, Melvin M. "Comprehensive Planning and Social Responsibility." See Chapter 7.

Wetmore, Louis B. "Preparing the Profession for Its Changing Role." In Erber, ed. *Urban Planning in Transition*. See Chapter 1.

Wilson, James Q. "Planning and Politics." See Chapter 2.

Wood, Elizabeth. *Social Planning: A Primer for Urbanists*. New York: Pratt Institute, 1965.

CHAPTER 9. A CHANGING AGENDA FOR URBAN PLANNING

Altshuler, Alan A. *The City Planning Process*. See Chapter 8.

———. "The Goals of Comprehensive Planning." See Chapter 8.

Barr, Donald A. "The Professional Urban Planner." See Chapter 2.

Benne, Kenneth D.; Chin, Robert; Bennis, Warren; and Corey, Kenneth E., eds. *The Planning of Change*. New York: Holt, Rinehart and Winston, 1976.

Bolan, Richard S., "Mapping the Planning Theory Terrain." In Godschalk, ed. *Planning in America*.

Dakin, John. "An Evaluation of the 'Choice' Theory of Planning." *Journal of the American Institute of Planners* 29 (February 1963):19–27.

Davidoff, Paul. "Advocacy and Pluralism in Planning." See Chapter 8.

Davidoff, Paul, and Reiner, Thomas A. "A Choice Theory of Planning." See Chapter 3.

———. "A Reply to Dakin." *Journal of the American Institute of Planners* 29 (February 1963):27–28.

Dyckman, John W. "Social Planning in the American Democracy." In Erber, ed. *Urban Planning in Transition*. See Chapter 1.

Fowles, J., ed. *Handbook of Futures Research*. Westport, Conn.: Greenwood Press, 1978.

Friedman, John. "Notes on Social Action." *Journal of the American Institute of Planners* 35 (September 1969):311–18.

Galloway, Thomas D., and Mahayhi, Riad G. "Planning Theory in Retrospect: The Process of Paradigm Change." *Journal of the American Institute of Planners* 43 (January 1977):62–71.

Gans, Herbert J. *People and Plans*. See Chapter 1.

Godschalk, David R., ed. *Planning in America: Learning from Turbulence*. Washington, D.C.: American Institute of Planners, 1974.

Grabow, Stephen, and Heskin, Allan. "Foundations for a Radical Concept of Planning." See Chapter 3.

Greenstone, J. David, and Peterson, Paul D. *Race and Authority in Urban Politics.* See Chapter 3.

Gronbjerg, K. A. "Disciplinary Tunnel Vision in the Study of Poverty and Social Welfare: Consequences for Social Policy." *Journal of Applied Social Sciences* 3 (1978):1–18.

Holleb, Doris B. *Social and Economic Information for Urban Planning.* vols. I and II. Chicago: Center for Urban Studies, University of Chicago, 1969.

Howard, John T. "City Planning as a Social Movement, a Governmental Function, and a Technical Profession." In Perloff, ed. *Planning and the Urban Community.* See Chapter 8.

Hudson, Barclay. "Comparison of Current Planning Theories." See Chapter 8.

Klosterman, Richard E. "Foundations for Normative Planning." See Chapter 7.

Krumholz, Norman. "A Retrospective View of Equity Planning." See Chapter 8.

Merriam, Charles E. *Systematic Politics.* Chicago: University of Chicago Press, 1945.

Meyerson, Martin. "Building the Middle-Range Bridge for Comprehensive Planning." See Chapter 8.

Moynihan, Daniel P. *Maximum Feasible Misunderstanding.* See Chapter 2.

Perloff, Harvey S. *Planning the Post Industrial City.* Washington, D.C.: Planners Press, American Planning Association, 1980.

Piven, Frances Fox, and Cloward, Richard A. *Poor People's Movements.* See Chapter 8.

Rein, Martin. "Social Policy Analysis as the Interpretation of Beliefs." *Journal of the American Institute of Planners* 37 (September 1971):297–310.

Rothman, Jack. *Planning and Organizing for Social Change.* See Chapter 6.

Solomon, Arthur, ed. *The Prospective City.* See Chapter 3.

Walker, Robert A. *The Planning Function in Urban Government.* See Chapter 8.

Webber, Melvin M. "Comprehensive Planning and Social Responsibility." See Chapter 7.

Wetmore, Louis B. "Preparing the Profession for Its Changing Role." In Erber, ed. *Urban Planning in Transition.* See Chapter 1.

Index

Jack Meltzer is dean of the School of the Social Sciences at the University of Texas at Dallas. He was the first director of the Center for Urban Studies at the University of Chicago and has worked extensively as a private consultant specializing in planning and in urban and economic community development.

THE JOHNS HOPKINS UNIVERSITY PRESS

METROPOLIS TO METROPLEX

This book was composed in Palatino text and display type by
Brushwood Graphics, from a design by Gerard A. Valerio. It
was printed on S. D. Warren's 50-lb. Sebago Eggshell Cream
offset paper and bound by the Maple Press Company.